EAST COAST
WHISKEY FLOW
MAINE
VERMONT
NEW HAMPSHIRE
NEW YORK
MASSACHUSETTS
CONNECTICUT
RHODE ISLAND
NEW JERSEY
DELAWARE
PENNSYLVANIA
MARYLAND
WISCONSIN
MICHIGAN
OHIO
ILLINOIS
INDIANA
WEST VIRGINIA
VIRGINIA
KENTUCKY
TENNESSEE
NORTH CAROLINA
SOUTH CAROLINA
MISSISSIPPI
ALABAMA
GEORGIA
FLORIDA
XXX
UNITED STATES OF AMERICA
LIBERTY
QUARTER DOLLAR

PRAISE FOR LEW BRYSON'S *WHISKEY MASTER CLASS*

"In whiskey, Lew Bryson is not only a god, he is a hero. With this book, he'll grow the base of whiskey knowledge and will help eliminate know-it-all know nothings."

—Fred Minnick, editor-in-chief of *Bourbon+*; author of *Bourbon* and *Bourbon Curious*

"Lew writes about whiskey the same way our family is proud to make whiskey—with honesty, craft, and a lot of heart. Whether you've been a whiskey fan for years or just getting into it, you'll learn something new from Lew's explanation of making whiskey. And damn sure you'll have some fun while doing it."

—Fred Noe, Beam Seventh Generation Master Distiller

"Lew Bryson knows more about whiskey than anyone I've met. But that's only one reason to read *Whiskey Master Class*. He writes with clarity and humor in a way that will engage novices and connoisseurs alike. I learned a lot, and you will too."

—Clay Risen, author of *Single Malt: A Guide to the Whiskies of Scotland*

"Lew is a true whiskey guy. To enhance your knowledge in the magical world of distilling, my friend Lew Bryson is the perfect place to start. His many years in the whiskey business and his insatiable *thirst* for knowledge ensures his fans and readers continue to gain great insights and understanding. Lew makes drinking good whiskey great!"

—Colum Egan, Master Distiller Bushmills Irish Whiskey

"As far as I'm concerned, everything Lew Bryson writes is pretty much a master class—deeply informed, as clear as white dog straight from the still, and as brightly illuminating as the August sun beating down on a rickhouse roof. So, when he sets out to teach an actual master class—let's just say that there is nobody, whether a complete newcomer or the most seasoned old-whiskey hand, who won't walk away from this fine book with a new, deeper understanding of the topic."

—David Wondrich, author of *Imbibe!* and *Punch*

"Lew uses a cozy, conversational style of writing that makes the reader feel as if they are sitting in front of a quiet fire with an old friend, enjoying the perfect dram. It belies his decades of experience of writing on all things beer and whiskey, and makes Lew's technical explanations feel less like an impenetrable fog of science and more like a welcome footnote. This is a must-have for anyone looking to enjoy whiskey just a little bit more."

—Todd Leopold, Leopold Bros. Distillery & Malthouse

"Like all great educators Lew wears his knowledge modestly and dispenses his deep wisdom with a deceptively light touch. His is one of the great voices in the whisky world. Listen to it."

—Dave Broom, author of *The World Atlas of Whisky*

AMERICAN Whiskey MASTER CLASS

The Ultimate Guide to Understanding Bourbon, Rye, and Other American Whiskeys

LEW BRYSON

HARVARD
COMMON
PRESS

Quarto.com

First Published in 2025 by The Harvard Common Press, an imprint of The Quarto Group,
100 Cummings Center, Suite 265-D, Beverly, MA 01915, USA.
T (978) 282-9590 F (978) 283-2742

EEA Representation, WTS Tax d.o.o., Žanova ulica 3, 4000 Kranj, Slovenia. www.wts-tax.si

The Harvard Common Press titles are also available at discount for retail, wholesale, promotional, and bulk purchase. For details, contact the Special Sales Manager by email at specialsales@quarto.com or by mail at The Quarto Group, Attn: Special Sales Manager, 100 Cummings Center, Suite 265-D, Beverly, MA 01915, USA.

29 28 27 26 3 4 5

ISBN: 978-0-7603-9620-9

Digital edition published in 2025
eISBN: 978-0-7603-9621-6

Content in this book previously appeared in *Whiskey Master Class*
(Harvard Common Press, 2020) by Lew Bryson.

Library of Congress Cataloging-in-Publication Data available

Design: Cindy Samargia Laun
Illustrations: Nicole Bustamante, @nicolebustamante.art

Printed in Guangdong, China TT062026

Foreword

by Fred Minnick, author of *Bourbon Curious*

I WILL NEVER FORGET the moment I cornered Lew Bryson, then the managing editor of *Whisky Advocate.*

We were inside a large industrial building that had been cleared for bourbon distillers to set up tasting booths along the walls and a buffet table in the middle. I had just grabbed a nip of whiskey from Heaven Hill master distiller Parker Beam and was assessing the crowd. And there he was—beard and all—Lew Bryson.

This was around 2010, when I was a burgeoning freelance writer trying to make it in the whiskey world. I was writing for smaller publications, but my goal was *Whisky Advocate.* At this point, I was like that little cartoon dog jumping up to Lew. "Hey, can I write for you?" Lew likely received about six pitches a month from me.

He rejected them all via email.

Now that he was in the same room as me, I gripped my Glencairn glass and eyeballed him from across the room. What pitch could I drop on him here? Would he be more accepting of me in person? Could I be so lucky that he feels sorry for me and gives me a gig out of the kindness of his heart? What could I possibly say that would get me within those sweet tabloid-sized glossy pages of the holy grail of whiskey writing—*Whisky Advocate?*

I extended my hand, introduced myself, and gave a pitch I had just heard from Buffalo Trace. "Let me tell you about Leak Hunters. They are these guys who go through the warehouse looking for leaks and they plug them with cedar. I'd love to write a feature about those guys!"

Lew, a good few inches taller than me, looked down, rubbed his chin and said, "I like it. But how good is your writing?"

I landed the assignment and wrote a few articles before my "Leak Hunters" was published, but that stalking moment near the buffet line began my seven-year journey with Lew at *Whisky Advocate.* And although we disagree on the Oxford comma (throw that thing away, Lew!), he molded me into the American whiskey writer I am today and helped me form my unique voice, instead of following the format of other writers.

No magazine editor before or since influenced my work like Lew.

And it wasn't just me. Lew mentored all of us. He edited the great British beer and whisky writer Michael Jackson, Jim Murray, Jonny McCormick, Liza Weisstuch, David Broom, Davin de Kergommeaux, and more.

There's not a prominent whiskey writer, from the 1990s to 2017, that didn't learn from Lew's red pen or his tracked changes. He made all of us better.

When he left the magazine editing role and pursued a life of writing books and speaking, we all were happy for him but selfishly missed his sage advice and, of course, his laugh. And when his first whiskey book came out, Lew outsold all of us for the next couple years. The reason why? His book was incredible, outlining every single step in all whiskey- or whisky-making nations.

But this new one you're reading now—*American Whiskey Master Class*—is truly special. It's uniquely American and a genuine "master class" for those wanting to learn. If you want to take a deep dive or just glance through it, this book will make you a smarter whiskey person, and Lew will mentor you just like he did me.

Yeah, I miss those days.

The beautiful thing about whiskey is that every dram offers a new treasured memory. I miss talking whiskey with Lew: over email, on the phone, or—the best—in person. Reading *American Whiskey Master Class* takes me back to those times.

I can tell you that this book will help you build knowledge to create new memories, so you know what you're sipping on and how to talk about it—both from a historical perspective and by way of the classic tasting notes.

Lew's the best overall whiskey teacher I've had in my life.

And now, he's yours.

Contents

PRICE PER CASE $12.00
OLD ECONOMY GRAND
PENNSYLVANIA STRAIGHT RYE WHISKEY
LINFIELD
STRAIGHT RYE WHISKEY
FOUR YEARS OLD
ESTABLISHED 1810
OLD OVERHOLT WHISKEY
BOTTLED IN BOND
PENNSYLVANIA
ONE PINT
100 PROOF
HIRAM GREEN
CORN WHISKEY
RUFFSDALE
Aged in Wood
REVERENCE AND AFFECTION

1

A Great Story

American whiskey has blossomed over the past twenty years. I've been writing about American whiskey since 1997, and I've watched it happen. When I started writing about it, "American whiskey" largely meant bourbon made almost exclusively in Kentucky, Tennessee whiskey, some commodity-grade blended whiskey used for bulk cocktails and rustic punches, and tiny amounts of rye and corn whiskeys.

Now bourbon has blown up and dared to experiment with different grains and different barrel treatments, and it's spread out of Kentucky. Tennessee whiskey no longer means only Jack Daniel's and George Dickel. Rye whiskey has made a triumphant comeback on the shoulders of an army of bartenders.

It doesn't stop with these familiar types. Wheat whiskey has returned from extinction, and corn whiskey is slowly gaining respect. An old idea, light whiskey, has shown promise. There is a large number of smaller distillers who have championed the idea of American single malt whiskey, taking on Scotch whisky head-to-head. There is a smaller but determined band who've taken the challenge of making whiskey reminiscent of Irish single pot still whiskey. They've also gone completely off into the blue and experimented with rice, sorghum, millet, quinoa, buckwheat, triticale, and, I'm sure, even more grains that I've yet to have the opportunity to taste. And yes, blended whiskey is still around, and may even be getting a turn to shine.

There is, therefore, a *world* of whiskey variety, all being made inside the borders of the United States. Yes, all fifty states—there is whiskey being made in Alaska and Hawaii—plus the District of Columbia, Puerto Rico, and Guam. You can't stop whiskey!

What does all that variety mean? It's about the market, of course, making what people want to buy, and it's about the creative drive of distillers to make something new or test themselves against the proven greats.

But you're a drinker, not a distiller. Variety means opportunity for you: What whiskey do I want today? And when you put that whiskey in the glass, it's down to you, the whiskey, and the moment. It's about aroma, and flavor, and perception. So . . .

What do you smell...what do you taste when you take a sip of whiskey?

Trying a bourbon? Scents of maple or blackberry or coconut may come from the glass. Rye? Maybe mint or spicy-bitter notes zip across your palate. Wheat whiskey? Some sweet citrus or fresh-sliced bread notes please the tongue. Old-school corn whiskey? Fresh notes of sweet corn, maybe roasted on the cob, will fill your nose. American single malt? Sweet cereal, perhaps with wildly varied smoky character, will please you. The myriad small distilleries are more innovative and might deliver aromas of barbecue, strawberries, peanuts, and peppermint.

All of these aromas and flavors are different, and these whiskeys are singular enough that you can often tell what you're drinking just by the flavors and aromas. But those more exotic fruity and spicy flavors and aromas also have something in common: Not one of them is an ingredient in the whiskey. No blackberries, no peanuts, no mint, and certainly no coconut have been added!

Where do they come from? The answer to that question is found in the answer to larger questions: What is whiskey, and how is it made? There are flavors and aromas being made (or taken away) at every step, and every step is necessary to the way the whiskey tastes.

One of the jobs of a whiskey writer is tasting whiskey and then describing it to readers. Writers speak of "teasing apart" the aromas to figure out what is in there, a process of deconstructing the whiskey, figuring out what went into it and how it was made.

That's what this book is about, but from the other side. We're going to take a look at how American whiskey makers go about creating, building, and integrating flavor and aroma.

Some of this will be things you already know. Even thirty years ago, informed whiskey drinkers would have known that whiskey was aged in oak barrels, though they may not have known what kind, or why, or what that did to the whiskey. They knew that whiskey was made with a still, and they probably had a vague idea of how a pot still worked. Very few of them had ever been to a distillery; very few distilleries offered tours.

Today's whiskey drinkers are much more sophisticated, more engaged. They want to know all they can about their chosen drink. "Transparency" is their watchword. They want to know where the whiskey is made and go there to see it being made. Tell us, they ask, what grains are being used, where they are from, and in what ratios they are included.

Don't stop there: Tell us what yeast is used, how the mash is made, and maybe even what kind of fermentation vessel is used. Then they want to know more about the still: what kind it is, how it is shaped, and how the distillation is done. Take them in the cooperage and show them the barrels. Take them to the warehouse; they must see how it is constructed and where it is sited.

Today's whiskey drinkers know a lot more than their predecessors did thirty years ago. But unless you're in the industry, or you're a dedicated whiskey writer like me, or you're an exceptionally well-read, well-traveled whiskey drinker, I can almost guarantee you'll find things in this book you don't know—things that are new to you. I know that I learned some things writing it, and I've been at this for quite a while.

It might be the components of water chemistry, the thermal path of fermentation, the history and chemistry of sour mash, or the intricacies of still design. It might be the influence of the design and position of the warehouse, the size and shape of the barrel, or the climate where the whiskey is aged. Maybe it's the difference between bourbon and corn whiskey.

Or maybe—and this was one of the main reasons that I wrote the book—for you it's the forest and not the trees. I find that in whiskey appreciation, as is the case in many a hobbyist's interest, people tend to put an emphasis on one or two factors that they find particularly interesting or simply easier to grasp.

Bourbon aficionados may obsess over the "mash bill," the ratio of the different grains that make up the whiskey's formulation. Rye drinkers are getting to be picky about "Kentucky" versus "Monongahela" style. American single malt chasers are curious about smoke and malt types. The small number of corn whiskey fans want to know about the source of the used barrels and the type of corn. Fans of the less easily-defined craft whiskeys want to know where it's made, and what kind of still, and what kind of grain, and what's the distiller's dog's name?

WHISKEY OR WHISKY?

One of the biggest arguments about whiskey is how to spell it.

It's generally "whiskey" in America, though some small brands, and even big brands like Maker's Mark, Old Forester, and George Dickel, drop the "e." It's "whisky" in Scotland and Canada, and some people think it makes a difference.

The spelling doesn't make the difference. "Whisky" and "whiskey" are pronounced the same, and they mean the same thing. It's exactly like the difference between "neighbor" in America and "neighbour" in Canada: It's a letter, nothing else; you still live beside them. But this book is about American whiskey, so we'll be using that spelling (except when referring directly to Scotch or Canadian whiskies, like that). And spelling . . . is all it is.

It doesn't hurt to mention that it's *all* whiskey. I've heard people say, "I like whiskey, but I also like bourbon." That's like saying, "I like cake, but I also like chocolate cake." Bourbon, rye, single malt, Irish, Canadian, Japanese, even Indian and Swedish: It's all whiskey. Or whisky, which, again, is just a different spelling.

I'll also be saying "bourbon" and "bourbon and rye" a lot. Unless I'm clearly talking specifically about those two whiskeys, assume I'm talking about American whiskey in general. It's easier than calling the whole roll of thirty-five types.

NEW YORK DISTILLING COMPANY

All of those things can be important. But none of them are the be-all and end-all of how those whiskeys taste. You need to keep your eye on the big picture, the whole process. The rule of thumb in American whiskey is that 50 percent to 70 percent of flavor and aroma comes from the barrel. That leaves a lot of room for other things, and the truth is that the barrel will give much different results depending on what goes in it. Even the barrels can be quite different these days.

To really understand a whiskey, you have to know where every bit of that whole 100 percent comes from and how it differs from another whiskey.

What Is Whiskey?

To understand *that*, we should talk briefly about what is whiskey and what isn't.

In the simplest terms, whiskey is a drink made from fermented grain that is then distilled and aged in wooden barrels. But it turns out that "the simplest terms" can get you in trouble. For instance, in the United States, unlike in most other major whiskey-producing countries, the regulations don't put any minimum on the amount of time that is considered aging. On the other hand, there are limits on the alcohol percentage of the spirit coming off the final distillation; it cannot be higher than 80 percent alcohol by volume (ABV).

You can depend on these basics in American whiskey. There are other, unaged grain spirits that are distilled higher than 80 percent: We generally call them "vodka." Whiskey does have to be made from grain. Despite what people may tell you, there is no "potato whiskey" or "sugar whiskey." That's what we call a "distilled spirits specialty." If it's distilled to under 80 percent alcohol by volume, from 100 percent grain and aged in wood, it's whiskey.

How did that come to be the definition of whiskey? In the late medieval period, when Arabic texts on the science of distillation collided with scholarly European monks who could read them, it happened in the colder climes of Ireland (or maybe Scotland—it's not 100 percent certain). The most common source of alcohol for distilling there was beer, the drink of northern Europe. Whiskey, or *usquebaugh* as it was originally called in Gaelic (pronounced, roughly, "ish-ka b'ah"), found a foothold among the monks of Ireland and Scotland and eventually spread to small farmers.

Those Scottish farmers, and the middlemen who brought their spirit to market, started aging it in used barrels. That "aging" was usually the amount of time it took to smuggle the spirit out of the hills. It wasn't always legal, but it was easier than selling grain. It took eight mules to carry the grain used to make one mule-load of whiskey, and the whiskey was worth more. Once legal distilling became widespread in the 1820s, an industry was born.

Distilling in the New World took root after the immigration of Scots-Irish and German distillers. Germans had a tradition of grain spirit made largely from rye. The rye whiskey makers in Pennsylvania, and later the distillers who developed bourbon in Kentucky, were largely German. The man George Washington hired to run his rye whiskey distillery at Mount Vernon after retiring from the presidency, though, was a Scotsman.

There is nothing like going to where whiskey is made, and talking to the people who make it.

Whiskey took hold as a good drink—and a nonperishable drink, unlike beer and wine. It didn't go flat, or stale, or turn sour, and it was a reliable source of income for farmers. Malt whiskey never really caught on in America like it did in the United Kingdom. We had that rye heritage, and rye was a crop that grew even on the hardscrabble soils of the Appalachian Mountains.

But we also had corn, an incredible resource of the New World. We'll talk more about that in Chapter 3, but the key here is that corn was a whole new grain for distillers to play with, and they soon found that it made great whiskey . . . with a bit of work, and a bit of wood.

Whiskey distilling industrialized in the 1800s, becoming very big business indeed. Rum had been the favored drink of early America, made in the West Indies or New England with plentiful molasses from the sugar plantations in the Caribbean. With the trade conflicts that accompanied the wars of America's independence and early history, rum lost its attraction as whiskey became cheaper, self-sufficient, and even patriotic. Distilleries dotted the country, with deep concentrations in Kentucky and the mid-Atlantic states, and in the grain-covered vastness of the newly plowed prairies.

That's how it would remain until the arrival of Prohibition in 1920. Once the Drys had their way, whiskey was allowed legally only in "medicinal" doses, which a doctor or pharmacist could prescribe for "reasons" like calming the nerves.

Gangsters stole whiskey from locked warehouses, often by the truckload. It was sold on the streets and in illicit speakeasy bars, usually after being "stretched" with various flavorings and additions of water. We also turned to illegally distilled and highly adulterated spirits, the "bathtub gin" of movies and novels, or smuggled whiskeys from Ireland, Canada, and Scotland. Not a great time for a whiskey drinker.

The arrival of Repeal in 1933 meant the bourbon and rye could flow again, but the new distilleries were bottling as quickly as they could, with painfully short aging times. Bill Samuels Jr., the former head at Maker's Mark, once told me that the old distillers referred to sales in those days as "swappin' dollars," taking in just enough to pay for supplies and meet payroll, and doing the same thing the next quarter. The good days wouldn't return until the 1950s, after the industry had temporarily converted to bulk industrial alcohol production to support manufacturing during World War II.

The revival was short-lived. The 1960s saw the rise of vodka and light rum; rum would taper off, but vodka still hasn't stopped growing. Whiskey sales fell precipitously, and by the 1980s there was a glut of aged whiskey. Distilleries closed, they shrank, they clung to the marginal markets they could find. Rye whiskey nearly disappeared except in niche markets in Maryland and Wisconsin, and corn whiskey was reduced to a novelty. Only bourbon held on, most strongly in the South.

The slow growth of single malt Scotch and the premium alternative it offered to the ubiquitous blends showed the way for American distillers. Select bourbons like Blanton's, the Jim Beam Small Batch Collection, Wild Turkey Kentucky Spirit, and Elijah Craig began to attract interest. This led the way to the restoration of the Labrot & Graham Distillery (that would become Woodford Reserve), the revival of Four Roses as a true bourbon, and even the slow resuscitation of rye whiskey.

Perhaps the greatest signal of whiskey's return to glory is the way the new small distillers have embraced it. Just over three thousand of these craft distillers are open in America in 2025. At least two-thirds of them are making whiskey, and they're making whiskey in a robust number of varieties, some in tribute to forgotten styles that haven't been made in more than one hundred years, some in ways that have rarely, if ever, been seen before.

Whiskey is a great story, a true story. Now learn the rest of it: how it's made.

YES, BLACK AMERICANS MADE WHISKEY

Whiskey is a very American product; at least, whiskey the way we make it here is. Much of it is made with corn (over half, by volume), a wholly American grain.

Technically, corn is Mesoamerican in origin, but the hybridization and genetic engineering that have made it the vast yellow river of grain it is today was mostly American—as in United States of—American. The new, charred white oak barrels are an American standard compared with the used barrels most of the rest of the world's whiskeys age in.

It's an uncomfortable truth for some that whiskey is also very American in that its roots entwine deeply with African American slavery in antebellum America. That's been openly acknowledged only relatively recently. The first discussion I recall had to do with George Washington's mill and distillery at Mount Vernon.

When the decision was made to reconstruct the distillery in 1999, part of the project was the history of the original operation. Washington's distillery was one of the largest commercial distilleries in the new country, for the short time it was open, with a production of just under 11,000 gallons (41,639 liters) in 1799, the year of his death. Those 11,000 gallons were produced on five wood-fired copper stills by the distillery manager and his son, a hired assistant distiller, and six enslaved African Americans named Hanson, Peter, Nat, Daniel, James, and Timothy.*

As whiskey production grew in the nineteenth century, it followed the same split as the rest of the country. The North industrialized production, with the rye distillers in the Monongahela Valley leaning heavily on the iron and steam that was driving that region. The South continued to treat whiskey more as an agricultural product, tended and propelled by enslaved labor. That changed after the Civil War, when industrial distilling came to the South.

Few people talked about those previous circumstances, that origin, in more than occasional speculative terms. Then whiskey writer (and *New York Times* reporter) Clay Risen wrote a piece in the *Times* in June 2016, "Jack Daniel's Embraces a Hidden Ingredient: Help from a Slave." Risen noted that the previous "official" story had been that the young Jack Daniel had learned to make whiskey from another white man, a preacher named Dan Call.

But there was a 1967 biography, *Jack Daniel's Legacy*, by Ben A. Green, that added a crucial detail.

(Continued on page 18)

The man in the middle is George Green, the son of Nathan "Nearest" Green; the man in the white hat beside him is Jack Daniel.

As Risen wrote: "Call told his slave to teach Daniel everything he knew. 'Uncle Nearest is the best whiskey maker that I know of,' the book quotes Call as saying." Nathan "Uncle Nearest" Green (no relation to the biographer) was that man.

It was a known thing, on the page in black and white, and according to Risen's article, it was informally known in the area around the distillery in Lynchburg, but somehow, we refused to know it, to integrate it. It reminds me of how *everyone knows* that the Biblical hero Samson lost his strength when Delilah cut off his hair, when it actually says right there on the page: "And she made him sleep upon her knees; and she called for a man, and she caused him to shave off the seven locks of his head." (Judges 16:19)

That may have been just an interesting story, even when the Jack Daniel's parent company, Brown-Forman, decided to weave the Uncle Nearest story into the Jack Daniel's history. But a Black woman, author and entrepreneur Fawn Weaver, read the piece, and it spoke to her, and she decided to dig more deeply into it.

It was a momentous decision. She rented a house in Lynchburg and quickly found historical traces, and descendants, of Nathan Green throughout the area. She met with executives from the distillery, and they were moved by her research. (I'm not surprised; I met Weaver at a bourbon event in New Orleans, and she is a captivating and convincing speaker.) Nathan "Uncle Nearest" Green was officially recognized as one of the Jack Daniel's master distillers.

But Weaver had further, bigger ideas. She found investors and launched an Uncle Nearest brand of whiskey. Nathan Green would have his own whiskey, not his name on someone else's. The brand was sourced, but Weaver had a working distillery in mind. After all, Nathan Green hadn't bought whiskey; he'd *made* it. Nothing less would do.

She found investors and raised the money to buy land and build the Nearest Green Distillery, north of Shelbyville, Tennessee, about half an hour from the Jack Daniel Distillery. This Black-owned business is helmed by an all-woman leadership team, including the master blender, Victoria Eady Butler.

That's one huge success story; even better, the whiskey is good (sourced for now, but their own should be in bottles by the time this goes to print). But the ongoing story is how more of the history of enslaved distillers is coming to light. Black men and women are building distilleries and making whiskey, assisted by programs like the American Craft Spirits Association's Spirits Training Entrepreneurship Program for Underrepresented Professionals (STEPUP) Foundation.

Nathan Green's mentorship made good whiskey for Jack Daniel's. Today, thanks to Fawn Weaver, the name and memory of Nathan Green has inspired a new generation of Black distillers who will make whiskey in their own names.

**mountvernon.org*

Uncle Nearest 1856

100° warmth, baked corn, dried fruit aromas. Lively, almost busy palate: more fruit, a bit of anise, background oakiness. Finish is sweet corn and fruit, framed by oak. Great balance.

Making Whiskey

Making whiskey, even average whiskey, is about flavor creation and flavor control, and there are a lot of different ways to do it.

Even the so-called legacy distillers, the familiar old names, have different ways of going about making good whiskey; the craft distillers have a wide variety of ways to do it, limited only by imagination and regulations. But all of those ways rely on putting together a varied mix of elements from four categories.

The four categories are *material, process, environment,* and *people.*

Material is the actual stuff that goes into making whiskey: grain, water, yeast (and bacteria), yeast nutrients, barrels, and sometimes, through a loophole, a small amount of added color and flavor.

Process is what gets done to the materials. Grain is at the heart of things and must be ground, turned into a coarse flour, to be used. Before that, it may be malted, or gelatinized. The ground grain is hydrated and cooked in a process called mashing. Then it's fermentation, followed directly by distillation. The spirit is cut to "entry proof" (the alcohol level at which it first goes in the barrel to age, legally no higher than 125°/62.5 percent ABV; some distillers go lower) and barreled prior to months or years of aging. The whiskey may be finished, a secondary aging, in a different type of barrel. It's then dumped, filtered, and proofed before bottling.

Environment is more subtle. It's what's around the whiskey from start to finish. It's the climate the trees and grain grew in, the weather that affected the function of the still, or the heat and cool of the warehouse. Altitude is becoming more and more important as distilleries pop up along slopes. It's the location, the *terroir*, of the distillery and the warehouses.

Finally, *people* make the whiskey, putting experience and attention into it. Here's how it happens.

Whiskey is an agricultural product. It starts in the fields. Grain is grown and harvested, then evaluated. Grain fit for distilling is top-quality stuff, be it barley, corn, wheat, rye, or anything else. It must be free of rot, have the right levels of protein and nitrogen, the right moisture content, and most importantly, it has to smell clean and right.

The grain is cleaned and processed. For barley, that usually means an extra step called *malting*, forcing the grain to sprout before heating it to kill the sprout. This causes the creation of *enzymes*, chemical catalysts that will transform starches to sugars as the grain or grains that go into the whiskey are carefully cooked, or *mashed*. (Grains like corn or rice are often cooked before the mash to gelatinize the starches, making them more accessible.)

The cooking makes that transformation happen by breaking loose the starches in the grains and allowing the enzymes to chemically transform them. The different enzymes work best in specific temperature ranges, so this part requires careful control.

Now the mash, a thin cereal porridge full of sugars, is cooled and usually pumped directly to fermentation tanks for American whiskeys, although some distillers strain out the solids, a process called *lautering*. In *sour mash* fermentation, some portion of the spent grain from the previous distillation is added to the fermenter. Yeast is added, and fermentation begins. The yeast attacks the sugars and consumes them, creating alcohol, carbon dioxide, and a variety of flavor and aroma compounds.

The resulting *distiller's beer* (with the unfiltered grains), or *wash* (strained liquid), goes to the still. If it's a pot still, it is *charged* with a capacity load and heated until the alcohol starts to vaporize. Alcohol vaporizes at a lower temperature than water, which is how distillation creates spirits. The first distillation, in the *wash still*, gets rid of a lot of the water. The second distillation, in the *spirit still*, is about *cutting* the spirit run to capture its alcohol heart.

There are compounds other than alcohol that vaporize at those lower temperatures that aren't desirable, referred to as *heads* or *foreshots*. These cook off first, and when the distinctive smell of the heads no longer taints the stream coming off the condenser, the distiller makes the first cut and starts collecting the cleaner alcohol and desirable aromatics (the *hearts*) in usable amounts. These are captured until they peter out, when other undesirable compounds start to join them in moving up the still, the *tails* or *feints*. The second cut is made, and this is also put aside. Some of the set-aside heads and tails cuts will be redistilled to recover all the alcohol; eventually, the leftovers will be disposed of (often burned for heat). There may be an additional third distillation to further "clean" the spirit.

In a *beer still* (or "stripper still"), a continuous flow of beer enters the tall column about two-thirds of the way up, dropping down through a series of perforated plates, while live steam makes its way up through the same plates. As the alcohol is heated, it's stripped out of the beer and rises near the top, where it is collected and sent to a *doubler*, a rudimentary type of pot still, and then to a condenser. The leftover beer, still containing the grain solids and dead yeast, drains to the bottom; this is the *sour mash* that goes in the fermenters to feed the yeast and set the optimal pH level of the mash.

The "new make," or "white dog," the just-distilled spirit, is clear as water and smells mainly of the sweetness of the grain, accentuated by the sweetness of the alcohol. Now it is *proofed*, where water is slowly added to bring it down to the proof, the percentage of alcohol desired for barreling. The proofed spirit is poured into a barrel; American whiskey regulations require that it is no more than 125° proof (62.5 percent ABV).

The barrel may be a new charred white oak barrel (required by regulation for whiskeys like bourbon, rye, or wheat) or a used oak barrel that once held other whiskey or wine or a fortified wine, like sherry or port. The barrel is closed with a wooden or silicon plug, called a *bung*, and stored in a warehouse to age.

Over the next however-many years, the whiskey will push into the wood as the summer heat makes it expand and pull back out as the cold of winter makes it contract. The warehouse may be heated and cooled to create that effect on a more rapid, consistent basis. The spirit is extracting color, flavor, and aroma from the wood; it is slowly reacting with oxygen to create new aromas; and the layer of barrel char is filtering undesirable flavors and aromas out of the spirit. The blender, the warehouse manager,

(Continued on page 24)

MILLING: ROLLER VS. HAMMER

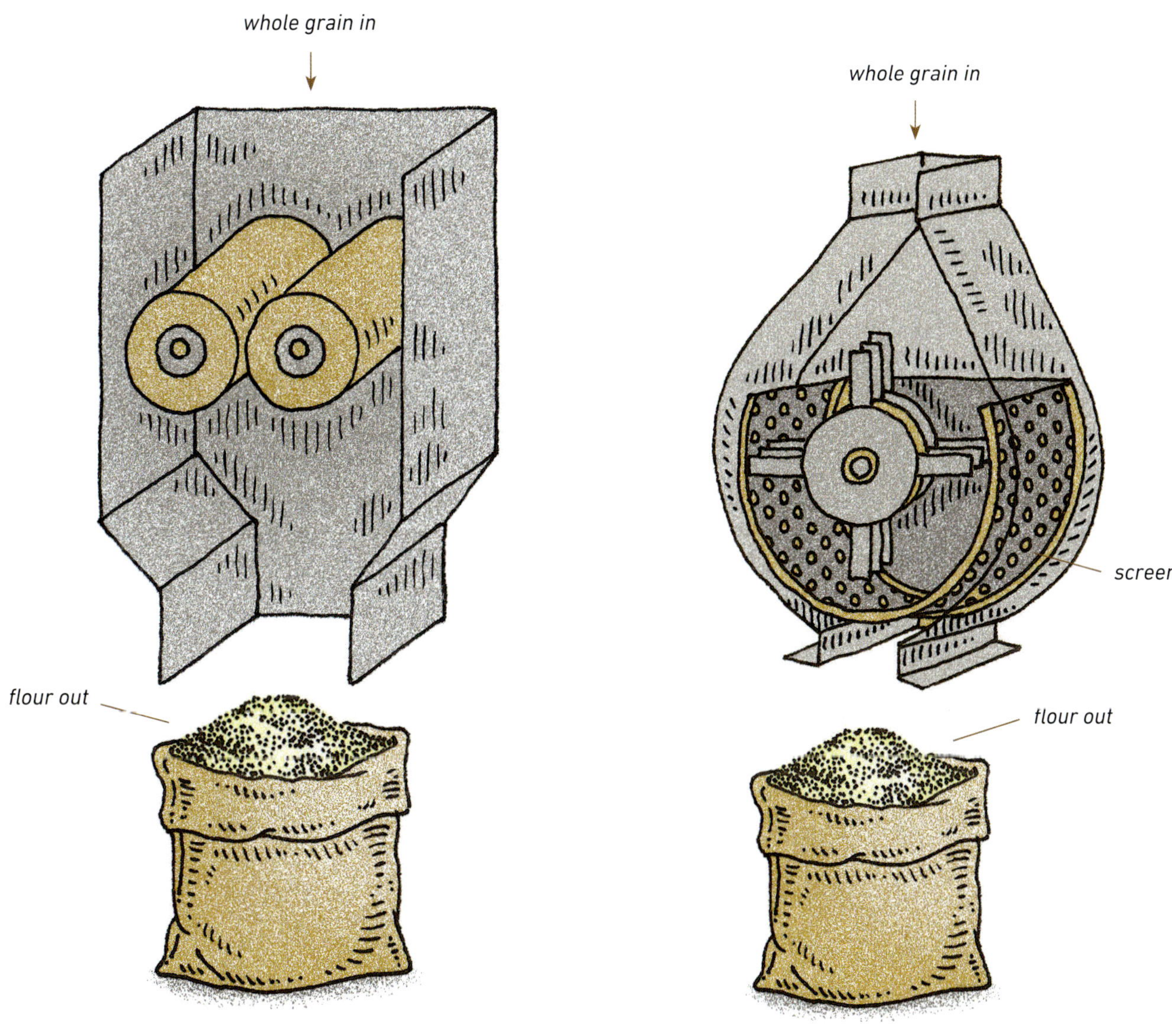

cut away of roller mill

hammer mill

MOONSHINE

You have probably heard of moonshine, the colloquial name for illegally made (and therefore untaxed) spirits. They are usually unaged and not made from all grain: Corn sugar is a common shortcut. Some are better than others, and you may hear stories about moonshine that is "finer than store-bought whiskey."

Pardon my French, but poppycock. Moonshiners may take pride in their product, but they're not doing any more work than they have to, and then only to be slightly better than their local competition. No one makes 'shine for the purpose of making fine whiskey; they do it to make some relatively easy money. Thanks to the high taxes on spirits in many states, illicit distillation can be a profitable sideline, if you can keep it hidden.

And you have to keep it hidden pretty well, because if you get caught, it's a large fine plus jail time. It doesn't matter if you're "only making it for friends," or giving it away. If you make spirits without a license in the United States and most countries (except New Zealand), you are committing a crime. There have been some recent court rulings that may lead to a change in that, but unless you've got a lawyer on retainer, I wouldn't count on that.

Real Moonshine

Unaged, unnamed, untaxed, illegal: the real thing, from central Pennsylvania. Clear, smelling sharply of alcohol and sugar. Hot, a bit rough, cornmeal sweet, short hot finish, surprisingly clean.

What about the bottles of "moonshine" you see on store shelves, usually flavored with fruit or spices, from a variety of sources? That's a catch-22: They're legal because they're licensed, but because they're legal, they're not *really* moonshine. That's part of its very definition: It's called moonshine because it's made by the light of the moon, under the cover of darkness, because if you get caught, it's the hoosegow for you. "Legal moonshine" is an oxymoron, like "deafening silence."

It is a fun segment of the industry, though it's not *always* whiskey. We'll have a look at it later. But the moonshine part is a marketing story, a nudge and a wink.

What is interesting is that those flavorings are a callback to the way whiskey was made back in the very dawn of distilled spirits. Flavorings were added because distillation was such an arcane process, the spirits were often made palatable only by the additions. In the real world of moonshine, if you come across the very fringy type, sold in Mason jars or simple plastic jugs, you'll often encounter flavorings for just that reason.

My advice? Stick to store-bought.

A small, crude moonshine still

and the distiller will keep tabs on the barrels, tasting a representative sample over the years to see how they are developing.

When the whiskey is ready, properly aged and tasting the way it should for the style that's being made from it, the barrel is removed from the warehouse and *dumped*. (That's what emptying barrels is called throughout the industry; in fact, they get dumped into a "dump trough.") It may be only lightly filtered to remove any bits of barrel char, or chilled and more tightly filtered to prevent any protein haziness in your bottle or glass. Some whiskeys are allowed by regulation to have small amounts of "traditional" flavors and colors added at this point, but for bourbon, any such additions are forbidden.

The whiskey is usually blended with other barrels at this time, or it may go for a single-cask bottling. Once the desired flavor and character are achieved and the blender or distiller is satisfied, the whiskey is proofed to bottling strength (or left as it came from the barrel, for a cask-strength whiskey). Then it is bottled, labeled, boxed, shipped, and sold, perhaps to you or me.

That's how whiskey is made. It is a product that is a result of natural ingredients like grain and water; processes like fermentation and distillation; chemical and physical interactions with oak over a number of years; and decisions made by human beings all along the way.

Whiskey flavor doesn't come from any single place. There are sources that have more effect than others—the barrel, the grain, the yeast, for example—but many, many things contribute to the final totality that is each bottle of whiskey, and the next, and the next.

It doesn't matter if it's a $20 bottle from the bottom shelf or a $12,000 bottle locked and chained in a display cabinet. It's still materials, process, environment, and the people who put them together. Is water a minor source of flavor? It's a major part of the whiskey, and you can't mash or ferment without it. Does it matter if the barrel is in a warehouse on a hill or in a valley? Air flow is greater on the hilltop, which affects evaporation rates. Does it matter what strain of corn or rye you use? Blind tastings can show small but definite differences.

Understanding these flavor-creation inputs is the key to understanding whiskey. When you learn them, you can talk about whiskey in a more informed way and ask questions from a more informed vantage. You're more likely to understand the answers, too.

The importance of the building blocks of flavor is not equal. Neither is it absolute, because their importance depends on the whiskey being created. Yeast is crucial to every whiskey, but particularly to whiskeys with rye in the mash, because which yeast is used determines the amount of rye "spiciness" that will be expressed. The uniformity of the new, charred oak barrel is important to bourbon and rye, but an American single malt may use different types of used barrel. The type and strain of grain is important to a craft distiller because it can represent a critical advantage and point of difference.

Perhaps most importantly, *none* of the ingredients or processes are unimportant; all must be considered. From the type of barrel and the time spent in it, to the temperature of the fermentation and the shape of the still, down to where the oak for the barrel grew and the weather on the day the grain was harvested, whiskey is solid proof of the butterfly effect. That's what makes it wonderful. There are always new whiskeys waiting to be made.

If you're ready, let's start taking this stuff apart, piece by piece. We'll start with the rules, regulations, traditions, and expectations that make the types of American whiskey distinct and different, and the free-flowing innovation that characterizes craft distillers. And then, we'll make some whiskey.

Frozen yeast samples at Wilderness Trail Distillery (Danville, KY)

Genuine Small Batch
Dad's Hat
PENNSYLVANIA RYE WHISKEY
CRAFT WHISKEY OF THE YEAR
Whisky
45% ALC/VOL
90 PROOF
BERNHEIM ORIGINAL
KENTUCKY STRAIGHT
WHEAT WHISKEY
7 YEARS AGED
SMALL BATCH
BERNHEIM ORIGINAL
Maker's Mark
S IV
KENTUCKY STRAIGHT BOURBON
WHISKY
Handmade since 1953
Made by the Maker's Mark Distillery Inc., Star Hill Farm,
Loretto, KY., under the personal supervision of ROB SAMUELS
750 mL · 45% ALC./VOL.

2

Meet the Traditional Whiskeys

When you inspect the selection at a whiskey bar or a good liquor store, you'll see that there are two major types of American whiskey. Bourbon is dominant, and rye has come back into its own. The traditional whiskey makers, the "legacy" distillers as some call them, make the vast bulk of these whiskeys by volume, and the names are the most familiar: Jim Beam, Jack Daniel's, Heaven Hill, Buffalo Trace, Four Roses, Wild Turkey. Many of these distillers have grown in size recently—some quite strikingly—as whiskey sales have increased strongly. They have been joined by newer, smaller distillers over the past thirty-odd years.

As whiskey caught on, distillers brought back older styles that had vanished, or maybe clung to existence with only a couple brands, like corn whiskey, wheat whiskey, or light whiskey. It's been an exciting, heady time.

There have also been a lot of experiments with other grains, and an emerging American single malt category; we'll cover them in the next chapter.

The thing to remember, of course, is that *all* whiskeys are very similar at their heart. As we noted in the last chapter, they are all fermented grain beverages that have been distilled and then aged in wooden barrels. The differences come from the grain, the mashing and fermentation, the distillation, the aging, and then the selection of barrels for bottling.

The major whiskey groups are traditional, but those traditions led to regulation. The federal government has "standards of identity," a set of actual regulations that lay down the differences between bourbon and corn whiskey, for example. There are quite a few of these differences: The standards of identity define *thirty-five* types of whiskey that can be made in America.

We won't be going through each of them! That's largely because some of them are of historical interest only, and no whiskeys—that I know of—are currently being made to those specifications.

Another reason not to address each one separately is because there's a lot of overlap. For example, sixteen are different types of blended whiskey. Every one of those types is slightly different, but they are more similar among themselves than to those from the other types. The same goes for the seven straight whiskeys and the six "whiskeys": They're quite similar indeed, except for the dominant grain, and the barrel requirements for corn whiskey (which I *will* address).

That's not to say the standards of identity are not important. The building blocks of flavor that we'll look at in this chapter are largely based on those regulations and the traditions they stem from. They are not inconsequential.

We'll start with the oldest type of whiskey that can be said to be "American": rye whiskey.

Rye Whiskey

American rye whiskey is the first one we'll talk about because it's older than bourbon. Rye came here with European settlers and was being made before the Revolutionary War.

Quite a bit before, actually. The earliest written mention of rye used to make spirits in the American colonies was in a letter dated April 13, 1648. Cocktail and spirits historian David Wondrich told me about the letter.

"The first mention of distilling rye in America is in correspondence between people in the Massachusetts Colony in 1648, where one of them asks about the 'German recipe' for making rye whiskey," he said. He forwarded a digital copy of the letter to me; it's held at the Massachusetts Historical Society in Boston.

The letter is from Emanuel Downing in Boston, to John Winthrop "at Pequoyt," and notes, "I have even now sold my horse to James Oliver for 10 [pounds?] to purchase the still, I pray remember me about the German receipt for making strong water with rye meall [sic] without maulting [sic] of the Corne[sic]..." (*Corne* is used here in the sense of grain, as you'd see it in the word *barleycorn*.)

Downing then writes to Winthrop again, most immodestly, in October 1648 that "I haue [sic] wrought in stilling these 3 moneths [sic], the water I mak [sic] is desired more & rather then [sic] the best spirits they bring from London."

Note that "German receipt." Rye spirit was being made by this time in central Europe, in Bohemia, and in the cluster of small states that is now Germany. It's still made there; they call it "Korn" or "Kornbrand": grain brandy, most often made from rye or wheat.

Korn is an unaged spirit that might be flavored with spices or fruit. I grew up in Pennsylvania Dutch country, where this would have been common. That tradition lived on in "cherry bounce," a concoction that was kept under the bar in a couple country inns I used to frequent. A jar of cherries, a scoop of brown sugar, and maybe a cinnamon stick, topped up with blended whiskey. The bartender would pour shots off the top on occasion for regulars. A whiskey-soaked cherry was a special reward for a particularly witty story or difficult task performed.

Rye was a well-liked grain for whiskey partly because it grows well in marginal soil (and so vigorously that it will choke out most weeds). The other part is because it makes very tasty whiskey, even in relatively small additions, even before aging. It's hard to argue with rye whiskey as a choice when no less an American than George Washington decided to make it in retirement at Mount Vernon.

Rye moved west with the settlers who set up in the Monongahela River Valley in southwestern Pennsylvania. Settlers grew it in the rocky soil, harvested it, and in time-honored tradition, mashed and distilled it for easier transport. This Monongahela Rye, the first geographically famous whiskey from the young country, would be almost entirely rye and malted rye. Barley malt had more enzymatic power for converting starches to sugars, but it was not common on the frontier.

Neither was money, which led to trouble when the new nation decided to impose a tax on spirits. The Whiskey Rebellion was the result, and although it eventually ended in a relatively peaceful manner, thanks to the wise mercy of President Washington, some of the more dissatisfied farmer-distillers decided to leave the Mon Valley, looking for more freedom. They rafted down the Ohio River to join the settlers in Kentucky, who were making a whiskey with a grain from the New World: corn. This new whiskey, which came to be called bourbon, would challenge and ultimately dominate rye whiskey in the American market, and in American culture.

Rye was still in for a good long run, though. Rye whiskey distillation was one of the earliest drivers of industrialization in the Monongahela River Valley, with large distilleries like Overholt, Gibson, and, well, Large (in West Elizabeth, Pennsylvania). These distilleries were major sources of income for the area and made quite a few fortunes.

Prohibition hit rye particularly hard, as Canadian whiskies, with their rye-flavored character, were smuggled in to slake a dry nation's thirst. When Repeal came, rye struggled to come back against them. It almost died out, reaching a nadir in the mid-1990s, when total rye whiskey sales dipped below twenty thousand cases a year. An ad hoc alliance of bartenders, whiskey writers, and craft distillers brought it back from the teetering edge of extinction, though, and now rye has regained a solid place on the back bar.

STRAIGHT REFERS TO AGE

I'll tell you truthfully: I've learned to not trust what everyone tells me about whiskey, or what I think I know about whiskey. You have to keep digging. One of the things you'll hear is that "the word *straight* on an American whiskey label refers to age; once a whiskey is two years old, it can be labeled as straight. It's not about purity." I know I've said that in the past. It is about age, but...that's not the whole story.

One of the touchstones of American whiskey is that unlike every other major whiskey region—Scotch, Irish, Canadian, Japanese—American regulations do not allow the addition of color or flavor to the whiskey outside of the direct process: no added caramel color, no direct additions of wine or other spirits, no fruit juices. If you do add that, your product becomes something else and must be clearly labeled as such; for example, "straight bourbon infused with natural flavors."

Except that it *is* allowed, in some cases. If you go digging in the Code of Federal Regulations (CFR), Title 27, "Alcohol, Tobacco Products and Firearms," buried way down in "Labeling and Advertising of Distilled Spirits," Section 5.23: "Alteration of class and type," you can find this little land mine. I've *added emphasis* in a few places.

"There may be added to *any class or type* of distilled spirits, without changing the class or type thereof, (i) such harmless coloring, flavoring, or blending materials as are an essential component part of the particular class or type of distilled spirits to which added, and (ii) harmless coloring, flavoring, or blending materials (HCFBM) such as caramel, *straight malt or straight rye malt whiskies*, fruit juices, sugar, infusion of oak chips when approved by the Director, or wine, which are *not an essential component part* of the particular distilled spirits to which added, but which are *customarily employed* therein in accordance with *established trade usage*, if such coloring, flavoring, or blending materials *do not total more than 2½ percent by volume* of the finished product." (27 CFR § Section 5.23 [2020])

And yes, "any class or type of distilled spirits" does include whiskey. Most whiskey. Let's figure this out.

Like many weird little things in the CFR, this is explained and explicated in the Beverage Alcohol Manual, the BAM, the federal government's guide to the ins and outs of the standards of identity as laid out in the Code of Federal Regulations. The BAM gives an example of the use of HCFBM in whiskey in Chapter 7, "Coloring/Flavoring/Blending Materials."

"Traditionally, to ensure consistency in color and smoothness, caramel color and blending sherry are added to blended whisky. Consequently, provided the total addition of caramel and blending sherry does not exceed 2½% by volume of the blended whisky, these coloring and blending materials are considered 'harmless.'"

The example says "blended whisky," and sadly, in the American market these days, blended whiskeys are cheap, commodity brands that are largely whiskey-flavored alcohol. But the example isn't the *only* way this exemption can be used, as you can see in a table in the BAM in that same chapter.

If you look at the table to see which spirits are allowed to include HCFBM, you'll see a whole list of blended whiskey types. But you'll also see check marks in the YES column on corn whiskey, wheat whiskey, and . . . rye whiskey.

Many of us learned that rye whiskey was allowed to have these "customary" flavorings or colorings back in 2014, when Mark Gillespie interviewed the owners of Templeton Rye on his *WhiskyCast* podcast, and they brought that up as something they do, in a nod to the roots of the whiskey they were emulating. It was a shock, but at the time, most people didn't notice that corn, wheat, and malt whiskeys could also do that.

However, you won't see those check marks next to *straight* corn, wheat, malt, or rye whiskeys. So yes, in this case, "straight" on the label is indeed a promise of purity; if the label says "straight rye whiskey," the whiskey is at least two years old and free of HCFBMs.

And bourbon? Straight or not, no colorings, flavorings, or "blending materials" are allowed in any whiskey labeled as "bourbon," harmless or not. Period. It is an exception, in a way that remains true to the distillers who pushed for whiskey regulations like the 1897 Bottled-in-Bond Act.

Old Overholt Bottled in Bond Rye

Unfiltered bonded rye. Bitter rye oils first, quickly followed by sweet grain, vanilla, rye bread. Bitter/sweet, oily on the tongue. Long warm finish, bitter rye, spicy oak, sweet corn. A carousel of flavors.

Bourbon

Rye's competition, that new whiskey, "bourbon," came out of Kentucky, though there are some claims from Virginia of a corn-based spirit being made there much earlier. I don't put a lot of stock in them; there's mention in letters from the 1600s of a "liquor" made from "corn," but both of those were much looser-defined terms at the time (Chaucer refers to rain as "switch licour," or "sweet liquor," in the opening lines of *The Canterbury Tales*), and there is no solid evidence of a still. Kentucky has the full receipts, so that's where we'll place it.

No one is completely sure where the word *bourbon* comes from, or exactly who first decided to age it in charred oak barrels, or even who decided to make it from corn. There are some hints and partial clues, though.

Evan Williams, namesake of Heaven Hill's flagship bourbon, is often mentioned as the first bourbon distiller, in 1783. Noted bourbon historian Michael R. Veach doesn't buy it. In his *Kentucky Bourbon Whiskey* (2013), Veach points out that Evan Williams wasn't even in North America yet, let alone Kentucky. He cites "the existence of a receipt for Williams's passage from London to Philadelphia on the ship *Pigoe* dated May 1, 1784."

There are other contenders, but again, Veach disposes of those claims by virtue of the lack of actual records. The liquor industry is tracked to the nth degree by government records because liquor has been taxed almost since it was discovered. No government in Kentucky in the 1770s and 1780s; no taxes, no records.

We will most likely never know, at least with any degree of certainty, who the first person was to distill corn into whiskey. This shouldn't be surprising; we don't have the name of the first person to brew beer or blow glass either. Even Emanuel Downing, our Massachusetts rye distiller, is only the first person we have a written record of making rye whiskey. We don't know that he was the first person to make rye whiskey in America; after all, he was asking someone else for the recipe on how to do it.

Someone made bourbon, though, and it's not surprising. When Europeans, and then Americans, got to a new land (new to them, at least) back in this era, one of the first things they did was look for something to ferment.

The native grain, maize (American corn, and that's the last time I'll use the word *maize*), was a natural. It grew well in Kentucky's rich soil, and still does. Cornfields still blanket the area. Once it's harvested and dried, it can be easily stored, on or off the cob. The large stalks can be fed to livestock. Corn was, and still is, the basis of cheap and filling food: cornmeal mush, cornbread, corn fritters, and the ubiquitous grits, and cornmeal makes a great filler for blood and offal sausages.

It is not the easiest grain to ferment and distill. It is low in the enzymes needed to convert its bountiful amounts of starch to sugars. But cook the corn and add barley malt, and you'll soon be stirring some sweet mash.

Whiskey was practically currency on the cash-poor frontier, and it was bartered or traded for the manufactured and imported goods the farmer-distillers needed. As they got better at growing corn and at making whiskey, some of these distillers inevitably began to trade whiskey in bigger markets. The way to get whiskey to those markets was barrels.

The barrel is a remarkable invention. Even though an oak barrel is quite heavy—a standard 53-gallon (200.6 liter) barrel weighs about 110 pounds (50 kg) empty; a 20-gallon (75.7 liter) barrel weighs about 60 pounds (27 kg)—it still weighs a lot less than the number of ceramic jugs needed to carry a similar amount of whiskey.

But wood isn't inert, like ceramic. A barrel will keep the flavor of whatever was stored in it: flour, nails, whiskey...dried fish. There is lore (i.e., made-up stories that people just keep telling) that because barrels retained that smell, distillers would build a fire inside a used barrel to burn that smell and taste out, because barrels were too expensive to use new ones all the time. That's the reason why bourbon barrels are charred...we're told.

Michael Veach to the rescue again. In *Kentucky Bourbon Whiskey*, he quotes an 1826 letter from a merchant in Lexington, Kentucky, to a distiller in Bourbon County, Kentucky, John Corlis, about barrels of whiskey to be purchased. The merchant, clearly someone with some experience with liquor, suggests that if Corlis charred the barrels to a depth of "say only a 16th of an inch, that it will much improve it . . . "

Veach explains that this was an aging tweak already widely used for brandy and cognac, popular imports in the French-influenced New Orleans, the main overseas trading port for Kentuckians, both import and export. Did the Lexington merchant know about cognac aging and the charred barrel trick? Did he make the leap that this was what made cognac so rich?

Again, we don't know. But it looks like a good case can be made for the thought that this was at least when it was happening, if not the very first time. It wasn't long after that when people started talking about the color of bourbon, the brown glow, or the hint of garnet that would lead to the title of Irvin S. Cobb's novel about the whiskey industry, *Red Likker* (1929).

(Then again, when I talked to Andrew Wiehebrink, a wood specialist we'll talk to more in Chapter 10, he casually mentioned that the charred oak barrel was a relatively new idea. "The char system wasn't even set until the 1950s," he said. "I read a 1908 ACS [American Chemical Society] paper about aging whiskey, and there wasn't a mention of char, not one." I'll guess I'll chew on that in the next book.)

To me, this cognac connection leading to a deliberate aging of bourbon makes a lot more sense than the usual tale about people noticing that the barreled whiskey tasted better after floating down the Ohio and Mississippi rivers to New Orleans on flatboats. Floating a flatboat from the Falls of the Ohio at Louisville, Kentucky, to New Orleans takes only about a month, and it's not likely that the whiskey would taste *that* much better.

But why do we call it bourbon? There are several theories. There's a Bourbon County in Kentucky (that used to be part of a bigger county in Virginia). But bourbon whiskey was made in other places, and there's no real evidence that the Bourbon County stuff was better, as some have suggested.

Maybe it was because the aged whiskey, the "red likker," was sold on Bourbon Street in New Orleans? Before you dismiss that, that street has been called Bourbon Street since 1721. It could well be. Or, as Veach suggests, was it a marketing idea to make it appeal to the French expatriates in New Orleans?

The truth is we just don't know. Let's stick to drinking it, and we can talk about what it tastes like and why, and note that it's all the result of a number of things that came together over the course of about fifty years in Kentucky and New Orleans. By the 1840s, everything was in place and we had a whiskey.

Unfortunately, by the 1880s we had screwed it up. Some blenders (called "rectifiers" in those days) were starting with cheap whiskey—or plain neutral spirits—and adding flavoring and sugars to it using various recipes, then labeling the result as "old bourbon." Actual bourbon distillers were horrified and realized that action had to be taken to protect their product's integrity. A group of distillers petitioned the government to regulate their industry.

The initial result was the Bottled-in-Bond Act of 1897, which set up a definition for "bottled in bond" spirits; bourbon would be chief among them. To be labeled as bottled in bond, a bourbon had to be the product of one distillery, with all the whiskey in the batch distilled in one six-month distilling "season," under the supervision of the same master distiller, and aged in a bonded warehouse under the scrutiny of a U.S. Treasury agent. Additionally, it had to be at least four years old and bottled at 50 percent (100° proof). This represented a government (and industry) guarantee that the bourbon was pure, unadulterated, and sufficiently aged.

Some reputable distillers, however, found this too restrictive and asked for further regulation. The initial result was the Pure Food and Drug Act of 1906, but it was a compromise that no one was really happy with. In 1909, President William Howard Taft (opposite) undertook to create a regulatory definition of whiskey (and isn't that the kind of work presidents should be doing?). The Taft Decision, issued on December 27, 1909, was the core of what would become the "standards of identity," the current definition of American whiskey.

Briefly, Taft said that:

- Whiskey had to be made from grain.
- A product that was all aged-grain spirits was to be labeled "straight whiskey."
- If high-proof unaged grain distillate ("neutral spirits") was flavored with a percentage of whiskey, it had to be labeled as "blended."

A critical addition would be made in 1938 when the requirement for new, charred oak containers for aging would be added. Amazingly, the requirement that American whiskey be *made in America* was added only in 1964.

Compare these to the modern requirements, the "standards of identity" as they are put forth in the Code of Federal Regulations, Title 27, Subpart C,

Section 5.143, and enforced by the Alcohol and Tobacco Tax and Trade Bureau (commonly shortened to TTB.) To my amusement, this defining *American* regulation spells "whisky" without an "e" throughout. A recent change to the regulations acknowledges that either spelling is acceptable.

There, bourbon, along with rye, wheat, malt, rye malt, "or [name of other grain] Whisky" (I'm absolutely not kidding; it says "[name of other grain]" right in the regulation) is defined as being:

- Distilled from a fermented grain mash of not less than 51 percent corn in the case of bourbon (or rye, wheat, etc. for those respective whiskey types)
- Distilled to a proof no higher than 160° (80 percent alcohol by volume; ABV)
- Aged at a starting strength no higher than 125° proof, in a charred new oak barrel (though no *minimum* period is given for the aging; the standards actually say "stored")
- Bottled at no less than 80° proof, with no coloring or flavoring added (see sidebar about allowed additions on page 30)
- Further, if it is aged for more than two years in the oak, it is allowed to be labeled as "straight whiskey"; if it is aged fewer than four years, it must have an age statement on the label; if it is aged at least four years, it may have an age statement, but it is not required.

I believe that these regulations have a more direct impact on the flavor and character of American whiskey than do most other countries' whiskey

regulations. The charred, new oak barrels are generally considered to be the source of at least 50 percent of the aroma and flavor of bourbon; most industry people believe it to be closer to 70 percent.

Many world whiskey regulations allow coloring additions. Bourbon does not, although other types of American whiskey do. There are more details on what's allowed, what isn't, and how you can tell if anything's been added in the "*Straight Refers to Age*" sidebar (page 30). The regulations mean that bourbon and "straight" American whiskeys are transparent for consumers in terms of contents. I'd like to see more transparency on origin; bottlers can choose to largely duck saying where the whiskey in the bottle was made.

The way the regulations are written also means that there is a fair amount of overlap in the flavor profiles of the different American straight whiskeys. The new charred barrel and the prohibition of additives mean that the main differences among these whiskeys stem directly from the base grains, and those can be relatively subtle differences; for instance, in the case of a bourbon with a high amount of rye in the mash versus a rye whiskey with the regulatory minimum of 51 percent rye in the mash.

Wild Turkey 101

Aromas of hot honey atop skillet corn bread, lightly dusted with baking spices. All that hits the palate, with refined warmth. Finish shows some red fruit; could be a bit longer. Classic.

That's not surprising, because the regulations essentially read like this: "This is how you make bourbon; to make other whiskeys, make them *like* bourbon, but with different grains." Bourbon is the big daddy of the category in terms of sales and in cultural impact as well. This big, burly workhorse has ruled the American whiskey category for decades, and I don't expect that to change any time soon.

Tennessee Whiskey

Tennessee whiskey used to be pretty simple. There was Jack Daniel's, there was Dickel (at least, after 1959, when the distillery opened), and that was it. What set them apart from bourbon, we were told, was what Jack Daniel's called the "Lincoln County Process," where the new distillate passed through ten feet of sugar maple charcoal before going into the barrel.

But "Tennessee whiskey" was not, and is not, part of the federal standards of identity. Tennessee whiskey, as Jack Daniel's is made—

(Okay, let's get this out of the way: George Dickel is a relatively well-known brand, is the second-best selling Tennessee whisky (as they choose to spell it on their labels), and makes some flat-out excellent whisky, but Jack Daniel's outsells Dickel by a huge margin. Really, when you talk about Tennessee whiskey, you're talking about Jack Daniel's.)

This description is going to be more about a somewhat amusing regulatory dance than about flavor and aroma, but it's important. It matters to people. It matters to the makers of Tennessee whiskey, because it's their heritage, and their identity, and their brand. It matters to drinkers, because it's something we like to...*discuss*. "Discussing" the difference between bourbon and Tennessee whiskey with a bartender got me thrown out of a bar once, before I'd even had a drink.

Let's have a look at it. Tennessee whiskey checks all the regulatory boxes as "bourbon": the 51+ percent corn, final distillation and barrel entry proofs, new charred oak barrel, no additions of color or flavor, age guidelines, all that. The difference is that pre-barrel filtering through charcoal, "leaching" as they used to call it, back before the marketers saw "leaching" and said, "Ew."

But even that doesn't mean it's not bourbon. As my colleague and friend Chuck Cowdery pointed out in his eponymous blog back in 2018, the charcoal leaching takes place *before* the spirit touches the barrel, which by the regulations means it is not yet whiskey, let alone bourbon whiskey. "You can't change the classification of something unclassified," he said.

So it is bourbon. Except it's also *not* bourbon. In the years during Prohibition and after Repeal, the Jack Daniel distillery was owned by the Motlow family; some of you may remember that Lem Motlow's name was on the label until 2011. With Repeal, in 1934, came new definitions of whiskey, which, importantly, *required* a whiskey to be labeled as the classification it fit.

Repeal didn't pass in Tennessee until 1937, and when it did, Lem's brother, Reagor Motlow, was ready to go to war. He petitioned the federal government to make a classification for "Tennessee whiskey," because they'd never labeled their whiskey as "bourbon," and neither had Mister Jack himself. They didn't want to be forced to do so.

After a time, in 1941, the Internal Revenue Service, in their capacity as the governing body for taxation of spirits (and therefore the keeper of the regulations pertaining to their definition), issued a letter on the subject. There's a copy on Cowdery's blog (along with more on the whole Reagor Motlow story), and it's pretty succinct, only two paragraphs. They note the label that was submitted, along with "an explanation of your distilling and leaching processes."

It's the second paragraph that's the meat of the letter. After analysis and "careful consideration," the Alcohol Tax Unit laboratory reached a conclusion: "In the view of the nature of this process and of the results of the analyses, it has been concluded that the whiskey in question has neither the characteristics of bourbon or rye whiskey but rather is a distinctive product which may be labeled whiskey."

 **George Dickel Bottled in Bond**

2019, 2nd release. Big nose: roasted corn, stone fruit, berry pastilles. All that in the mouth, plus dry oak, anise notes, a light sweetness. Beguiling finish, begs another sip. Sophisticated bonded whiskey.

Whiskey is the catch-all regulatory term for spirits that didn't specifically meet any of the narrower category definitions. That suited the Motlows, and they took that "whiskey" classification and legally, properly, parked "Tennessee" in front of it, since that is where their particular whiskey is made. Since then, the Tennessee legislature has made "Tennessee whiskey" a defined product, centered on the charcoal leaching process, but the federal regulations have never done so.

Meanwhile . . . does the Lincoln County Process, the charcoal leaching, actually make a difference? I got to taste new make at Dickel once. There was the first-run spirit off the column still: rough, full of coarse corn notes. Then after that had passed through the doubler: cleaned up, more focused, more like clean cornmeal. Finally, the filtered spirit as it was ready to go in the barrel: pure, essential, like a corn eau de vie. There wasn't just a difference—there was a clear difference.

If you're still in any doubt about Tennessee whiskey versus bourbon, let me add a couple more quotes from a story I wrote for the Daily Beast website back in 2021.

Nicole Austin, master distiller at Dickel: "Making it in Tennessee and using the Lincoln County Process makes it a Tennessee version of bourbon. It is its own thing and it is also bourbon. Both can be true."

(It's worth noting that Austin has overseen the creation of a George Dickel *bourbon* that is blended from selected barrels of Dickel whiskey, no difference in the process, just a difference in the individual barrels. And it's delicious, and definitely different.)

Chris Fletcher, master distiller at Jack Daniel's: "Tennessee Whiskey does completely qualify as bourbon. We . . . believe the charcoal mellowing process is a long-standing tradition that deserves its own designation, which is what the Tennessee Whiskey Law passed in 2013 does. In short, charcoal mellowing doesn't *prevent* us from labeling our whiskey as 'bourbon whiskey'—it *allows* us to label it as 'Tennessee Whiskey.'"

If that's not enough, Robert Hall, the CEO at the Ole Smoky distillery in Gatlinburg, concurs: "The James Ownby whiskey that we developed is both a straight bourbon whiskey, because its mash is primarily corn and it has been aged . . . in charred new oak barrels, and a Tennessee whiskey, because it has been mellowed through the Lincoln County filtering process."

The next time you get into the old "is Tennessee whiskey bourbon" argument, remember two things. First, don't get into the "is Tennessee whiskey bourbon" argument! But secondly . . . if you do? You're both right. Have a drink and talk about something else.

Old No.7 BRAND
JACK DANIEL'S
Old No.7 BRAND
Tennessee
SOUR MASH
WHISKEY
1,0 Litre 40% Vol.
DISTILLED AND BOTTLED BY
JACK DANIEL DISTILLERY
LYNCHBURG, TENNESSEE, USA
QUALITY & CRAFTSMANSHIP SINCE 1866
JASPER NEWTON
"JACK" DANIEL
HERE AT THE JACK DANIEL DISTILLERY, WE'RE PROUD TO HONOR THE INDEPENDENCE & INTEGRITY OF THE MAN WHO ESTABLISHED OUR DISTILLERY AT THE CAVE SPRING HOLLOW. TRUE TO MR. JACK'S WHISKEY-MAKING TRADITION, WE STILL MELLOW OUR WHISKEY DROP BY DROP AND STAND BY JACK'S CHARGE.
"EVERY DAY WE MAKE IT, WE'LL MAKE IT THE BEST WE CAN."

THE SMALL GRAINS

Bourbon is required to be a minimum of 51 percent corn, and the other main types of American whiskey also have a dominant grain: rye, wheat, malt. It's plain that other grains have to make up the rest of the recipe, the mash. Those other grains are referred to as "the small grains."

I haven't been able to learn if that's a distilling usage meaning that they're the non-dominant grains in the mash, or if it's the agronomic term for crops that are literally "small grains," like wheat, oats, barley, and rye; not corn, which is a larger kernel on a much larger stalk. It may well be both, or as one distiller told me, just not something they ever thought about.

As we'll discuss in Chapter 4, a certain amount of barley malt is needed for the enzymatic push to convert starches to sugars, somewhere between 5 and 15 percent. Some distillers add pure enzymes directly and skip or reduce the malt. Does it make a difference? Some tasters say they find flavor from the malt, whereas others do not; maybe it's a subtle part of the overall character. But mostly, malt's a functional ingredient.

After malt, the most common small grain in bourbons is rye, added for its distinct punch of flavor. Aficionados differ over the amount of rye they prefer in a bourbon; "high-rye" mash bills have their adherents, while some like more corn. New Riff, in Covington, Kentucky, has a high-rye bourbon mash bill with 65 percent corn, 30 percent rye, and 5 percent malt. George Dickel uses 84 percent corn, and 8 percent each of rye and malt.

Rye might be the most common third grain in bourbon, but a significant—and prized—number of bourbons use wheat instead, among them Maker's Mark, Old Fitzgerald, Rebel Yell, Weller, and, oops, almost forgot, the always hyped Van Winkle.

Why do these bourbons use wheat? Some of the reason is that it isn't rye. "Wheaters" don't have that rye bite but instead deliver a softer palate, one where the corn has more of a chance to shine through. Wheated bourbons also have a light aroma of whole wheat bread and may taste sweeter than a high-rye bourbon.

As we entered a period of innovation in the early 2000s, some "4-grain" bourbons emerged with both rye and wheat along with the malt and corn. There had been 4-grain bourbon before Prohibition, but none in the modern era until these. Some are good whiskeys in their own right, but I don't feel like there's a "4-grain character" that identifies them. It's fun, and we were interested to see them.

Non-bourbon straight whiskeys may, of course, have corn as a small grain. Efforts to revive the Monongahela style of rye whiskey include mash bills with significant percentages of malted rye as a small grain. Hotaling's Old Potrero rye is 100 percent malted rye.

They may be "small grains," but they can have a large effect on the aroma and flavor of the whiskeys they grace.

Corn Whiskey

Corn whiskey is a bit of an oddity in American whiskeys.

It is very focused in its makeup, requiring at least 80 percent corn in its mash bill; many corn whiskeys are 100 percent corn. More importantly, it's an outlier in American whiskey aging requirements in two ways: Uniquely, it doesn't have to be aged, and if it is, it cannot be aged in new charred barrels. The Beverage Alcohol Manual (BAM) says of corn whiskey: "*if* stored in oak containers stored at not more than 62.5% alcohol by volume (125 proof) in used or uncharred new oak containers and *not subjected in any manner* to treatment with charred wood" *(emphasis added).*

I'll repeat: "if stored." To a lawyer, like the ones who undoubtedly wrote the BAM, that clearly means that it does not have to be stored (aged) at all, and it means that to some distillers as well.

Every other type of straight whiskey is "stored . . . in charred new oak containers." Blended whiskeys are made, at least partly, with whiskeys that are stored in charred new oak. (There is a category of "distilled from a bourbon/rye/etc. mash whiskeys" that are also aged in used wood; see the sidebar on page 46.) And of course, straight corn whiskey has to be stored in oak for at least two years, but again, the BAM specifies "used or uncharred new oak containers."

This, I assume, is a tribute to corn whiskey's early origins, prior to the common use of freshly charred barrels. It results in a whiskey that is rich in corn flavor, with very little wood influence. Bourbon, naked, if you will. I'd suggest you try some corn whiskey if you haven't. Like the unaged new make spirits that have become available for purchase in the past ten years or so, corn whiskey is a chance to taste whiskey the way it tasted at the dawn of the industrial age, some two hundred years ago.

Don't give it *too* much respect; it's a drink, not a transcendental experience. Sometimes I drink it the way H. L. Mencken drank corn liquor at the Scopes Trial in 1925. "Ten minutes after I arrived a leading citizen offered me a drink made up half of white mule and half of coca cola." A hundred years later that fizzy blend's still tasty; you could do worse.

The classic Mellow Corn is a favorite of some of us; pure, sweet, fun. Craft distillers have been experimenting with corn whiskey too, and I've had some very good ones recently, including a barrel sample at Liberty Pole Spirits in Washington, Pennsylvania, that was so good I got a bottle of it.

Mellow Corn Bottled in Bond

Corn whiskey isn't bourbon. Try Mellow Corn, and you'll get corn—stewed, ground, baked—and some spicy notes of pepper. But there's no real oak character in this whiskey.

Wheat Whiskey

Wheat whiskey had disappeared from the American shelves well before I started drinking whiskey in earnest in the mid-1990s. The only information I was able to find about availability before that was a few late-nineteenth-century labels.

The reason we even talk about wheat whiskey is Heaven Hill's Bernheim Original wheat whiskey, which they introduced in 2005. Made with a mash bill of 51 percent wheat, 37 percent corn, and 12 percent barley malt, Bernheim made a small but significant initial impact simply by virtue of its uniqueness.

However, I quickly found that when I took a flask of Bernheim to non-whiskey events and sampled people on it, it made friends much more quickly than bourbon or Scotch. Bernheim, and other wheat whiskeys I've had since, is quite mellow, with a mild character that balances the bite of new charred oak with the soft sweetness of wheat. The recent introduction of a Bernheim Barrel Proof bottling puts some robust power and full flavor behind the brand.

Wheat whiskey is still a niche, and a small one, though Journeyman Distillery has also garnered some attention with their Corsets, Whips & Whiskey bottling (the name is a reference to their building in southwestern Michigan, which once housed a large factory that made stays for corsets, and buggy whips . . . out of turkey feathers). CW&W has won a slew of awards, including back-to-back "Whiskey of the Year" from the American Spirits Council of Tasters (ASCOT) Awards (a blind judging competition that I help judge). It's not just a great wheat whiskey; it's a great whiskey.

Bernheim

A 7-year-old wheat whiskey, over 51 percent wheat. Bright, fresh nose of cinnamon and sassafras root with oak framing. Lean, warming on the palate, firm oak spice with a restrained sweet finish.

BERNHEIM
ORIGINAL®
KENTUCKY STRAIGHT
WHEAT WHISKEY
7 YEARS AGED
45% ALC./VOL. (90 PROOF)
SMALL BATCH
BERNHEIM ORIGINAL
KENTUCKY STRAIGHT WHEAT WHISKEY

Blended and Light Whiskeys

Blended American whiskey and light whiskey are two whiskey types that aim to have less whiskey flavor. No, really, that's the whole idea. Let's have a look, because there's actually a small revival of these types going on.

We'll visit blended whiskey first. This is from the "standards of identity."

Blended whiskey is a mixture that contains straight whisky or a blend of straight whiskies at not less than 20 percent on a proof gallon basis, excluding alcohol derived from added harmless coloring, flavoring, or blending materials (it's our old pal, HCFBM!), and, separately or in combination, whisky or neutral spirits.

In other words, to be labeled "blended whiskey" in America, all you have to do is put one part straight whiskey in your blend, along with four parts "whisky of any type or neutral spirits." I don't know of any distillers who are blending four parts "whisky of any type." There might be, because there are an awful lot of distillers and whiskeys out there, but I'm unaware of them.

Most blends are legacy products, like Seagram's 7 Crown, or Kessler, or Four Queens, made with neutral spirits. Neutral spirits are what's referred to in the trade as GNS, which is "grain neutral spirits." They're fermented from grain, usually corn, and distilled out to about 95 percent ABV; no color, and no flavor or aroma other than the vague perceived sweetness of ethanol.

A distiller can buy bulk GNS from a huge manufacturer for an equivalent cost of less than a dollar per 25-ounce (750 ml) bottle. If that's 80 percent of your "blended whiskey," then the cost goes way down . . . along with flavor and complexity. A distiller *could* put more than 20 percent whiskey in a blend, and there are offshoots of the blended whiskey category that are made for that, the "blended bourbon whisky" (and the rye, rye malt, wheat, malt, and corn variants) that specifies "not less than 51% . . . straight bourbon whisky." There are a tiny number of these, and I'm somewhat interested in seeing what happens with the category.

But blended whiskey brands aren't as big in the United States as they were. The only American blended whiskey of any size is Seagram's 7 Crown, which still puts up a respectable two million cases a year. It was selling eight million cases in the 1970s. We like more whiskey in our whiskey these days.

Light whiskey is quite different from blended whiskey: No neutral spirits are blended in. It's all whiskey, but not the usual American type; it's a rough equivalent of Scotch grain whisky. From the Beverage Alcohol Manual: "whisky produced in the U.S. at more than 80% alcohol by volume (160 proof) [but less than 95% alcohol by volume (190 proof)] and stored in used or uncharred new oak containers." There's also a "blended light whisky" classification that is light whiskey with up to 20 percent straight whiskey that would be very close to the idea of blended Scotch, but I don't know of any being made. Pity.

The "light" doesn't refer to alcohol level or color, though light whiskeys are generally light in color; it's about the amount of flavor. I've been told by people in the industry that light whiskey was developed in the 1960s to compete with the growth of white spirits like vodka and gin, and blended Scotch. It never caught on (I haven't seen a lot of evidence that anyone really tried that hard to sell it), and some barrels aged a long time.

When whiskey got hot again, and folks started poking around in distillery inventories, looking for something to sell, someone tasted these old barrels of light whiskey and found them to be quite good. It's not surprising to me; one of my favorite Canadian whiskies, J.P. Wiser's 18 Year Old, is very similar to an American light whiskey. It's mellow, rounded, sweet with caramel but not cloying, a real all-afternoon drinker.

There are several light whiskeys on the market now, though it remains to be seen if they'll grow past that. Will blended whiskey make a similar surge, maybe by upping the percentage of straight whiskey in the blend? Time will tell. I'll try it.

There is one other whiskey category that's similar to these, so I'm going to tuck it in here: spirit whiskey. It's the very last American whiskey category in the BAM, and it's not alphabetical. Someone decided it was going to be last. To paraphrase: "Spirit whiskey is a blend of neutral spirits and not less than 5 percent whiskey, straight whiskey, or a combination . . . but less than 20 percent whiskey."

Spirit whiskey is barely whiskey-flavored. I only know of one on the market: Kansas Clean Distilled. It tastes sweet, and has a clean but creamy texture, and that's about all. Like I said: Someone decided it was going to be the last whiskey category.

DISTILLED FROM BOURBON MASH

There's another collection of types of whiskey that are much alike, and the lead category is "Whisky distilled from bourbon mash." There are similar classifications for rye, malted rye, wheat, and malt. If a whiskey is distilled from a bourbon mash, why wouldn't it be bourbon?

It's because the mash isn't the only thing that makes the whiskey. The BAM defines "whisky distilled from a bourbon mash" as "whisky produced in the U.S. at not exceeding 80% alcohol by volume (160 proof) from a fermented mash of not less than 51 percent corn and stored in used oak containers." That's pretty much a bourbon, but aged in used barrels, which sounds interesting, maybe something I'd like to try.

And I have, kind of; Crown Royal made a whisky with a label that was originally approved by the TTB, proclaiming "Crown Royal Bourbon Mash." As I understand it, it met the definition of the category, except that it was produced in Canada. But it also clearly said "Blended Canadian Whisky." The TTB decided to cancel the approval, and the whisky is now called "Blenders' Mash." (The taste? Sadly disappointing, mostly like a washed-out bourbon.)

There are a handful of these "bourbon mash" whiskeys on the market. In late 2024, for example, Woodinville Whiskey (Woodinville, Washington) released a very limited "distilled from bourbon mash" whiskey that was aged in second-use, re-charred barrels. I heard it was pretty good. But you won't find a lot of these whiskeys.

You may have noticed that there's no "whiskey distilled from a corn mash." That's because corn whiskey aged in used oak containers . . . would be corn whiskey. No need for a separate classification.

Everything Else

I say "everything else," but we're going to talk about American single malt, "moonshine," flavored whiskeys, state-specific whiskeys, and the craft outliers in the next chapter. What we're talking about here are odd little classifications that rarely get used, but not never. Turn on your flashlights—let's go exploring.

Here's an odd one. We've been obsessing a bit over the 51+ percent rules for the various grain-defined whiskeys. "Straight whisky"—just "straight whiskey," nothing else—dodges that: "whisky produced from a fermented mash of *less than* 51 percent of any one type of grain and stored in charred new oak containers for 2 years or more" *(emphasis added).* For instance, then, a mash bill of, say, 40 percent corn, 40 percent oats, 10 percent malt, and 10 percent raw barley. Why not?

There are also some so-called blended straights out there, what the BAM refers to as "a blend of straight whiskies," and there are two variants. If all the straight whiskeys in the blend are from the same state and contain HCFBMs, that's a blended straight. And if they are from different states, but do *not* contain HCFBMs? Still a blended straight.

If all of the straight whiskeys in the blend are from the same state and it doesn't contain HCFBMs, it's *not* a blend of straights. That's just a straight whiskey. And to my frustration, the BAM is silent on what a blend of straight whiskeys from different states that contains HCFBMs is called. Or if it's even allowed.

A blend of straight bourbons, though, that's pretty simple. That's a blend of all straight bourbon whiskeys; nothing about what states they're from, just a blend of straights. And all the usual variants, a blend of straight ryes, wheats, etc., works the same way.

And that's it! We're done here. My head hurts. Let's put the BAM aside and go have some fun with the new American whiskeys.

Lost Lantern Whiskey
Far-Flung Burbon II

A blend of straight bourbons. Five bourbons (one from a distillery, Rich Grain, that has closed), five states at barrel proof: 126.6°. Rich warehouse reek: mature oak, dark caramel, nice citrus top notes. Youthful, lively, full-bodied. Long finish, oak-framed and sweet. Hail the blend!

Ole
Smoky
Tennessee
Moonshine
750ml
35% ALC./VOL
(70 PROOF)
NEW YORK
AGED FOR THREE YEARS
RAGTIME
RYE
NEW YORK STRAIGHT
RYE WHISKEY
NEW YORK
FROM LOCALLY GROWN RYE
SKREWBALL
PEANUT BUTTER WHISKEY
TO THE MISFITS, BLACK SHEEP AND SKREWBALLS
WHISKEY WITH NATURAL FLAVORS
ROCKY MOUNTAIN
Stranahan's
ORIGINAL
SINGLE MALT WHISKEY
IN THE HEART OF DENVER
HANDCRAFTED AT HIGH ALTITUDE
ELEVATION 5,280'
COLORADO
SINGLE MALT WHISKEY
REFINED, COMPLEX & BOLD
OUR ORIGINAL WHISKEY RECIPE USES 100% MALTED BARLEY AND PRISTINE ROCKY MOUNTAIN WATER DOUBLE DISTILLED IN SMALL COPPER STILLS & WE LET IT REST IN VIRGIN AMERICAN OAK CASKS
SINGLE MALT

3

Meet the New Whiskeys

When you inspect the selection at a whiskey bar or a good liquor store, you'll see that there are two major types of American whiskey. Bourbon is dominant, and rye has come back into its own. Look past them, though, and you'll see that there are some whiskeys that you probably would not have seen twenty years ago. Some of these are new ideas from legacy distilleries; some are new ideas from new distilleries. They're an exciting segment of the category.

We're going to tick through them, like the last chapter, but these might be a bit less familiar, and maybe a bit more interesting for that reason. We're going to talk about American single malt, commercial moonshine (also known as "white whiskey"), beer-based whiskey, flavored whiskey, the new regional whiskeys like Empire Rye, and that wild west of whiskey experimentation we just call "craft whiskey." Last chapter I joked that you should bring a flashlight to explore the odd little leftovers of the traditional whiskeys. This time, maybe bring a compass and canteen, because we're headed for the fringes.

American Single Malt

One of the biggest, and the most interesting (to me, at least), of these new categories is the one that's calling itself "American Single Malt" (ASM). As you might guess from the name, it's a whiskey that's similar to single malt Scotch.

American Scotch? When you think about it, why didn't we do that before? We have plenty of used barrels; American distillers used pot stills, and they still use plenty of malt. We did try it, kind of. There were malt whiskeys made in America in the 1800s, but they never really caught on like bourbon and rye did. Maybe the competition from established Scotch (and Irish) brands kept them from getting a foothold; I'm not really sure.

Things have certainly changed. Small American distillers like St. George Spirits in Alameda, California, started making malt whiskeys back in the 1990s. They were made in tiny amounts, a handful of barrels a year; you get the impression that they made them largely for themselves. Easy to believe a distiller wanting to test themselves against the titans of the whiskey world.

By 2010, there were hundreds of these small distilleries, and significant numbers were making malt whiskey, and starting to call it "single malt." I was not generally impressed, but as Michael Faraday was supposed to have said when asked what possible use his early discoveries about electromagnetism might be, "Of what use is a newborn baby?" The whiskeys continued to improve as their distillers got more experienced, and as the whiskeys were able to mature further.

The ASM category is now producing whiskeys that can rival their Scottish counterparts, and drinkers are taking them seriously. They're taking themselves seriously, too. There is an American Single Malt Whiskey Commission (ASMWC), a group of distillers with support from peripheral industry players, like maltsters and coopers.

The Commission formed in 2016, and after meetings and discussions, proposed a new regulatory definition for ASM. They aimed to differentiate it from the "Straight Malt Whisky" category in the standards of identity, which was one of the "bourbon, but insert 51 percent other grain here" types of definitions. They diverged from an exact copy of Scotch, too. That's not what they want to make; they want to make their own whiskey.

The ASMWC proposed the definition, and the TTB put it up on their website for inspection and comments; the comment period closed in September 2022. This was a major change to the regulations, the first new whiskey category in years, and the TTB took their time. They approved the American Single Malt Whiskey category in December 2024, just as this book went to final edits.

Let's have a look at this new American Single Malt Whiskey category.

- Fermented mash of 100 percent malted barley produced in the United States

- Distilled to no more than 160° proof (80 percent ABV), entirely at one distillery

- Stored in used, charred new, or uncharred new oak barrels with a 700-liter (184.9 gallons) maximum capacity, stored only in the United States

- Stored for a minimum of two years to be labeled Straight American Single Malt Whiskey

- No neutral spirits allowed to be added; no HCFBM allowed except for caramel coloring, which must be disclosed on the label

- Bottled at minimum 80° proof (40 percent ABV)

What I find interesting here are the similarities and differences, the overlap and exception, with Scotch whisky regulations and the American standards of identity. The all-malt mash, the single distillery, the entire process taking place in one country, the minimum 80° proof bottling, and no additions other than caramel coloring are all in the Scotch whisky regulations (with the exception of the U.S. instead of Scotland). The 160° (80 percent ABV) distillation limit, two-year minimum for "straight," and no neutral spirits added are standard for U.S. whiskey definitions.

That's the overlap. What's not here is just as interesting. Like the standards of identity, there is still no minimum aging requirement (except for the "straight" labeling requirement), and there is no limitation about the type of still; single malt Scotch must be made in a pot still. Unlike the standards of identity for malt whiskey, the "oak casks" do not have to be new or charred; they may be, but it's not required, which is a big difference for U.S. whiskey. If you're curious about the size of the barrels, I'm assuming that the upper limit, 700 liters (184.9 gallons), reflects the high end of standard used cooperage, the Madeira "drum" of up to 650 liters (171.7 gallons). An American standard bourbon barrel is 53 gallons (200 L).

So *is* ASM simply an American single malt Scotch? There are clear differences, if the distillery wants to make them. Like single malt Scotch, ASM is made of 100 percent malted barley, at a single distillery, made from mash to maturity in one country (albeit a *much* larger one!), and must be bottled at a minimum 40 percent ABV. But it does not have to be made in a pot still, and it must have a terminal distillation proof of 80 percent ABV. There's also a clear option to use new charred barrels that isn't specifically disallowed for Scotch, but is rarely used.

And yet . . . the use of "single malt" seems to invite the comparison. The reason there's a category of Scotch called "*single* malt" is because of the long tradition in the Scottish whisky industry of blending whiskies from different distilleries, often a dozen or more. To bottle a malt that comes only from the production of a single Scotch distillery—and just as a reminder, that's what "single malt" means, not that it's produced from a single type of grain—is a decision that steps a bit out of the usual tradition of blending.

We don't have that tradition here, or at least, we don't anymore. There was some inter-distillery blending going on pre-Prohibition, but it largely died out. Start-up distilleries will often buy aged whiskey stocks from established distillers and may blend them with their own, younger whiskeys, but that's not the same thing, in intent or in flavor. Virginia Distillery (Lovingston, Virginia) has released blends of Scotch malt whisky and their own malt whiskeys, but they're always clearly labeled as such.

It may seem a bit artful to call an American malt whiskey a "single malt." I'm frankly surprised that there hasn't been at least a token legal challenge to that from the Scotch Whisky Association, which is usually quite active in defending what they perceive as their intellectual property. I'm not saying that I think that "American Single Malt" does infringe on such properties, but that I'm surprised that no lawyers have at least tried it on.

Still, I've always said that the proof is in the glass. If the whiskey is good, and it's a good malt whiskey, I guess I'm more concerned with that. And the more American single malts I try, the more convinced I become that this is a category with a promising future.

Cedar Ridge The QuintEssential

Two mashes (malt and peated malt) distilled and aged separately in used whiskey barrels, then finished in a variety of used barrels, all of it blended into a solera-type vat. Huge dried fruit/grass nose, hint of smoke, a bit heavy. But malt sings sweet and light on the palate, with fruit, oak, and an undercurrent of smoke that swells a bit in the long, long finish. Accomplished.

White Whiskey

As I mentioned awhile back, the standards of identity don't give a minimum age requirement for American whiskey, like Scotch, Irish, and Canadian whiskeys have. It notes in the definition that the spirit must be "stored in oak barrels" (as I'm writing this, the online version of the BAM still says "oak containers"), but it doesn't give a minimum time for that storage. Pabst Brewing makes a whiskey that literally—puckishly—says on the label "Aged 5 seconds," which is all it takes to legally make it "whiskey."

Unless they're corn whiskeys, at least 80 percent corn, these essentially unaged spirits legally must be stored in oak for at least . . . well, at least five seconds. I've wondered if passing the whiskey through a 30-foot-long oak-lined pipe would count.

When craft distilling was getting started in the last twenty years, new start-up distillers had to sell something to get some cash moving. Some made gin; some made vodka. Some also made runs of new make whiskey, put it in a bottle, and urged people to make cocktails. Did they put it in a barrel for five seconds? Dunno, that's between them and the TTB. But a few weeks in a used barrel wouldn't hurt, that's for sure.

While those twenty-years-ago bottles of white dog were often barely palatable, distillers have gotten much more skilled and experienced. Today's white whiskey is much better than it used to be. I got some samples from Michael Myers at Distillery 291 in Colorado Springs, Colorado, for a story I was writing: Colorado Whiskey (a corn, malt, and rye malt mash) and Colorado Rye White Dog (distilled from a rye malt mash). It was quite nice; I made highballs with it and whiled away the afternoon.

Myers is bullish on white whiskey and thinks it will have its day. Is he nuts? Do people really want white dog, white lightning? Think a moment. What kind of tequila do you drink? Is it always reposado, or añejo? Don't you like some blanco? I know I do. And white rum is pretty popular, but I like an aged rum too. If it's well made, how is white whiskey so different?

A lot of the stuff labeled "moonshine" out there is unaged or minimally aged whiskey mash spirit. But a lot of it is also flavored, and even if you call it "flavored whiskey," it's not. Which is as good a segue as any into the next section: flavored whiskey. Which it's not. Let's go.

Distillery 291
Colorado Fresh Whiskey

Minimally aged, colorless. Fresh-cut meadow grass, cut sweet corn, a bit of green pepper. Light on the tongue, peppery, herbal. Finish is a bit oily, peppery. Begging to go in a cocktail.

WHISKEY STARTS AS BEER

The first time I heard someone at a whiskey distillery identified as the brewer, it confused me momentarily. But the milling, mashing, and fermentation of the wash for whiskey are a lot like the same processes for brewing, and so a distillery needs a brewer.

It's said that whiskey and beer go together so well because whiskey starts out as beer. It does, but there are some crucial differences. Whiskey wash is rarely—not never, but rarely—brewed with hops, the leafy cones that add bitterness and aroma to beer. Another difference that I found interesting is that the wort isn't boiled in making whiskey, whereas a brewer almost always boils the wort for at least an hour when making beer.

There are other differences that are more a matter of choice. Malt whiskey makes use of a fairly simple malt palate, almost always using all basic pale malt, which is then fermented with a house yeast strain. But brewers regularly use a wide variety of malts: dark malt, crystal malt, caramel malt, honey malt, chocolate malt, Pilsner and Munich malts, and so on. These are all processed differently from pale malt, resulting in different colors, aromas, flavors, and residual sugars in the mash.

Brewers mostly use malt, but like distillers, they also use other grains, and for mostly the same reasons. They'll use corn as an abundant source of sugars (they also use rice, which a few distillers have started using). They use wheat for the lighter body and subtle flavors. They'll also use wheat and rye because they deliver such high loads of flavor and aroma when used with particular yeasts (see the "Wheat Beer and Rye Whiskey" sidebar on page 102). And like the distillers, they've experimented with grains like spelt, buckwheat, and millet.

Overall, brewers and distillers have diligently trotted along in their parallel paths, both making great drinks from grain, but in distinctly differently ways. But sometimes, somebody crosses the streams.

These are a small set of whiskeys, made at small craft distilleries, that are distilled from a beer mash; a formulation that includes the ingredients of a beer type, like stout (dark malts, raw barley), or tripel (candy sugar, malt, and a special yeast strain), or IPA (lots of hops), or a Belgian white (malt, raw wheat, spices, and bitter orange peel). Charbay Distillery, in Ukiah, California, has been making beer-based whiskeys since 1999.

These beer distillers reflect thoughts that some outside observers have had for years about whiskey making. I remember writer Michael Jackson wondering why Scottish distillers didn't do more with yeast or barley varieties, especially with the examples of brewers right before them.

"Traditionally, distillers have greatly overlooked the process of making the 'beer' that is to be distilled," said Tim Obert, at the currently shuttered Seven Stills Brewery & Distillery in San Francisco, where he made beer mash whiskey. "The school of thought is that you are just creating sugars to convert to alcohol that will then be distilled and matured. We feel strongly that this primary beer is a drastic contributor to the finished spirit."

Mike Reppucci, the founder of Sons of Liberty Spirits in Rhode Island, has been making beer mash whiskeys since 2011. "We use a variety of malts," he said. "In Uprising Single Malt Whiskey, which is a stout mash, we use pale malt, de-husked chocolate malt, flaked oats, crystal 45 and roasted barley.

"The earlier you start imparting flavor in the process," he continued, "the more well-balanced and integrated that flavor will become. We start by carefully selecting the grains to act as our base layer for our whiskey."

Then come two steps that not all distillers follow. "We separate out all of our wort from our grain solids," Reppucci said. "We decided to just distill the wort to ensure that we got a clean expression of the beer itself without the potential of any sharp, bitter tannic notes coming through the still."

Once the wort has been strained of grain solids, Sons of Liberty does a full boil of the wort, like a brewer. The boil kills any wild yeast or bacteria in the wort. In fact, the whole process is done with brewery-level sanitation. Distillers often are less concerned about sanitation, since at some point everything will be boiled or exposed to live steam. But the wild microbes may create off flavors, and most brewers—and Reppucci—want nothing to do with that.

Obert has different reasons for the boil. "We feel that by taking the beers through the full lauter/boil process," he explained, "we are able to capture key flavor profiles, mainly caramels produced via the melanoidin effect that are often missed in traditional whiskey production."

Do the flavors from these beers translate through the distillation process? "The whiskey from the Stout mash has distinct notes of baker's chocolate and cacao that totally come from the grains," Reppucci confirmed. "The whiskey from the Belgian mash has really nice baker's spice notes that I believe comes from the fermentation, along with spice from the 20 percent rye malt we use."

Beer mashes are an alternative way to get new flavors into whiskey. Using a full variety of malts, barley and otherwise, may be nontraditional, but it's not necessarily against the regulations. There's certainly nothing to stop a whiskey maker from using a different yeast or boiling their wort. Distillers are always finding new ways to make this old beverage.

Sons of Liberty Uprising

Sweet young malt touched with chocolate; more chocolate on the palate, with warming oak and vanilla, and sweet malt. Finishes a lot like a good stout: chocolatey and dry.

Flavored Whiskey

I'm not much of a fan of flavored whiskey; there's enough flavor in regular whiskey for me. But I do not look down my nose at anyone who likes the stuff. If that's what you like, well, good on you. Pick one that has a realistic character to the flavor and is not grossly sweet. At the very least it's more sales for the whiskey company, and that's always good in the long run.

But let's get one thing straight: Legally, there's no such thing as "flavored bourbon," or flavored straight whiskey of any kind. As I explained in Chapter 2, the rules on bourbon are firm: no kind of added coloring or flavoring in bourbon (straight bourbon), as well as straight whiskeys of other types as well.

You might see a label that says something like "straight bourbon whiskey with peach flavor added" or "bourbon whiskey blended with cherry liqueur," but the BAM is pretty clear on this. If you add coloring (the BAM uses FD&C Yellow #5 color as an example) or flavoring to bourbon, the resulting product is no longer bourbon. "The product is now a *distilled spirits specialty* and must be labeled with a statement of composition such as, "STRAIGHT BOURBON WHISKY WITH FD&C YELLOW #5 ADDED," *(emphasis added).*

Note that the wording says "straight bourbon whiskey," but legally it is no longer a bourbon; it is bourbon and something else, and that's a distilled spirits specialty. Does that make a difference? It does to me; it says, "Don't mess with bourbon."

So we'll talk about your non-bourbon, non–straight whiskey flavored whiskeys. You're going to have to thread the needle to get there, and some of the dodgy language I'm using is because of the possibility of adding HCFBM to a whiskey category that allows it. But that's not supposed to "flavor" the whiskey; it's supposed to make it more like a traditional whiskey. Flavored "whiskey" is supposed to taste like something else: honey, or peppers, or peanut butter.

If you're wondering how the flavor gets in there, it's pretty simple. The whiskey is made just the way we've been telling you, mash to maturity, and then a flavoring is added. It might be an infusion, a syrup, or an essence. If there is additional sugar added, as there often is, you've made your whiskey into a liqueur or cordial, and if you've diluted the spirit below 40 percent ABV, you'll hit some regulatory barriers to calling it "whiskey" in many countries, including the U.S. It's tricky, and most people who want a flavored whiskey really want a whiskey cordial.

Let's talk about a flavored whiskey, a whiskey cordial, that I do like: rock and rye. This is a cordial made with at least 51 percent rye whiskey, and bottled at no less than 24 percent ABV. It's very sweet, made with an addition of rock candy and fruit or fruit juices. That's right: rock candy and fruit. There are usually spices added too, and with all that, and whiskey, it's not surprising that some people swear by rock and rye as a cough cure.

Old school rock and rye will have actual chunks of orange and lemon in it, preserved by the alcohol and high sugar content, and you may see chunks of rock candy in there or a crust of sugar on the fruit. The oldest distillery in Pennsylvania, Charles Jacquin et Cie, in Philadelphia, makes the Original Jacquin's Rock and Rye, with a gorgeous Jazz Age label on this brand that dates to 1933. That's one with the fruit in it. I've been in Pennsylvania dive bars late at night and seen guys poking in empty Jacquin's bottles with knives, trying to get the orange slice out.

There's even been a bit of a revival of rock and rye in the craft world. Hochstadter's Slow & Low is a nice one, albeit without the actual fruit chunks, and comes in nifty little 100 ml (3.4 ounces) cans as well as bottles. New York Distilling makes Mister Katz's Rock & Rye, with flavors of sour cherry, citrus, and cinnamon.

Flavored whiskey, or whiskey cordials, can be fun, and they can be really good. As to whether it's still "whiskey," I'll leave that to the regulations, and a little bit to your personal opinion. Be polite and enjoy yourselves.

Skrewball

Wow, what is this doing in my house? Labeled "Whiskey with Natural Flavors." 70°, definitely not a "whiskey." Roasted peanut aroma is enormous, like a great peanut candy. Quite sweet, lots of peanut with some boozy vanilla; finish much the same, a bit sticky but not cloying. Well-executed.

Craft Whiskey, Craft Distillers

I'm not crazy about the term *craft whiskey* any more than I like the term *craft distiller*. It's imprecise; what makes a whiskey a craft whiskey? Is it the type, the size of the distiller, or who owns it? It directly implies that the legacy distillers can't make excellent and interesting whiskey, which is ludicrous. Most of all, who decides what's a craft whiskey and what isn't?

I write a column for *Craft Spirits* magazine, the house publication of the American Craft Spirits Association, so I'm clearly divided on this. But that also means I've thought a lot about it. Why do we call them craft distillers and craft whiskeys?

Mostly, we inherited the term from parallels to *craft brewer*, a market of similar small upstarts that has been hugely successful; until quite recently, anyway. But that category is in the process of walking away from the term (in favor of *independent brewer*), because it is imprecise and doesn't adapt well to success. If a craft brewer is, essentially, a small new brewer, what does it become when it is successful and twenty years old?

Craft is clearly problematic. But I couldn't think of anything better, and there's definitely a group of distillers that are *not* the legacy distillers, even if they are quite varied themselves, and it's convenient to have a handle for them. Ones I've considered and rejected: *artisanal* (speaks to small production and higher prices); *boutique* (that's a clothier, not a distiller); *microdistillery* (obvious problem with successful growth, and who sets the numbers?).

Finally, I came back to *craft* because of a definition of the word I found when I was writing a column on this for the magazine: "to make or produce with care, skill, or ingenuity." I would add, "or all three." As I said in the column, the best part about it is that it's not just a definition; it's a challenge to do your best every day.

Craft distilling started . . . well, it's hard to pin down. Germain-Robin started a small brandy distillery in 1983. St. George Spirits was making malt whiskey in the very early nineties, followed shortly by Anchor Distilling's malted rye whiskey and Clear Creek's peated malt whiskey, and then things took off. It's been about thirty years, but it really got going in the past ten.

It's more important to ask why it started. The craft brewers started because the big brewers, the "legacy" brewers, were making vast amounts of beers that were approximately the same: A relatively bland and simple light lager, with only tiny individual differences. The people who started these little breweries were inspired by the broad variety of beers still available in Europe, everything from stouts to pilsners to wild-fermented fruit beers aged in huge, old wooden barrels. They looked at that variety and said, "Why not?"

But while the legacy whiskey makers in America did make mostly the same kind of whiskey—bourbon, along with tiny amounts of rye and corn whiskey, and some blended whiskey—no one could seriously argue that the bourbons were bland, or all the same. What's more, the growth in Scotch single malts had inspired those legacy distillers, and they were bottling some longer-aged whiskeys with real emphasis on stand-out quality. Bourbons like Booker's, Elijah Craig 12 year old, Wild Turkey Rare Breed, Blanton's, and Woodford Reserve were starting to get attention.

Maybe that was why craft distillers started, because things were getting interesting again. I've told people that when I started writing about whiskey, back in 1996, it wasn't a great time to start writing about whiskey. That's true because whiskey, especially American whiskey, was still struggling to come out of a long decline. But it was also an incredibly exciting time because of that struggle, and the innovation and striving for quality that made it work.

People ask me why whiskey recovered, and I tell them it was because people wanted to know more about what they were eating and drinking, and whiskey had a great, authentic story. It was captivating, and I think that's a lot of what inspired craft distillers to take a swing at it.

To come back to where we started, I think they were also inspired by the craft brewers. If you're not old enough to remember that time, I can't express how strange it was for a small brewery to be making beer and having that beer show up on tap and in the cooler. It was something Americans hadn't seen in years: real choice in beer, outside the four or five major brands. It broke a very solid dam, despite the legacy brewers' best efforts to stop it, and co-opt it.

And that is the third reason I think this succeeded. The legacy distillers saw how badly the big brewers failed to stop this wave of small brewer-led innovation, and they responded in a completely different manner. They joined it and rode the wave. Brown-Forman rebuilt an old distillery and started making whiskey in pot stills. Jim Beam did experimental batches of whiskeys made from different grains, like red rice. Heaven Hill even tried a line of white dog.

It may have created competition for the craft distillers, but it also normalized the idea of innovation and variety and difference much more quickly than it happened on the beer side of the market. Add in the way the Scotch and Irish whiskey makers jumped in as well, and you had a perfect storm of opportunity, interest, and acceptance.

Who are the craft distillers? They're not just new distillers; some of them have been making whiskey for more than thirty years. They are small distillers with big ideas. They are people who want to make whiskey in their home country, in their hometown.

They may want to make whiskey very similar to something they had that made an impression. Steve McCarthy, one of the early pioneers, was making fruit brandies and eaux de vie at his Clear Creek Distillery in Portland, Oregon. He tells the story of how he found himself on vacation in Scotland, trapped in his hotel by days of lashing rain, with only a pool table and a supply of Lagavulin single malt for diversion. Inspired by the whisky, he came up with McCarthy's Oregon Single Malt, made from Scottish peated malt but aged in Oregon oak barrels.

Craft distillers often use heirloom or hybrid grains, maybe grown by very local farmers; they might even grow it themselves. They use nontraditional grains, like triticale, spelt, or quinoa. They use hybrid stills, or stills of their own design. Leopold Bros. in Denver uses a three-chamber still, an old design once popular among the Pennsylvania and Maryland rye whiskey distillers, the first one made in almost one hundred years. Others are following in their footsteps.

Craft distillers may make bourbon without the sour mash technique; twenty years ago, I could write that every bourbon distiller used sour mash without fear of contradiction, but that's no longer true. They use a variety of wood, and they may bathe the barrels with music as they age; there are distillers who put their barrels to age in shipping containers, and there are distillers who put their barrels *on ships* to age.

Darek Bell, the cofounder of Corsair Distillery in Nashville, told me once about operating in "the shadow of Jack Daniel's," as he put it. Craft distillers have to realize that they're not going to be able to make a business on making whiskey that's just like Jack Daniel's, he said. Packaging costs money, marketing costs money, advertising and promotion cost money.

"But," he said with a smile, "creativity is free." Craft distillers have to break traditions and traditional expectations in order to compete, in order to make their mark. For instance, Bell has done wide experimentation with smoking grain with different woods and peats and herbs.

Distillers can drill deep on the local angle, like Cedar Ridge in Iowa, where they make much of their state's excellent quality corn crop. They can dig into history, like Leopold Bros. and their three-chamber still, or Mountain Laurel Spirits, near Philadelphia, where they use a historical mash bill for their Dad's Hat Monongahela-style rye. They may hitch up with a brewer to make whiskey from dark beers, heavily hopped beers, wheat beers, and more. They try new barrels, like Bainbridge Organic's Yama grain whiskey, aged in Japanese Mizunara oak, or any of the number of craft whiskeys aged in 10- or 30-gallon (37.9 or 113.6 liter) barrels.

Several distillers use only organic ingredients; others use exclusively non-GMO grains. (To be fair, so do Four Roses and a number of Scotch distillers.) Some do their own malting and may smoke the malt with local peat or varied woods; one uses corncobs to smoke the corn for their whiskey. And some try truly unique ideas, like the new Redemption Sur Lee Rye, which adds backset, sour mash, to the aging whiskey in the barrel.

That's the similarity of craft whiskey: difference. Craft whiskey is seeking to do something different. They do it for the challenge, they do it for fun, and they do it for profit, in the end, because difference is what sells these whiskeys. Craft distillers give us the chance to find out "what if." And that's often worth the price of admission to their wild, wonderful circus.

Balcones Baby Blue

Bourbon made with Hopi blue corn. Nose is sweet, corn pudding, honey notes; some spice in a light, sweet rush on the tongue; cocoa notes as it fades. A small distiller favorite of mine.

Westland Distillery barrel hall (Seattle, WA)

REGIONAL WHISKEYS

If you're a Scotch drinker, you're probably familiar with the whisky regions: Highland, Lowland, Speyside, Islands, each with their own characteristics. You may also know that these are very loose regional similarities, with exceptions, and are largely a marketing creation . . . but there is something to them.

Does American whiskey have a similar regionality? It certainly did at one time. Pennsylvania and Maryland were rye whiskey territory, extending to some degree into New York and Wisconsin. Kentucky, Indiana, Illinois, Tennessee, and Missouri were bourbon country. Other whiskey makers were scattered about, but these were the powerhouses.

Prohibition leveled this playing field most brutally, doing such damage that the rye distillers never recovered and the bourbon distillers of the Midwest were knocked back to Kentucky, alongside their filtered rivals in Tennessee and the quiet giant of Seagram's in Indiana. The Pennsylvania rye brands were folded into Kentucky portfolios and became much more bourbon-like, with mash bills that most often only met the 51 percent requirement for rye, along with a big dose of corn.

Enter the craft distillers. One of the drivers of the craft distillers' motivations (and marketing dreams) was a restoration of old whiskey regions. Pennsylvania distillers wanted to reclaim the Monongahela mantle. Maryland distillers dug deep into what exactly it was that led journalist H. L. Mencken, the famed "Sage of Baltimore," to declare that a friend "always ate rye bread instead of wheat because rye was the bone and sinew of Maryland whiskey—the most healthful appetizer yet discovered by man."

Research led to a variety of recipes and techniques and processes, and is ongoing. At this point, discussions I've been privy to have largely agreed that "Maryland rye" is definitely a rye whiskey that is made in Maryland; similar agreement has been reached on "Pennsylvania rye." That's it for now, and nothing is official yet.

A definition of Monongahela rye whiskey remains elusive, but the hunt is exciting (and delicious). There is something of a Venn diagram that includes circles labeled "sweet mash," "heated warehouses," "rye malt," and "no corn." No one can quite agree on where they intersect, or don't, probably because, as I like to say, the distillers back then were busy making whiskey, not regulations.

State distillery guilds are looking at certification programs to add a name to whiskeys made in the state. New York has gone further with their "Empire Rye" classification, looking to make it more than simply geographical.

Empire Rye must meet all the federal standards of identity for rye whiskey. In addition, 75 percent of the mash bill must be New York–grown rye (malted, raw, or a combination). There is a barrel entry proof maximum of 115° proof, and the whiskey must be aged for a minimum of two years. Finally, it must be mashed, fermented, distilled, barreled, and aged at a single New York distillery. I've had a few Empire ryes, and they are good whiskeys.

There is one other regional whiskey that's happening because of conditions. It's nothing official, but I think it should be: high-altitude whiskey. There are a growing number of distilleries in the Rocky Mountains that are at altitudes over 5,000 feet. As I'll discuss in more detail in Chapter 11, that means significant differences in atmospheric pressure and humidity that affect distilling times and barrel aging.

Does that give the whiskeys made at high altitude enough of a similar character to be able to group them? I don't know, but as always, I am willing to volunteer to do that research.

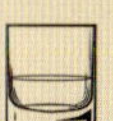

Black Button Empire Rye

96°, a mash of 6 percent malt and 94 percent heirloom Danko rye grown just south of Rochester, New York. Pristine, almost polished rye grain nose, notes of red plum and pepper, maybe a hint of cumin. Full, spicy-sweet palate, throat-coating finish. Delightfully different.

4

Amber Waves of Grain

Whiskey is made from grain. There are more involved legal definitions of whiskey in several countries. Various distillers' associations define whiskey, in ways that are understandably self-referential (and often self-serving). There are cultural definitions, which may overlap with the legal and business definitions. Then there are personal ones: What whiskey means to each of us, the drinkers.

Despite the regional differences in those definitions, in barrels and stills and aging, they all agree on one thing: All whiskey is made from grain, from cereals. Not fruit, vegetables, honey, cane, or milk (really, milk); those are sources for other spirits. If you're going to call what you make or sell or drink "whiskey," it has to be distilled from fermented grain. (There are spirits made largely from sugarcane in Asia that are called "whiskey," but only in their native countries. The rest of the world doesn't consider them to be whiskey.)

This is an odd thought at first. Grain is dry, not like fruits or honey or pressed sugarcane. Even when you cut it open, what you find are hard, insoluble starches, bound in a matrix of proteins, none of which will ferment. But that grain also has a sprout, with a chemical trigger that can convert those starches to sugars, and that's what we want for whiskey. Of the four major grains used to make whiskey—barley, corn, rye, and wheat—barley is the one with the quickest pull on that trigger, the one that's easiest to convert. We'll start with it because that eagerness to convert makes it the key to making all types of whiskey.

Barley and Malt

Barley *(Hordeum vulgare)* has been a partner of humankind for at least twelve thousand years, one of our earliest cultivated crops.

The history and mythology of the Fertile Crescent, the rich Middle Eastern area that is the origin of human civilization, is bound to barley cultivation. Barley was made into everyone's daily bread, though it was not a loaf that we'd probably find appetizing. Barley has only about one-tenth the amount of gluten that wheat does and makes a crumbly bread that doesn't really "rise like wheaten bread."

What barley does have is a lot of diastatic enzymes, the protein catalysts that enable starch conversion. These Sumerian barley-eaters eventually discovered that if barley got wet and sprouted, it became softer, a very simple version of the process we now call malting. That's a vital step on the way to converting starches to sugars, which leads directly to fermentation, beer, and finally whiskey.

We know these Sumerians also learned that next step of converting the barley starches to sugar: by cooking them with water, some version of the process we call mashing. We know this because they worshiped a deity, Ninkasi, the goddess of beer and brewing, and a hymn to Ninkasi survives. The hymn is praise, but also instructions to make beer. One verse goes: "You are the one who soaks the malt in a jar, The waves rise, the waves fall."

Beer was a daily drink in Sumeria, and a regular part of their diet. But the alcohol, and the way it made them feel, also made beer a religious experience—and made Ninkasi more important than just another goddess of the hearth. If the Sumerians had taken the next step and discovered distillation, maybe Ninkasi would have ruled the pantheon!

They're not far wrong, for a people who were just discovering civilization, agriculture, and science, because barley is something of a miracle. It is a grain that almost seems designed to be fermented. Barley's low gluten content doesn't make for great bread, but that means it doesn't get too sticky when it's ground up and mixed with water (FYI: Wheat definitely does). Plus, it has a substantial husk that makes a natural filter bed during mashing, holding back the spent bits of grain while the dissolved sugars run away with the water.

But most importantly, barley malts easily and consistently. While many grains can be malted, barley is by far the favorite, so much so that while other malted grains are named specifically—malted wheat, malted rye—malted barley is known simply as "malt."

Best of all, malting barley yields a rich surplus of the enzymes needed for starch conversion, the diastatic enzymes mentioned above. This surplus of diastatic power is so large that other nonmalted grains can be ground up with it, and the starches in the whole mixture will convert to sugars. That's the reason you'll find about 15 percent malt in most bourbon mash bills.

Barley grows in a range of climates, though it's not as well adapted to truly cold climates as is rye. There are two major types of domesticated barley: two-row and six-row, named for the number of kernel rows on the ears. Most barley is grown for animal feed, with only the exceptional barley going to brewers and distillers.

Six-row barley ready for harvest

The six-row strains tend to grow better in North America, and they have a higher diastatic power—a greater ability to convert those starches to sugar. The two-row barley strains grow better in Europe and are favored for Scotch and Irish whiskeys. Agronomists are constantly creating new barley cultivars with improved traits for feed and beverage use. Distillers are generally looking for the highest yield of spirit per unit of grain.

Here's what's going on when barley malts. When grains are planted and sprout, enzymes are released that convert the hard, insoluble starches in the barleycorn into softer, soluble starches that are ready to be used for food by the new plant. But we don't want plants in the ground—we want beer and whiskey—so we trick the grain by simply wetting it down and letting its little chemical brain think it's time to sprout. This takes about two days.

You can feel the difference in the hardness of the grain as it converts. When I was visiting Bowmore Distillery, on the Scottish island of Islay, we spent time at their in-house maltings. I was shown an old-school method for checking the progress, called "chalking the malt." Workers would rub a grain against a dark plaster or stone wall. If the grain left a white mark, the starches were almost completely converted, and it was about ready.

When the malt maker (the maltster) judges that conversion is complete, the malt is heated in a kiln. It's a balance: You want to kill the sprout and drive off most of the water, but if it gets too hot, the malt will roast or, worse, those crucial enzymes will break down, and we need them later for mashing. Successful kilning leaves the grain, now called "malt," in a condition to be bagged, shipped, and stored until it's time to grind it for processing.

Barley shown here being raked and, opposite, resting patiently and sprouting

From Malt to Whiskey

The American single malt whiskeys are made from 100 percent barley malt. It may be partly or all smoked malt, depending on the distiller and the planned whiskey.

It's not just single malt whiskeys that use malt, though. Whiskeys like bourbon and rye usually have between 10 percent and 15 percent malt, primarily used for an enzymatic boost rather than flavor, though there is a small contribution to the flavor from the malt. Small distillers may use this more traditional malt addition, or they may add enzymes directly, depending on circumstances.

American craft distillers who emulate the Irish-style "mixed mash" single pot still-style whiskeys will use a mixture of malted barley and unmodified "raw" barley in the mash, which gives a fresh grassy and fruity character to the whiskey, along with a certain oiliness. There may be other grains in these mixed mashes as well: rye, corn, or oats.

One thing that's been baffling to me, as someone who has been enjoying and writing about beer longer than I have about whiskey, is the tiny number of whiskeys that take advantage of the wide array of malts that brewers use regularly. The malt distillers use is what brewers call "pale malt," the most common and simplest type. But brewers use malts that are roasted black, toasted brown, or "stewed" to crystallize; there are more than 100 different types of malt. But most whiskey makers use only one or two. The craft distillers are turning this around, driven by the flavors they taste in craft-brewed beer.

When you're making whiskey, you may use malt for the sweet, somewhat delicate flavor (and you may use unmodified barley for that Irish freshness). But malt's powerful enzymes ensure it a place in most distilleries.

Corsair Triple Smoke

Three measures of malt, three different smokes: peat, cherry wood, and beech wood. Big layer of peat on the nose, with beech wood bacon underneath and cherry notes on top. Malt on the mouth opens to the peaty bonfire with bacon on the side and the cherry on top. Lusciously smoky finish.

MICROMALTING

"Small, independent, and innovative" doesn't only apply to distillers. It also applies to the small wave of new malt makers who are bringing local malt options to local distillers.

Malting in earlier times was a process, like brewing and distilling, that could easily be done by farmers and artisans on a cottage level. One person making malt could supply their own brewery or distillery. Then as towns got larger, and brewers and distillers grew to supply them, maltsters grew beyond single-person operations as well. Founding father Samuel Adams had a family malt business (although it failed from neglect as Sam paid more attention to politics).

Malt houses, like many other agricultural processing businesses, consolidated and grew enormously, chasing market domination and economies of scale. I've visited malt houses so large we had to drive around them to get to different parts of the operation.

But back in 2012, I visited a malt house that was in someone's garage—a two-car garage, to be fair, but a garage. That was Valley Malt, in Hadley, Massachusetts, a business founded by Andrea and Christian Stanley. I still remember Andrea showing me a "small batch" of malt they'd done: cherry-smoked malted triticale, for Brooklyn Brewery. The full batch fit in a box Andrea held in her hands; that's pretty micro!

More small, independent malt houses have opened across America, and they are supplying distillers now, as well as brewers. The thing I like best about the micromaltsters—no, let me rephrase that: *some* of the things I like best about them—is that they can, and do, produce small batches of very specialized grains for distillers; they encourage and provide a market for local farmers to grow heirloom strains of grain and organically grown grain; and some of them are growing grain themselves.

Some distillers are growing and malting their own grain. Hillrock Estate Distillery in Ancram, New York, has their own on-site malt houses, malting their own grain (Christian Stanley helped them get the maltings set up).

Valley Malt has grown considerably since I visited in 2012. They're in a much bigger building, a former paper mill in Holyoke, and they have employees now. I've seen Andrea address professional conferences about micromalting and malting history. They still have very strong local connections to farmers, and when a farmer sells their grain to Valley Malt, they get more money. I like the graphic on their website, showing that an acre of farmland equals a pallet of local malt, which makes 544 bottles of locally distilled spirits.

Distilling is an agricultural process, and micromalting is a strong link between the farmer and the distiller.

SMOKING MALT

I like telling people that single malt whiskey is about as simple as it gets. It has only two ingredients after all: water and malt. (There's yeast, but it comes out before distillation. Is that an *out*gredient?) That's knowingly overlooking one of the most defining flavors of single malt whiskey: the smoky presence or clean absence of smokiness usually—but not always—driven by peat. That flavor enters the whiskey by smoking the malt over a smoky fire, so let's have a look at that.

Peat is decayed vegetation—like moss, leaves, grass, flowers—that accumulates over centuries in bogs and ponds. The water that's held in place by the moss keeps oxygen away from the plant matter, so it doesn't rot. More and more plants die and fall into the water, and the mass presses down. Given hundreds of millions of years and a lot more weight, it would become coal. But in about one thousand years, it becomes peat.

Like coal, peat can be burned once it's dug out of the bog and dried. It is a smoky and aromatic fire. When my wife and I were on our honeymoon in Ireland in 1989, a lot of homes and pubs still burned peat fires; the air was hazy and the reek was thick.

That smoke is the same smoke you'll find in peated whiskeys like McCarthy's and Westland. When the malt is still wet, just after the final turning, it's put in the kiln and a smolder of peat (or wood; cherry, mesquite, and alder wood are popular) is built beneath the slotted floor. The smoking goes on for up to twenty hours, after which the malt won't absorb much more smoke. I've stood in a malt kiln at this point; it's humid but not terribly hot, or even that smoky. The wet malt is absorbing the smoke, binding it to the husks.

The smokiness of the malt is measured in parts per million (ppm) of phenols, the aromatic compounds in the smoke. It's as much as 70 ppm or more in strongly peated malts. The phenols in malt versus the phenols in the actual spirit are at about a 3:1 ratio. Much of the smoke is locked in the husks and left behind in the mashing process. As with other number-driven descriptions, I prefer to be led by my nose and palate. This is a case where you're better off staying subjective. Drink the whisky and see how smoky it tastes to you.

Whiskies differ in how much smoke they put to the malt, but they also vary from using different peats, different woods. There are regional differences related to rainfall and temperature, but every bog has different plants growing in it. Some peats are therefore more floral, some more grassy, some more acrid, some more savory. It is now believed by some researchers that the "seaside" or "briny" character of some whiskies comes from the peat used in malting. (That's still somewhat subjective, and much is still open to debate.)

Corn

Corn is a hugely important grain in whiskey production, the biggest in American whiskey making.

It is the primary grain in America's largest-selling whiskey, bourbon, but it might surprise you to learn that the Canadian whisky makers, on the whole, use more corn than any other grain as well. Corn's a pretty surprising grain overall.

Zea mays is a giant grass that has its origins in the Americas. It is a heavily modified grain, believed to be bred from a beneficial mutation of a wild grass called *teosinte*, which can still be found in rural Central America. It's worth noting this because humans have worked with this grass and made it much more than it was. From a waving multi-stalked weed, corn has become the most important cereal crop in the world, grown on every populated continent and producing a bigger annual harvest than any other grain, including wheat and rice.

About 40 percent of that crop grows in the United States. Americans took corn from a highly productive grain in the 1800s—when 9 pounds (4.1 kg) of seed per acre would yield a farmer about 1,100 pounds (499 kg) at harvest—to today's amazing example of hybrid vigor. American farmers will now plant 19 pounds (8.6 kg) of seed corn on an acre and expect to harvest 11,000 pounds (4989.5 kg)—five and a half tons!—of yellow dent corn in the fall. Research plots are delivering yields up to 20,000 pounds (9071.8 kg) per acre from less than 50 pounds (22.7 kg) of seed, proving corn is still evolving.

HEIRLOOM STRAINS

The United States Department of Agriculture (USDA) has a program called the National Plant Germplasm System. It's a seed bank, designed to preserve the genetic diversity of a wide array of plants. That includes what are commonly called "heritage" or "heirloom" strains of grains.

You're probably more familiar with things like "heirloom tomatoes," which might be odd-looking or more fragile than the standard red balls we're used to but often have wonderfully rich or different flavors. The downside is that the heirloom plants may not yield as many tomatoes per plant, are more susceptible to modern blights, or have a significantly shorter shelf life. It's a trade-off.

Heirloom grains work the same way. They may not be as productive as today's standards but offer interesting differences in flavors. We'll talk about that more specifically in Chapter 6, where I talk to a distiller about why they chose to use an heirloom rye strain that had significantly less starch per ton of grain than modern varieties, starch being the main fuel for alcohol production. (Short answer: Less starch meant potentially more room for flavor.)

There's been a lot of interest in older strains of rye. Rye had fallen out of favor as a harvested crop in the U.S., being used mostly as an off-season cover crop to be plowed under as "green manure" to enrich the soil, but not harvested, cleaned, and used in food or whiskey. Rye was something you bought from Canada or Europe, and the varieties grown here for their utilitarian value maybe weren't the best for whiskey.

People wanted to find out. Farmers (and distillers and maltsters) requested samples from that USDA seed bank and grew up old strains like Abruzzi, Danko, and Rosen. After a few years of growing for seed and scaling up, there was enough rye to distill. There was a cross-generational moment in 2019 when Dick Stoll, who made whiskey with Rosen rye at the original Michter's Distillery in Schaefferstown, Pennsylvania, mashed and distilled a run of Rosen rye at Stoll & Wolfe Distillery in Lititz, Pennsylvania, about 10 miles (16.1 km)—and thirty years—apart.

Heirloom grains speak to the romance of agriculture and whiskey, the old days and old ways, but I'm not wholly convinced that straight-up heirloom grains are the full answer. I remember talking to Stephen Jones, the Washington State University plant geneticist who founded the university's Breadlab. They do a lot of work with heirloom grains there, but they're more interested in cross-breeding plants from those strains. They plant test plots every year, looking for grain that doesn't just taste better but is better for the soil and the farmer, and most importantly, is affordable.

Erik Wolfe and Dick Stoll

"High-priced ingredients don't help anyone," he said. "As plant breeders, we have to create grains that will be used. We don't do heritage strains because they're not the best use of the land. We breed them to strains that yield flavor, with much higher tons per acre. We need flavor for the producer, and we need profit for the farmer. No compromise."

To make whiskey from grain that is optimized for both flavor *and* yield should be the goal, and to do it with a grain that doesn't need gallons of chemical fertilizers and herbicides, a grain that a farmer will want to harvest because it's profitable. That's a goal worth working toward.

Stoll & Wolfe: Rosen Rye

Herbal, peppermint notes atop the full smell of rye grain; robust. Oily and warm on the palate, sweet herbal rye with hints of the mint. Long, warm finish with subtle oak. (A three-year-old barrel sample, distilled from Rosen rye grown on Erik Wolfe's cousin's farm, 2 miles [3.2 km] from the distillery.)

Corn to Whiskey

Yellow dent corn is the type most used in the whiskey business. It arrives at distilleries in trucks and rail cars, a yellow river of grain.

One of the easiest quality tests done on this incoming corn is to heat a random sample in a microwave. If the hot corn smells right, with no off aromas, the load is more than likely acceptable, though it is still tested for nitrogen and moisture content and visually checked for evidence of mold.

Corn is bursting with starches, but they're a different set of starches than in malt, rye, or wheat, so corn has to be milled and precooked before mashing. Some distillers cook the corn under pressure, and some just do a longer boil, though both gelatinize the starches, making the corn ready for the mash.

Corn also has a distinct, sweet flavor that stays with the liquid throughout the process, from mashing to fermenting to distilling. That flavor and abundant fuel for the creation of alcohol are what corn brings to the whiskey equation.

High Wire Jimmy Red

100 percent Jimmy Red corn, a South Carolina heritage strain. Bursts out of the glass: sweet orange, dusty corn, cinnamon. Corn, spice, vanilla flavors, and a long rippling finish. Light but luscious.

Fermenting bourbon mash

Rye

Rye has some strange habits. It grows almost as tall as corn, though it looks more like wheat and barley, with a classic grass-grain stalk and head.

It will grow almost anywhere it can get a toehold; I once saw rye growing in a half-inch-deep skiff of dust on a tractor blade. Farmers call these unplanned plants "volunteers," and you may see them sticking up above the other plants in a field of wheat or barley. Rye also acts up in the distillery, where it is notorious for causing billowing foam during mashing.

Well, what can you expect from an adolescent? Rye *(Secale cereale)* only recently joined barley around the human fireplace. Archaeological evidence for rye in active cultivation goes back only about 3,500 years, making it a newcomer, which is probably why the Roman historian Pliny the Elder was so dismissive of it. He complained that this northern grain "is a very poor food and only serves to avert starvation" and that it had a "bitter taste—most unpleasant to the stomach."

Pliny got the bitterness part right. But that bitterness is part of what makes rye so attractive to whiskey makers and drinkers. Rye has a full fan of tastes: bitter, mint, grassiness, pepper, and more. It was probably shocking to Pliny's wheat-accustomed palate, but in a glass, it's wonderful.

The other thing that makes rye attractive to farmers is its hardiness, which Pliny also noted: "It will grow upon any soil, and yields a hundred-fold; it is employed also as a manure for enriching the land." Farmers say rye will grow on rock, and rye is a dominating grass, growing so quickly that it barely needs weeding. Those long stalks make for a good cover crop, returning plenty of sun-spawned nutrients to the soil when they're plowed under.

That's largely how rye has survived in the United States, as a cover crop to hold soil in place during fallow seasons between cash crops. Rye was a popular crop in Eastern Europe and Scandinavia because it could grow on rocky soil or in cold climates, and that's why you find rye bread there. When those folks emigrated to early America, they found that rye grew in the stony soil of western Pennsylvania, and that's what they grew and distilled. Bourbon distillers add rye to their mash for the great dose of flavor that even a small amount of rye can give to whiskey.

"Rye whiskey" means different things in different places; by regulation, it may have a minimum of 51 percent rye in the mix. Some whiskeys are as much as 100 percent rye, thanks to rye malt or added enzymes; there are a handful of whiskeys made with 100 percent rye malt. But the reason it's in there, rye's ticket to the whiskey dance, is that punch of flavor it gives a spirit.

Wild Turkey Rye

Traditional Kentucky-type rye. Spicy and sweet, like Red Hots or old-fashioned hard candy. Corn is sweet on the tongue; rye is somewhat bitter. A real push-pull. Screaming for a cocktail.

SMALL BATCH
BULLEIT
95
FRONTIER WHISKEY
95% RYE MASH
Whiskey using a 95% rye mash for a superior

Wheat

Common wheat *(Triticum aestivum)* has been with humans almost as long as barley. It, too, was grown in the Fertile Crescent but overtook and surpassed barley in value and importance.

We eat wheat, while most barley is fed to animals. Wheat is second only to corn in volume of production. When it comes to whiskey, wheat is an important second choice to rye in making bourbon and, as noted in the chapter on traditional whiskeys, is slowly gaining acceptance as a primary grain in whiskey as well.

Wheat whiskeys, where wheat makes up more than 51 percent of the mash bill, bring an even softer palate. I've found that they're a great introduction to the barrel-forward flavors of American whiskeys.

You'll find a variety of opinions on what wheat adds—or doesn't add—to a whiskey, even among master distillers, but the strong sales of these whiskeys prove that whatever it is, it's popular. Call it softness, call it smoothness, or call it manners: That's what wheat brings to the table.

We have our cast of characters. Now it's time to put them in play, let them mingle, and get to work together. That's our next step in building whiskey flavor: mashing.

Bulleit Rye is sourced from MGP in Indiana; you can tell by the 95% rye mash bill.

Bardstown Bourbon Origin Series: High Wheat Bourbon

Respectable 106°; 6 years old. Nose is focused, direct: rock candy, vanilla, light citrus. Pillowy on the tongue: light corn bread, warm oak, that orange note. Finish is more oaky, but not heavy-handed. Nimble bourbon.

"Call it softness, smoothness, or manners: That's what wheat brings to the table."

Other Grains

Malt and corn are the most common grains used in making whiskey. Rye and wheat run a distant third and fourth, but they are still far more common than any other grains distillers may use to make whiskey. There are whiskeys being made with oats, blue corn, and hybrid grains like triticale, a wheat/rye cross. Millet and teff are also used, often in small proportions, occasionally as the dominant grain.

Different strains of the common grains are also used, like the Bloody Butcher and Wapsie Valley corn varieties or Golden Promise barley, most of them heritage strains that may not be as productive as today's standards but offer interesting differences in flavors.

I remember a distillery rep at the Distill America show in Madison, Wisconsin, cajoling me to try her vodka, made with Bloody Butcher corn; not big on the vodka, I told her, but she insisted. I gave in, and wow, there really was a difference. There was a clear creaminess and a fruity grain flavor.

There are also early varieties, almost fossils in their age, from the dawn of cultivation. There are strains and variants of wheat that can be used: emmer wheat, club wheat, spelt, freekeh, bulgur, all of them offering something different (both to distillers and to the farmers who supply them).

Rice is a huge crop worldwide and is made into spirits like baijiu and shochu in Asia, but is not widely used in America for making whiskey. There are some Asian-style rice spirits being made here, and barrel-aged to boot, but there are also some more traditionally American-type whiskeys being made from rice in Louisiana, such as Riz and J.T. Meleck. The latter is a farm distillery; they grow the rice, then they distill and age it. They raise crawfish, too, and there's one on the label.

I was able to taste some of the J.T. Meleck whiskey that my friend Sam Komlenic brought back from a visit to the distillery. After the first couple sips, I was sold. It was creamy, flavorful, clean, and showed great barrel character.

Finally, there are the so-called pseudocereals: quinoa, amaranth, and buckwheat, all of which are technically seeds, not grains. They have been used to make spirits that were fermented, distilled, and aged like whiskey, but until recently, they were not legally allowed to be labeled as "whiskey." The standards of identity have been amended to allow that labeling. Having tasted quinoa and buckwheat whiskeys, I welcome that addition; they make interesting spirits.

Catskill Distilling
The One and Only Buckwheat

80 percent buckwheat. Earthy aromas of hickory nuts and autumn leaves, a bit of cinnamon. Creamy mouthfeel, more nuts, sweet oaken vanilla, and more dry leaves at the end. Unique, compelling. Catskill is sadly no longer in business; the only other buckwheat whiskey I know of is Barrel 21 Distillery's, in State College, PA.

5

There's Magic in the Mash

When the grain arrives at the distillery, it's hard, dry, and about as far from the idea of a great-tasting glass of whiskey as we'll be in the entire process. The job is to somehow go from dry and dusty to wet and tasty.

To do that, you have to get at what's inside the grain, the starch that the plant has stored there to feed the seed when it sprouts. We've got to steal that, pulverize it, and wet it down so that we can turn it into sugar, pretty much against the seed's will. Once we have sugars, we can unleash the yeast, but we have to get at that starch first.

It's time to mill and mash. Milling is a fairly simple proposition: crushing the grain into a fine grist. Does the size of the grist affect the flavor? Dr. Pat Heist, cofounder of Wilderness Trail Distillery in Danville, Kentucky, compared it to coffee. "It's like a drip grind versus an espresso grind," he said. "You can get a slightly different flavor."

There are two types of mill in general use: the hammer mill and the roller mill. Roller mills are very easy to explain. You have two heavy metal rollers placed horizontally and very close to each other; the gap is adjustable. The rollers rotate in opposite directions in such a way that both are turning in toward the top of the gap. Grain is fed into the gap area, and friction pulls it in, where the rollers crush it. There may be an additional set of rollers below to crush the grain more finely and consistently.

Ground grains, or grist, falling into the mash tun

The hammer mill is a bit more complicated. There is a rapidly rotating frame inside a cage of steel that's pierced with a web of uniformly spaced and sized holes. On the surface of the frame are sets of freely rotating hammers, metal bars designed to slam into the grain as it drops around the outside of the frame. Very tight tolerances leave the hammers swinging just barely above the surface of the cage. The impact of the hammers smashes the grain against the holes in the cage, and the grains are broken and quickly pounded into flour.

Both mills develop similar grades of consistently sized flour from the four grains used in most distilling: corn, malt, wheat, and rye. Distillers have preferences, of course. Some feel that a hammer mill damages the grain and heats it too much. Others feel that a roller mill isn't as efficient as a hammer mill. It seems like they always like best what they already have, and that's probably a lot of it. There's no definitive scientific literature on the difference that either side could point to.

RECIPES

American single malt whiskeys have a very simple recipe: ***malt***. A single malt whiskey must be 100 percent barley malt. It may be a mix of malts—peated, unpeated, different strains—but all malt. But that doesn't mean the old "Malt Whisky" definition has gone away.

The current standards of identity treat "malt whiskey" like bourbon, only made with malt instead of corn as the main grain. The mash bill has to be at least 51 percent malt (other grains are allowed), and the whiskey must be aged in a new, charred oak barrel. Honestly, reading the standards often brings to mind the adage: "When all you have is a hammer (bourbon), everything looks like a nail."

Most American whiskeys have a mixed mash bill. Bourbon is made with anywhere from 51 percent to up to 80 percent corn, then 10 percent to 15 percent malt, and the rest rye or wheat. The corn is there for sugar and flavor, the malt is there for enzymes for conversion, and the rye or wheat is for its own flavor, a twist of spice, or softness. The different mash bills may lean heavier on corn for sweetness or rye for spice, but there's not really a lot of flavor from the malt. It's there for the enzymes.

Time for Some Magic

We've milled our grains, and the grist is ready to go. Wait, we're almost ready: Are we mashing with corn? We'll need to cook it beforehand to gelatinize corn's particularly well-integrated starches. That's not really a flavor-creation step—just a way to get the corn converted better.

Speaking of which, I don't want to raise any expectations. Mashing is a crucial step in distillation, but it is more of a preparatory step to flavor creation. Mashing converts the grain's starches into sugars; without sugar, there's no fermentation. And fermentation is where the flavors begin to be created. So we're going to talk about it in order to get to that.

With all the mash in the cooking vessel, the "mash tun," we have a green light for conversion. Conversion is an enzymatic process. Naturally occurring enzymes in the malt are activated by water and the right temperature. The brewer

(Continued on page 88)

"THAT'S THE SAME WHISKEY."

Is a mash bill the same thing as a "recipe"?

I do hear a lot of people saying that so-and-so bourbon from Distillery A is "the same mash bill as this-and-that bourbon, which costs $30 less; it's the same bourbon, different label."

Sure it is, and this pancake is the same as this waffle, this funnel cake, or these crepes—except they're not. They're all made from flour, sugar, eggs, milk, and butter, but they're prepared differently.

A mash bill isn't a recipe; it's just a list of ingredients. It doesn't matter if it's bourbon, rye, or single malt. Mix and mash them, and it may still be the same. But then you can use different yeasts, different fermentation times; you can use different stills or different still settings, different barrels, different warehouses or floors in the warehouses; and of course, you can leave them in the warehouse for different periods of time. Then the blender gets hold of them, and anything can happen.

Same mash bill, same whiskey? Don't you believe it. And if you're not convinced, just look at the world's single malt whiskeys and their diverse range of flavors: Scotch, Irish, Japanese, American, English, and Indian. All different, and all with *exactly* the same "mash bill," 100 percent malt. The other variables in the process make the difference. Case closed.

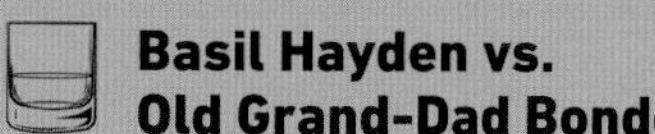

Basil Hayden vs. Old Grand-Dad Bonded

Same mash bill, yeast, barrel—different whiskeys. Basil: Oak and light cinnamon, oily rye on the tongue, quick finish. Grand-Dad: Vanilla, oak, bare hint of spice, explodes on tongue with sweet cinnamon and hammering oak. Hello, warehouse influence.

> "Same mash bill, same whiskey? Don't you believe it."

Whiskey making process

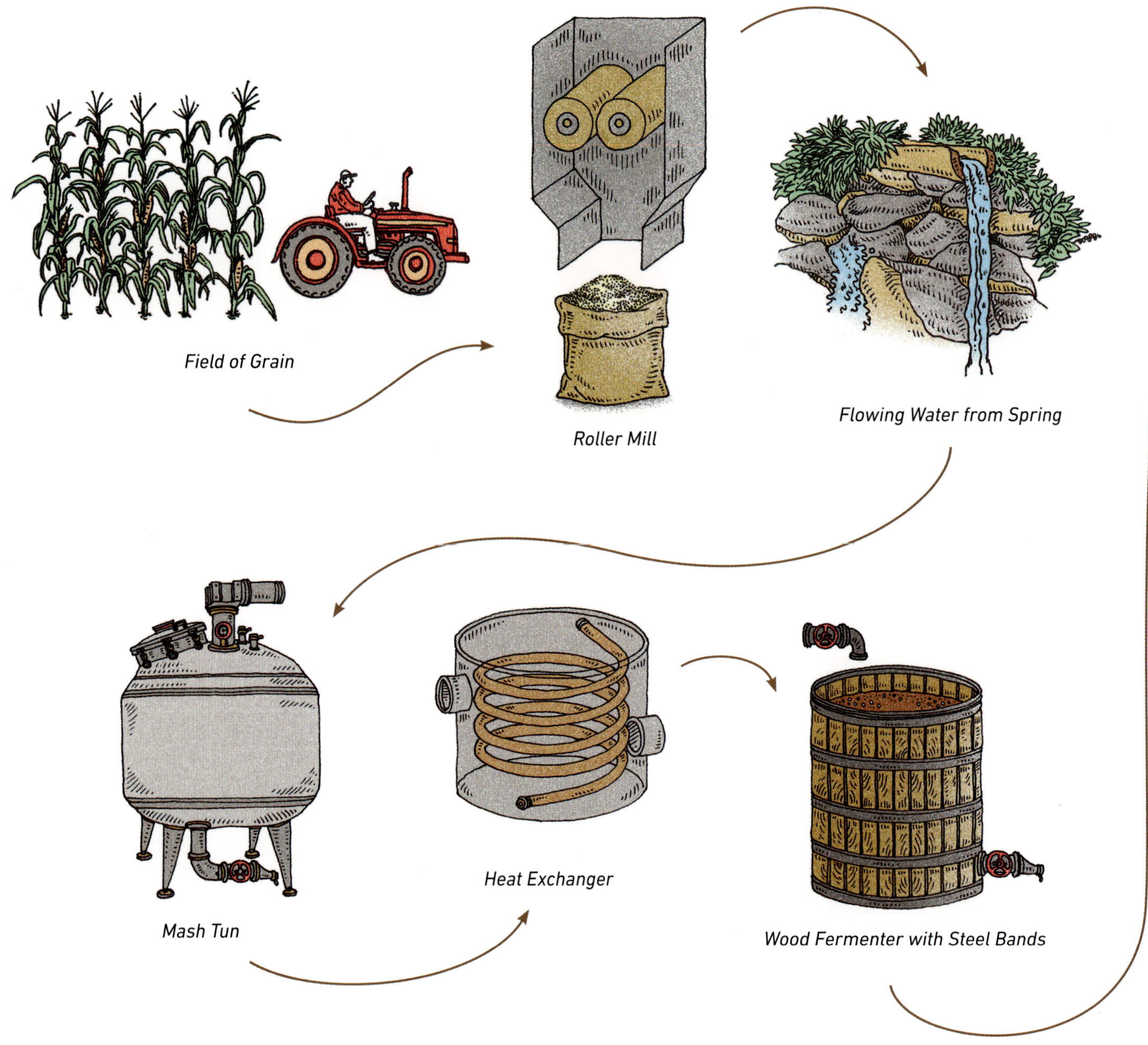

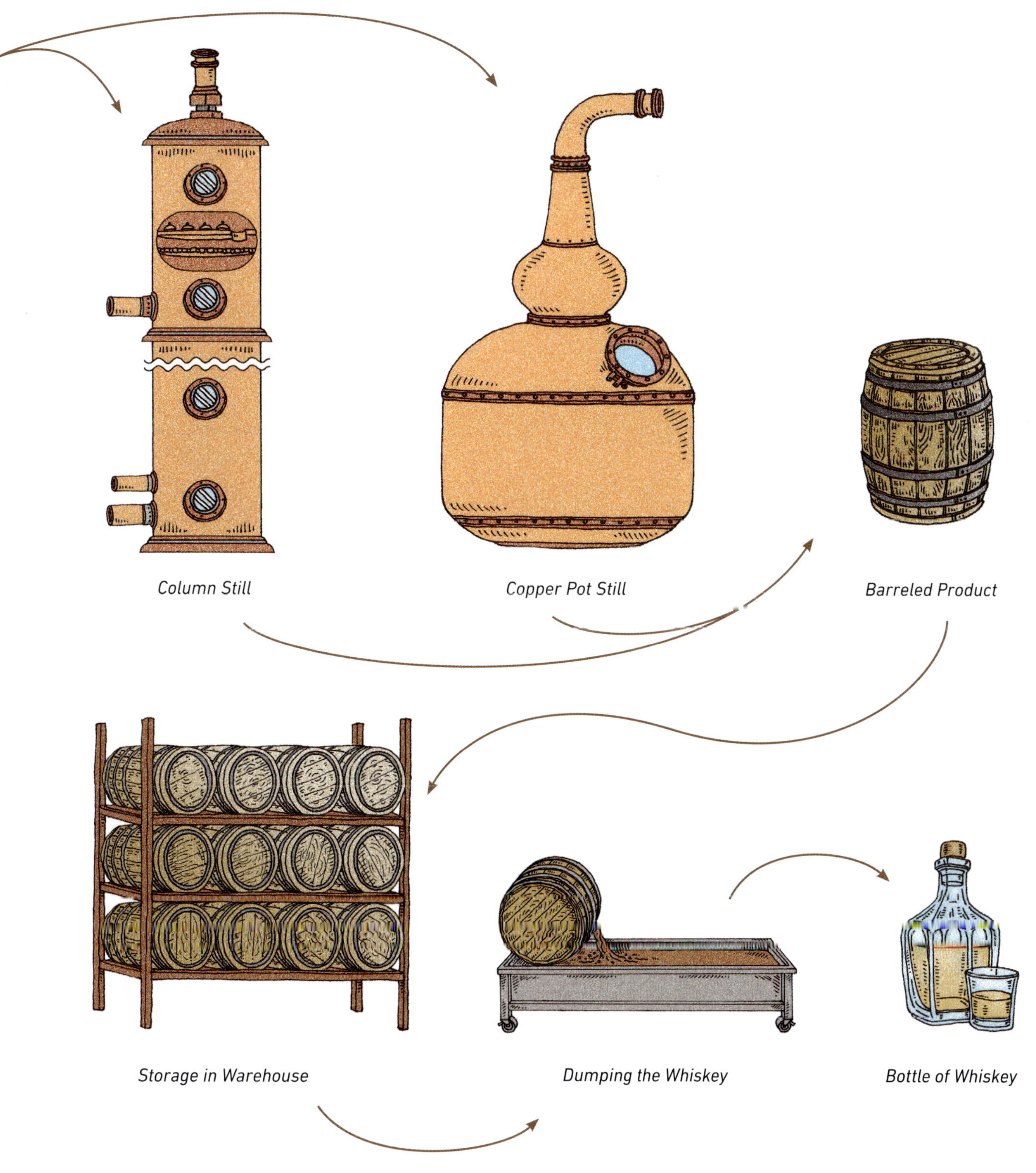
Column Still
Copper Pot Still
Barreled Product
Storage in Warehouse
Dumping the Whiskey
Bottle of Whiskey

“hydrates” the grist (now called the “mash”) by mixing in hot water. It may be set at the temperature needed to bring the mash to the proper temperature for the enzymes to work, in which case no further heating is needed. Or the distiller may raise the temperature of the mash in steps to activate different enzymes at different stages to increase efficiency.

It's precise work. If the temperature of the mash is too low, the enzymes aren't activated; too high, and they'll break down before they get their work done. But when that conversion happens, the thick, starchy mash suddenly turns slippery, thin, and slick with sugar. It's a stunningly evident, almost magical, physical transformation.

I'll mention that some distillers add enzymes to the mash. The enzymes are grown up using molds, in a similar fashion to the use of *koji* in sake. They are usually kept and applied in liquid form.

Why add enzymes? Some do it to boost the enzymes from the malt, but some distillers will set a mash bill without any malt—or with only token amounts—and rely on the added enzymes alone for conversion. Distillery consultant Liz Rhoades notes, in the section on sour mash on the opposite page, that some added enzymes can perform in wider pH and temperature ranges than the naturally occurring enzymes.

Adding enzymes is a common practice in Canadian distilling, and I know of a fair number of American craft distillers who do it. I used to balk at the idea, just because it's not traditional. But I've found no reason to believe that it changes the flavor or character of the whiskey, so I've become more relaxed about it. Completely relaxed, to be honest.

When the mashing is complete, there is a step that *does* have a major impact on flavor and aroma. In most single malt distillations, the sugary water, now called “wort,” is strained out of the grains through a false bottom in the vessel, called a “lauter tun.” The false bottom sits above the real bottom and has thin slits cut in it so the wort can drain out.

The husks of the grain make an effective filter bed. Sugars left behind in the spent grains and husks are usually washed out with two or three “waters,” fresh applications of hotter water. The initial run and the next one or two waters are collected, cooled in a heat exchanger, and sent for fermentation. The final water, the “sparge,” usually becomes hydration water for the nest batch of grist, preserving the last bits of sugar (and saving the energy to heat the hydration water).

But in making other American whiskeys, there is no filtering, no sparge. The entire mash—water, grain, husks, everything—is sent through the heat exchanger to cool, and on to the fermenter. It is called “beer” from that point on.

Sour Mash

Since we brought up American whiskey and mash, we need to talk about sour mash. Let's go back to Liz Rhoades, since she's something of an expert on it. She starts by talking about the acidity of the mash. "pH plays a key role during mashing," she said, "as the conversion enzymes responsible for turning starch into fermentable sugars have specific pH requirements. In the U.S. we are also allowed to modify pH, which most do (i.e., backset)."

When she says "backset," she's talking about sour mash. (It's also called "setback" by some older distillers, and no, I'm not kidding.) Modifying the acidity, the sourness, of the mash is one of the most important reasons sour mash is used. By the way, that also answers the question, if you ever wondered about it, of why there are no sour-mash Scotches: They're not allowed to alter the pH of their water. It also adds yeast nutrients to the mash, in the form of dead yeast.

Where does sour mash come from? The most common method is to take the leftover solids from the bottom of the still, called "slops" or "stillage," and add them to the mash. Distillers might also blend it with the grist for hydration going into the mash tun.

How does the mash get sour? Organic acids are created during fermentation. Fermentation causes acidity, and backset carries that acidity "backward" to the mashing process, where it's needed. That fermentation-created acidity is where sour mash affects the flavor of the whiskey, so we'll put that off till next chapter as well.

What about "sweet mash"? A lot of craft distillers have decided to forgo sour mash. They put only freshly made mash in the fermenter. If sour mash is so beneficial, why do sweet mash?

For one thing, tradition. Rye whiskey distillers in the pre-Prohibition era, and for a couple decades after Repeal—essentially until all rye whiskey production moved to Kentucky—used a sweet mash. For another, sour mash needs to be used as quickly as possible. It's a breeding ground for lactic bacteria and can go too sour pretty quickly. You're only going to use sour mash if you're using it regularly, and a lot of smaller distillers don't mash or distill every day of the week.

But another reason is that the ability of sour mash to suppress wild yeast and bacteria growth isn't as crucial or unique anymore. We'll talk more about that in the next chapter, too, but when sour mash lowers the pH of the fermenting mash, it creates an environment that gives the distiller's house yeast an advantage over the wild microbes that are about (especially in places with grain) and allows it to establish itself.

But with modern sanitation (particularly with stainless-steel fermenters) and brewing techniques, a sweet mash is much less risky these days. Get that fermenter cleaned and sanitary, cook a clean mash, and culture up a bomb-load of yeast, and the need for sour mash is minimized. It's another option distillers have, but it's no longer as sternly required.

The mash is set, it's cooled to the mid-70s Fahrenheit (mid-20s Celsius), and the yeast is ready and waiting. It's time to make some alcohol.

WATER'S SMALL, CRUCIAL CONTRIBUTION

Water is essential to making whiskey, but it's not a huge factor in flavor creation. It's more like a factor that can only make whiskey flavors terrible, unless you get it right.

Iron in water can ruin whiskey. It will turn black and taste wretched. One of the most important things about a water source for making whiskey is that it be iron-free. Kentucky's vaunted limestone water, Scotland's free-flowing springs, Ireland's mystic wells, Japan's forested streams, and Canada's plentiful lakes all provide iron-free water—as do the municipal water systems of nearby towns these days.

But it's not just iron. There's also *geosmin*, a word that sounded so odd when I first heard it that I assumed it was something folksy, made up. But it's real, an organic compound (C"12"H"22O") formed by bacteria that's found in water and in soil. It is a made-up word, but made up by biologists who identified it in 1965 and named it from the Greek words *geo* ("earth") and *osme* ("odor"): earth smell.

Geosmin is responsible for the earthy smell of beets and the musty, earthy smell of some lake water. It's a key part of *petrichor*, another interesting word; that's the smell that comes after rain falls on dry, warm earth. It can also most definitely get into whiskey, as people of a certain age can attest. I know I tasted it in my youth and thought it was part of the flavor of bourbon, which is why I became a Scotch drinker in grad school. That mustiness doesn't happen anymore. Distillers are aware of geosmin now and filter it out.

There can also be positive things in water. I asked Liz Rhoades about water; she's a very bright friend of mine who used to work for Diageo and now does consultation for distillers on fermentation and distillation. The first thing she brought up was mineral content.

"Limestone water has a higher content of calcium and magnesium," she noted. "Both of these minerals are key to yeast performance and also provide buffering capacity in the fermenting mash, keeping stress levels low. Therefore, an effect on flavor, typically in a positive way."

I talked to another distiller about limestone water: the late Dick Stoll, the still largely unknown last distiller at the original Michter's Distillery in Pennsylvania, where he made some truly legendary whiskeys back in the 1970s and 1980s. Dick worked with the same water I grew up with, about 20 miles (32.2 km) away: exceptionally hard water, flowing through a limestone aquifer, that would block your hot water pipes with calcium deposits.

Back in early 2018, I asked him what it was about the water at that location that made it good for making bourbon. "The alkaline in it, as opposed to acid," he said. "Our water there was either 7.15 or 7.2 pH, and everyone said that was better for fermentation. Much more than that, I can't tell you. It worked very well."

Water's contribution is subtle, but it's also absolutely essential. No water, no whiskey.

> "Dick worked with the same water I grew up with, about 20 miles away."

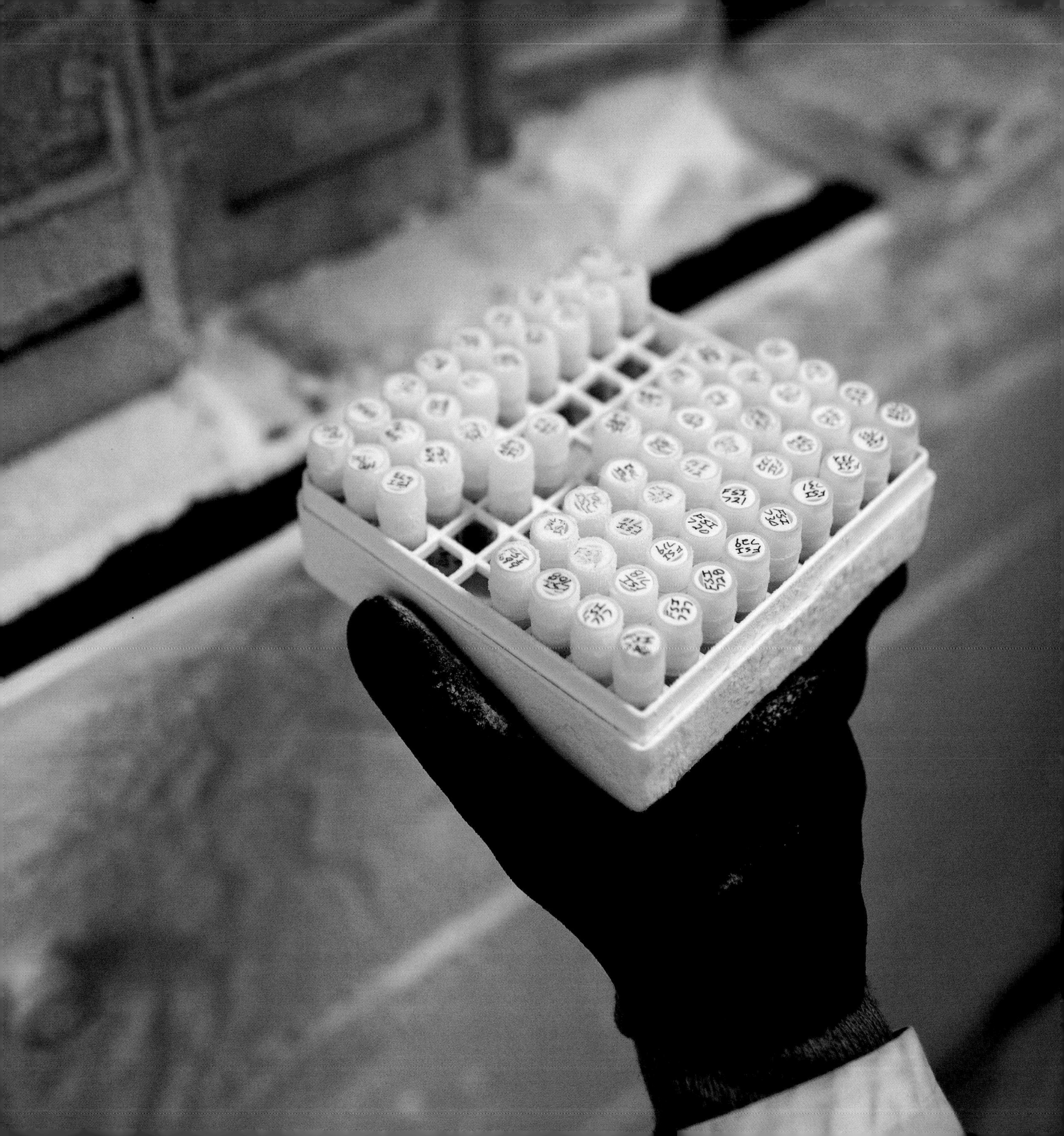

6

The Secret Partner

Yeast is the weirdest part of making whiskey. You can't get around that fact. What happens in the barrel is wrapped in some level of mystery—the "angel's share," the inescapable variety of the outcome—but I think distillers often overemphasize that, probably to soften the pain of losing so much whiskey every year.

Yeast, on the other hand, is another living thing that works with the distiller and does something the distiller simply cannot do for themselves: It makes alcohol out of grain. It's a partnership, or maybe it's something else.

I was talking about yeast to Conor O'Driscoll, the master distiller at Heaven Hill, in Louisville Kentucky. It turned out to be his favorite topic, and he hauled out a binder that was literally 3 inches (7.6 cm) thick and started leafing through it, showing me reproduction growth curves and metabolic pathways. The two of us were chattering away (he was chattering, I was mostly taking notes and asking him to slow down) when he suddenly stopped and cocked his head.

"I wonder," he said. "Has yeast merely figured out how to get us to feed it?" There was a brief, uncomfortable silence before we both laughed. But honestly, if yeast would only churn out good whiskey for me, I'd feed it every morning and twice on Sundays.

I teased you a bit in the last chapter, saying that mashing wasn't really a flavor-creation step so much as a necessary preliminary to the flavor-creating steps in fermentation. Here we are, so let's look at how yeast creates not just alcohol but a rich array of flavors, aromas, and precursors that will be transformed in the barrel.

Yeast samples are preserved for years at -196°F (-127°C).

FOUR ROSES: THE SEAGRAM WAY

Four Roses is owned by Kirin Brewery of Japan.

Before that, they were owned by Seagram, and Seagram always had a philosophy, laid down in its early years by founder Sam Bronfman, that blending was the key to consistent whiskey. Four Roses, then as now a well-respected straight bourbon, would be turned into a cheap blended American whiskey in a weird version of this obsession, although it continued to be bottled as a blend of straight bourbons for sale overseas. I remember the cheap Four Roses, and some older drinkers still can't get past that. One of the first things Kirin did was to end the blended Four Roses and bring Four Roses bourbon home to America.

The Seagram blending philosophy lives on, though, in the distillery's now well-known process of making ten different bourbons and blending them. There are two different mash bills, each of which is then fermented by one of five distinctive yeast strains. As I'll explain later, they age the whiskeys in single-story warehouses to keep the variation of aging conditions to a minimum, focusing instead on the differences coming from the yeasts and the mash bills. After all, why go to all that trouble making ten different whiskeys only to introduce more variables?

While the flagship Four Roses will have a "mingling" of all ten whiskeys, their Small Batch bottlings have a reduced number. The Single Barrels are a rare opportunity to see just what a yeast does to a bourbon. Try two with the same mash bill but different yeasts side by side, and you'll see why I've been telling you that every flavor-creating factor has to be considered.

These are the five different yeast strains, marked by their in-house letter identifier, and what they add to Four Roses' bourbons:

F: More floral, herbal, soft and full

K: Spicy, needs longer aging to develop

O: Fruity, complex, long finish

Q: Huge floral nose, quite fresh and delicate

V: A slightly fruity, well-rounded classic bourbon character

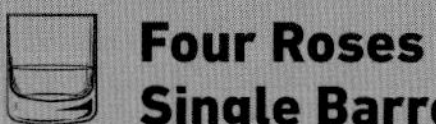

Four Roses Single Barrel

A private bottling from my collection, selected for the now-closed Avenue Pub in New Orleans; high-rye mash bill, K yeast. It's sure enough spicy, right from the top. Clove/cinnamon, orange circus peanut candies. Splashes of orange and spice and hot corn on the tongue, so lively it sings!

Distiller's Yeast

The yeast that distillers use for fermentation is broadly the same that brewers use for ale: *Saccharomyces cerevisiae*. It has been adapted to distilling by the age-old technique of maintaining the strains that worked the best, particularly ones that worked relatively quickly and weren't slowed or stunted by higher alcohol levels.

There are many different strains of distiller's yeast, with more coming all the time. Some strains mutate quite readily. Distillers have to be vigilant for mutations because they can quickly cause unwanted changes in flavor. That's how distillers find strains that give great flavors. Craft distillers are watching for those now, looking for the wonder yeast that gives new flavors and aromas to their whiskey.

Unlike brewers, who often harvest yeast from a current batch of beer and put it right into the next batch, distillers don't usually do that more than once or twice, largely because of the open fermentation vessels so many of them use. Open fermentation is less stressful for the yeast, but it makes contamination with wild yeast and bacteria more likely. Fresh yeast is pure yeast, so that's one way to deal with the issue.

Some distillers culture their own yeast, growing it up from samples they carefully keep cold and fresh. These are the house strains you'll hear mentioned, and bourbon distillers talk about how their

(Continued on page 97)

DONA JUGS

Some bourbon makers go a bit further when they culture their own yeast.

One of the first articles I recall reading about whiskey that was about more than "this whiskey is good, but this one is not" was a piece by the late bartender extraordinaire Gary Regan about "dona jugs." The *dona*—an odd word, maybe from the Latinate roots for "mother"—is a container and propagation vessel for yeast in which the traditional bourbon distillers would culture up their own strains.

It was a procedure wrapped in ritual and superstitious regularity; there were special rooms, special ingredients, and certain actions that had to be performed to make the yeast come out right. Gary told a story about Jimmy and Eddie Russell always cooking breakfast in the yeast room whenever they prepared a new batch of yeast from the dona—tradition, and not to be messed with.

The strains were kept cool in the dona jugs—in refrigerators now, but one hundred years ago, the jug would be dunked in a cool well or lake. The distillers would cook up a small mash—some insisted that hops were critical to the success, while others said no—and add some of the liquid yeast to it. The yeast would grow and be transferred to another, larger vessel and fed again until it was ready to make whiskey.

The origins of the strains involved even more mystery. Distillers would leave open buckets of the special mash in particular areas outdoors—under fruit trees, by fields or streams, or their own back porch—and hope to catch a good strain of yeast. If they failed and the mash went bad, they'd try again. When they succeeded and had a yeast that smelled right, it was off to the dona.

You'd think I'd wind this up with a wink and a sigh about the old days. But this still goes on in some distilleries. It's part of the traditions of whiskey making, and it's definitely a factor in whiskey flavor.

"There were special rooms, special ingredients, and certain actions that had to be performed to make the yeast come out right."

predecessors kept their strain alive throughout Prohibition. Others pay a yeast laboratory to store their yeast or to provide a strain from their library. Some simply toss in cakes or bags of distiller's active dried yeast. Then there's Four Roses, where yeast is an integral part of their entire philosophy.

Fermentation

Once the mash is cooled (too high a temperature will kill the yeast), the yeast is added. Each strain has different requirements for working at optimum, and distillers do what they can to provide them.

Every strain wants sugar and water (preferably slightly acidic), and they work best below 90°F (32.2°C).

Fermentation is a heat-producing reaction, so the temperature has to be monitored. If the temperature goes too low, the yeast will be stunted; too high, and the yeast will produce unwanted flavors and aromas and eventually die. Bourbon distillers used to close down over the summer, especially when demand was low. Lately more of them have chosen to spend the money to cool their fermenters rather than lose those months of production.

Yeast is also notoriously finicky about where it's working. Brewers have told me that the shape or size of the vessel can change how the yeast works. Some of that is about hydrostatic pressure on the yeast in a deeper vessel, but using forced circulation to move the liquid from bottom to top solves that problem. It's almost as if yeast has some sort of genetic memory of where it's supposed to be.

The amount of yeast that's initially put in the mash can also make a difference: A lot means a faster, cleaner fermentation; less can mean a longer, slower fermentation that may allow more wild yeast and bacteria a chance to get a foothold. Those can add their own flavors, some of them desirable, others not so much.

This is where sour mash comes in handy for American distillers, as explained in the previous chapter. According to my genius distiller friend Liz Rhoades, sour mash contributes to aroma formation in fermentation. "Sour mashing and lactic acid bacteria also can provide sweet, green/grassy, spicy, and meaty notes, further adding to the complexity of a whiskey."

Once the yeast is in the wash, or beer, it begins eating sugar and protein, and excreting alcohol, carbon dioxide (which blows off), and very important but minuscule amounts of aromatics, all while reproducing every twenty minutes or so.

That's an explosive amount of reproduction, which is how *S. cerevisiae* stays out ahead of the wild competitors and why it needs protein. Some distillers add yeast nutrients, which hurry things along, but healthy yeast is, like so many other factors, more about preventing off flavors than creating new ones.

Dr. Pat Heist is the cofounder of Wilderness Trail Distillery in Danville, Kentucky. He also runs Ferm Solutions, a company that provides yeast services to the industry. Heist has more than seven thousand

AROMA COMPOUNDS

Flavors and aromas are being created during fermentation.

Here's what's going on: Esters are fruity, aromatic by-products of fermentation that come in various flavors (e.g., isoamyl acetate: bananas; ethyl caproate: apples). Ethanol is not the only alcohol created during fermentation, even though it's usually the only one we want. It may not be the only alcohol carried over in distillation, either, if things aren't done right. These other alcohols may be collectively called fusel alcohols and are undesirable, oily flavors in high concentrations.

Steam-cleaning a cypress fermenter

yeast strains under refrigeration and more than twenty thousand bacteria. Some have never been used for making beverage alcohol, but he keeps samples of all of them.

About those 20,000 bacteria: "You can't avoid bacterial contamination," Heist said. "Most distillers don't even track bacteria, and they're surprised when they see how much is in there. Yeast and bacteria both produce sourness but with different acids. Those acids will [react] with alcohol to create esters in the barrel."

The type of fermentation vessel can have an effect on how clean the fermentation is. If the vessel is more difficult to clean (wooden ones), bacteria is more likely to survive and affect the fermentation.

The aromatics are being produced, and what they are will depend on what strain the yeast is and what's in the tank with it. Rhoades broke it down: "Essentially the major flavors produced by yeast can be bucketed in these major flavor camps: fruity, floral, solvent/chemical, sulfur-containing, fatty/buttery, and spicy."

It's quite a range, and the trick is keeping those flavors from escaping during fermentation, and then keeping these volatiles through distillation—or not.

Fermentation is hugely important, because it doesn't just create aromas and flavors. It also creates building blocks that will *become* desirable flavors and aromas through the distillation process and beyond, in the oxidation, heat, and direct interaction with wood in the barrel.

We'll work with that next, in the big, meaty middle of the book: distillation, the heart of making whiskey.

Old-school cypress fermenters at Woodford Reserve

CHEMICALS VERSUS AROMAS

All the rich, sharp, delicate, and pleasing aromas that are present in whiskey are the result of chemical compounds that are created by conversion, fermentation, or autolysis, or that come from the barrel through direct absorption or through chemical transformation in various pathways created by heat, time, and oxygen transfer.

The very thought of these is stunningly complex to this former history major.

It was intimidating to think about trying to explain them to other people. I can follow the paths if they're laid out for me, but I have to be honest: I don't really understand what a carboxyl group is or the difference between an organic acid, a salt, or an ester. I do understand polymers fairly well, but that's about it.

What to do and how to handle this? Then when I was interviewing Heaven Hill's Conor O'Driscoll, I mentioned the problem to him in passing. I'd realized that to explain the presence of spicy "rye" notes in a bourbon, I'd have to explain that they were largely the effect of the presence of 4-vinyl-guaiacol (4VG) and then note that the 4VG was a derivative of the ferulic acid found in either the wheat or rye cell walls, which was broken down by yeast, but only the right yeasts, and many whiskey yeasts were related to the strain brewers use for the spicy *weissbiers*. . . (This is all explained in full in just a few pages.)

Heaven Hill distiller Conor O'Driscoll in a brand-new warehouse

That's where he stopped me. "Why?" he asked. "Why do you have to name the particular precursors, or the esters they produce? I'm a chemical engineer; I'd like to know that, but every time you come across a name like 4-vinyl-guaiacol, it stops the reader. You're reading, and you see that, and you stop to think about how to say it. Do you really know what it is? Why not just say there's a spicy, clove-like note, and it's from the influence of the grain and yeast?"

It made sense. I've decided to write this without getting bogged down in chemical details that I don't really understand, and probably many of the readers won't understand. (Honestly if you do understand, you can probably figure it out from the breadcrumbs I drop.)

I'm going to just name the general families of flavor and aroma compounds and what part of the process they come from: fermentation, wood extraction, oxidation, and so on. Except that thing about the ferulic acid, because that's just really cool, and I love connections between my beer-writing world and my whiskey-writing world.

WHEAT BEER AND RYE WHISKEY

I promised you a little bit of chemistry to explain the spicy notes in rye whiskey: the peppery, clove-like edge that we find in rye whiskey and high-rye bourbon—usually.

Whiskeys have the same spice, and some very high-rye whiskeys indeed don't seem to have the spice at all—just the pleasant mint and grassy notes. I wondered about this for years, but I figured that somehow I wasn't getting it.

Then I called Todd Leopold at Leopold Bros. distillery in Denver for a piece on heirloom grains, and I learned something amazing about where that spice comes from. He started talking about why he was paying farmers a premium to grow Abruzzi rye for him. It's an old strain, and Leopold had read in several sources that it was the rye that used to be favored for Pennsylvania and Maryland rye whiskey production. But Abruzzi's starch content was noticeably lower than modern ryes: 62 percent compared with about 80 percent, which means less alcohol yield.

That's how commodity farmers and distillers looked at it, anyway. Leopold looked at it in reverse: 18 percent less flavorless starch meant the possibility of 18 percent more flavor. "I'm looking for older grains that have lower starch content," he said, "simply because that's a sign that there may be something else in that grain that is of interest to me as a distiller."

And that's when things took a twist. Leopold, who came to whiskey from craft brewing (and knew that I came to whiskey writing from beer writing), explained that as a brewer, he was trained how to control the spiciness found in German-style wheat beers, *hefeweizens*.

"The spicy note comes from 4-vinyl-guaiacol," he said, noting our old friend. "You control the formation of this compound by controlling its precursors . . . the chief of which is ferulic acid. Ferulic acid is found in some quantities in most varieties of wheat."

I asked Liz Rhoades about this, and she eagerly confirmed it. "Ferulic acid is bound within part of the cell wall material, which is greater in rye and wheat," she said. It's released during mashing and converted to 4VG during fermentation. But, she said, "this is where yeast selection becomes critical, as not all yeast are POF+ (phenolic off note-positive). POF+ yeast strains have a specific gene that allows them to make the conversion from ferulic acid to 4VG. POF- yeasts lack this gene and cannot make the conversion."

It turns out that Abruzzi rye is loaded with ferulic acid. "When we mash 80 percent Abruzzi rye with 20 percent of our floor-malted barley," Leopold said, "I got a fermented mash that smells like the hefeweizen I made for over a decade!

"Stunning, right?" he asked, as stoked as Rhoades was by all this spicy science. "The best part is that for years distillers have believed that the classic whiskey yeast strains are descendants of hefeweizen strains. I confirmed this. The classic American and Scottish strains are nearly all POF+."

If you, like me, always thought that rye grain was responsible for the spiciness in your whiskey, it's not technically so. It's only spicy if you use the right yeast. Want proof? "Make rye bread without any added spices," Leopold said. "It's not the least bit spicy.

"This is why we use Abruzzi," he said. "Not because it's old or cool or because I believe in nostalgia. I sourced the seed and had it grown for me because the compounds in Abruzzi are very different from modern rye. Growing 'old seeds' for the heck of it is not only pointless; it's very expensive."

Hope you enjoyed the chemistry. Back to the simpler world of flavors. But that was fun, right?

Distilling consultant Liz Rhoades makes distilling a science.

UNCLE NEAREST

7

Distillation: Making Cuts

When you're making whiskey, there are a few crucial steps, things that make whiskey what it is. There's malting and mashing, which break the sugars out of dry, starchy grain. Fermentation is the natural magic that creates alcohol from those sugars, harnessing a tiny single-celled fungus to do the chemical heavy lifting. Barrel aging gives whiskey its flavor and color and rounded maturity.

These are all necessary steps, but there is one thing that sets making whiskey apart from making beer, which is otherwise what you have here, even to the barrel aging. That's distillation, the hissing, steamy science and art of separating everything that is whiskey from the beer and leaving behind that which isn't. To understand what's going on, let's go back and take a look at how distillation began and how it grew into the core concept of making whiskey. We haven't done a lot of history in the book, but it's important to understanding distillation.

The stillhouse at Uncle Nearest

Purity of Essence

The first inklings of distillation come from the Greeks, but they seem only to have conceived of it as a way to desalinate water and perhaps make essences for fragrances. There is also archaeological evidence of possible distillation in China in the early centuries CE.

It is the Egyptians who are believed to have been the first to consistently distill alcohol. The word itself is derived from the Arabic *al-kuhl*, meaning "the kohl," the black powder used by early Egyptians for eye makeup. The etymology is uncertain, but kohl was derived by purifying metals, and it is speculated that the word spread to encompass other types of purification, including liquids like alcohol.

This was part of alchemy, the protoscience of material transformation. There is no solid evidence that alcohol was being distilled in China, Egypt, or Greece; that is, not for the purposes of recreational drinking. That would not occur until the 1400s in Ireland.

Distillation came to Ireland by way of Christian monks. Along with their faith and a desire to live holy lives in isolation from Europe's wars and dynastic politics, these monks brought with them an amazing amount of knowledge, mathematics and science gleaned from many sources. Judging from what soon came after, that knowledge included some of the texts of the Arab and Egyptian alchemists who were distilling and rectifying centuries before.

From the evidence in the records that survive, those philosophers were distilling for reasons other than refreshment: science, medicine, perfumery. All good reasons, to be sure, but the monks found the use that would turn distillation into a cultural phenomenon and profitable enterprise.

We don't know how these monks came to distill strong spirits from beer and then get the idea of drinking it in more than slight medicinal doses. We have dates for the first mention of it from the early 1400s. This would have been pot-stilled spirit made from a malt beer, almost certainly unaged, more than likely flavored with herbs, flowers, perhaps honey. We don't know if the monks knew about making the cuts as the spirit began to flow from the condensing arm, but the awful smell of the undesirable heads and tails should have quickly led to an understanding of what "the good stuff" was.

From these small, rudimentary beginnings would grow a knowledge that quickly spread across the mere 12 miles (19.3 km) of water to Scotland and the monastic communities there. There is a 1494 record from a Scottish monastery of the purchase of malt to make *aqua vitae. Aqua vitae*, or "water of life/vitality," was the Latin name the alchemists gave this spirit. The Gaelic translation, *uisce Beatha*, would become—after enough years of drinking it—linguistically massaged to "whiskey."

Soon farmers would gain the knowledge as well and have a new use for their crops. All it took was some copper and a bit of skill to hammer out a riveted vessel, and a farmer was now a distiller.

A distillery in the sixteenth century, vintage engraved illustration

The benefits of whiskey over beer were clear. Whiskey didn't sour or go bad and wouldn't freeze. It wasn't just a drink; it was a fire starter, liniment, cleanser, and medicine. It took up less volume and was much more valuable in trade. So much more valuable, in fact, that the whiskey a farmer made and sold could mean the difference between a reasonable profit and mere survival for his family.

Distillation was truly a disruptive technology. It took agricultural products that were millennia old—beer, wine, cider—and made something completely new out of them. We had to learn how to make it and how to safely drink it (in a chemical heads and tails sense; we're still working on the dosage part). We also had to learn how to incorporate it into national economies. Distilled spirits, once people learned what they were, created not just new industries but new sources of government revenue.

As is still the case today, the dance of taxation and licensing would bring about changes in whiskey and changes in distillation. Change what is taxed—malt, or the size or number of stills used by a distillery, for instance—and you will almost certainly change how people make their whiskey, if they can see a way to pay less in taxes.

British taxation sought out the growing spirits industry like a profit-seeking missile. Without a reliable gauge of the amount of alcohol being produced, alternative measures were found. In the late 1770s, for example, distillers were taxed based on the volume of the large pot stills used in the first run of the wash. Distillers responded by building the stills with the same volume, but much wider and shallower. The wash now boiled quicker; they could distill more spirit in a day, well beyond government estimates.

The whiskey in these big stills, run in Ireland and Lowland Scotland, suffered from a hard-driven distillation, losing more volatiles and flavor. That made the product of the illegal "sma' stills" (small stills) back in the Highlands even more prized once it got to market illegally.

A tax on malt in the United Kingdom was intended to bypass the failings of the still tax. Tax the grain used to make the whiskey, and size of the still doesn't matter. Taxation has had a big hand in shaping whiskey history. Increased whisky taxes in the United Kingdom led the Scotch whisky industry to focus more on the export market. A tax break for including American ingredients led to greater innovation in Canadian blended whiskies.

Meanwhile, a revolution was beginning in whiskey distillation. This was the continuous, or column, still. The main limit, the bottleneck of a pot still, is that it is a batch device. Put in a batch of wash, distill it until it's done, clean the still, and run the next batch.

But what if you could just continuously pour wash into the still, heat it, and get a constant stream of spirits? In the early 1800s, fuels, metallurgy, and physical chemistry all reached a point where such a still became possible. Different spirits industries used it in different ways, but the column still became the accepted alternative to the pot still: more efficient, capable of easily distilling to a higher proof, and still able to produce a flavorful spirit.

At that point, distillation processes were largely set, though the craft distillers are busily tinkering around the edges again, this time more for aesthetic reasons than for those of economics. Let's take a wide view of how whiskey distillation works before moving on to specific stills in the next two chapters.

MAN VERSUS MACHINE

Some distilleries have "digital probes" and "servo-actuated valves" run from a computerized control room. Others are worked by hand and eye and sweat and memory. Is one way better?

The relative merits of automation are a settled argument in most industries. Automation saves money, increases efficiency, and makes for a consistent product. But in the distilling business, tradition often trumps efficiency. Whiskey makers differ on the amount of automation they'll allow in the process, and they have good arguments for both sides.

Consider the case for automation. Wire your system with probes, switches, actuators. Record everything as the distillery workers make a batch of spirit from milling to distillation: temperatures, times, yeast counts, pH, alcohol levels, and so on. Test every batch of spirit as it comes off the final distillation.

When you find the runs that have come out the best, program your control system to recreate that run every time. You have now consistently repeated a great distillation run. You may miss the possibility of the occasional incredible run, but you've eliminated every one that might be below average.

And even when the machines are opening and closing, stirring and steaming, they're still mimicking what a very human person decided and did.

On the other hand, if your process is automated, do the people pushing the buttons from a control room know why they're pushing those buttons? The team that's working in the manually operated brewery and stillhouse knows what's going on, because they can smell it, they hear it and they feel the heat and the vibration. They've become attuned to the whole thing, and that, supporters argue, makes better whiskey and can improve it.

Can they make mistakes? Sure, they can make some, but making whiskey, even for experienced people with a long-settled regimen, is inherently a process fraught with chaotic elements. Barrels are handmade, and they may come to the distiller from a variety of sources. Grain varies; not as much as grapes do for a vintner, but it's there. The weather can affect mashing and fermentation; climate affects aging.

The whiskey will age differently in various warehouses or on different floors of the same warehouse. The blender has to bring it all together; what's one more random factor, really?

Once again, to automate or not, and any level in between, is not better or worse but just another choice for the distillers and their whiskey.

Boiling Points

At the heart of distillation is a simple, basic difference between two liquids' physical properties.

The reason we can make whiskey is because alcohol (ethanol) boils at 173.1°F (78.4°C) and water boils at 212°F (100°C). Distillers use this difference to separate the two. Put beer (whether you call it "beer" or "wash") in your still (whether it's a pot or a column), heat it to the boiling point of alcohol, and then capture the vapors that come off the boiling liquid. Condense them and—ta-da!—you have alcohol.

If only it were that easy. The process is never that precise and clean, and physically never can be. The amount of time it takes to heat all the alcohol past evaporation (which takes more heat out of the mix as it happens), the swirling differences in heat and pressure within the still, and mostly the physical chemistry of boiling two liquids in solution all have an effect, and it leads to a separation that is less than clean and precise.

But thank the dumb luck of humans, who live in a universe of physical laws we never made, for that dirty imprecision. If it *were* that easy, if fractional distillation of wash into alcohol and everything else were something precise and clean and simple, there would be no whiskey. There would only be vodka, gin, aquavit, and the like rolling out of the still at a constant 95 percent ABV (physical chemistry dictates that you cannot distill pure alcohol; just can't do it). Not a terrible world, but it wouldn't be as fine as this whiskey-filled one we have.

Worst of all, it would be a terrible waste of all the flavor we just spent the past three chapters building!

The distillation process has several goals, most of which are made possible by this manipulation of boiling points. Starting with your—let's just call it "beer," for simplicity's sake—at somewhere between 7 percent and 15 percent alcohol, roughly, the main goal is to get it up to somewhere between 65 percent and 80 percent alcohol. If you're making blended whiskey, you'll want it cranked all the way up to about 92 percent. That's Job One.

Getting there means leaving a lot of water behind. That's the second goal: taking out what we don't want. We certainly don't want all that water; if we did, we'd be brewers. But there are other things we don't want. There are unhealthy compounds—some directly toxic, some that have a cancer risk. These are easily, almost automatically removed though, so don't worry.

There are compounds that are simply unpleasant—meaty, heavy, sulfury aromas, smells of paint thinner and nail polish remover—that can be revolting in high concentrations, though some can add bracing body and structure in small amounts. These bad smells are removed through careful control of the distillation process and by the plentiful presence of chemically reactive copper in the shell and guts of the stills (and condensers) themselves.

The third main goal of distillation is to capture and keep the flavors that have been carefully built up over the stages of malting, mashing, and fermenting. These are the things that drive distillation, that feed the still. Distillery brewers have to consistently hit those marks to give the still operator the right materials to work with.

(Continued on page 112)

NEVER 100%

You may have, as have I, experienced Everclear, a beverage alcohol product (and I use that term most carefully) that is bottled in a variety of strengths, including one at 190 proof, a full 95 percent alcohol.

Everclear is a product of the Luxco company, a subsidiary of MGP, the company that makes so much good whiskey (that's usually bottled under other folks' labels). It is grain alcohol, literally more pure than vodka and with less flavor. Please take my advice, and do not, even on a dare, drink it undiluted.

Everclear is for putting alcohol in nonalcoholic drinks, or, I suppose, boosting the content of "adult" drinks. It's the essential component of all the variations on "jungle juice," the young drinker's blend of fruit drinks and alcohol usually served from a (hopefully) new garbage can.

Why on earth do I even bring up this comedy/horror show booze, particularly in a whiskey book? It's because of the question Everclear at 95 percent alcohol poses: "Why stop at 95 percent alcohol? *Why not 100 percent?"*

Well, it's science. It's not a particularly simple answer, but it is interesting and gets directly at the heart of distilling not being an exact process. Ethanol and water is not just a solution; it's a special kind of solution called an "azeotrope." (In fact, I've heard distillers refer to it in reverent or annoyed tones as "THE azeotrope.") An azeotrope is a mix of two liquids such that when it boils, the vapor has the same proportion of the two components as in the liquid.

With ethanol and water, that proportion is 95.57 percent alcohol and 4.43 percent water. That explains what's going on at lower proof distillations too. When we say that alcohol boils at a lower temperature than water, that's true: Alcohol boils at 173.1°F (78.4°C), water at 212°F (100°C). However, what's in the still is (almost all) a *mix* of alcohol and water, the azeotrope, so when we're running the still under 212°F (100°C), and it boils, we're actually getting *mostly* alcohol, along with about 4.43 percent water.

That's why distillation needs to be watched, and that's why you can't get 100 percent alcohol off a still. You can get up to 95.57 percent, but that's the most that's ever going to boil off the azeotrope. You can get close to 100 percent by adding benzene, but since it's poisonous and carcinogenic, better leave that to the chemists.

Finally, just to frustrate you even more in your quest for 100 percent, ethanol has a strong affinity for water; it really, *really* wants to form that azeotrope. So even if you do all that weird, somewhat dangerous stuff to get to 100 percent alcohol, unless you keep it hermetically sealed, it won't be 100 percent alcohol for long.

As always, my best advice: Stick to whiskey.

The problem is that the boiling points of those volatile compounds, the good ones and the bad ones, are scattered above and below the boiling point of alcohol. Distillers (and to some extent, the designer of the still) have to understand where those points are and how to work with them and the limitations of the still to keep what they want, cut or leave behind what they don't, and keep the spirit interesting, all while running the still as efficiently as possible.

Three goals, then: Concentrate the alcohol, remove the water and foul components, and preserve the desirable flavors, all in consistent proportions from run to run. No matter what kind of still you're using, no matter what complex or simple setup you have, those three goals remain the same.

Horses for Courses

If you've looked at the table of contents, you know that there are three chapters on distillation.

The two following this one are specific to the types of stills: one for pot stills and one for columns and other types. Obviously we'll dive deeper into still types in those chapters, but here is the place to note that the type of still is yet another choice.

Stills are a means to an end, hitting those three goals mentioned previously. The choice of still for a distiller is the result of several factors. Big American distillers have been running big column stills—also called "beer stills" or "stripper stills"—for a long time. They are efficient, they are easier to run and clean with grain-in beer than pot stills are, and the distillers have long since learned how to make excellent whiskey with them.

Smaller distillers often use pot stills, or pot-like hybrid stills. It might be because of flavor reasons; they've decided that the pot still gives them more of what they're looking for. It might be much more pragmatic; they aren't making enough spirit to efficiently run a column still. Oftentimes these small distillers will add a column still as they get bigger, but not always.

But don't doubt that good rye can be made in a pot still, or that good American single malt can be made in a column still. American distillers are quite versatile; give them copper, heat, and a steady source of beer or wash, and they'll make whiskey for you.

Column, pot, hybrid, or the three-chamber still we'll get to later: All of them can make whiskey, and all of them can make excellent whiskey. We won't be saying, "This still is better" or "This still is for making bulk whiskey." We'll be having a look at how each still adds—and removes—flavor.

For now, let's home in on how a still works. There are common threads to the process that run through all types of stills. The beer comes in and is usually preheated as it goes into the still to make the boiling quicker. This will often take place in a heat exchanger that simultaneously cools the vapors or the leftovers from the previous batch. The beer goes into the still, and the heating and separating begin.

The first run for a pot still takes hours, as gallons and gallons of beer have to boil. Columns take a couple minutes for the beer to make its way through the still. As the vapors rise, steamy and laced with alcohol and flavors, they rub up against the copper in the still and leave some of their stuff behind. That's where some nastiness goes away. The water and grain residue are left behind.

Some of the vapors run out of energy, literally, then condense and fall back into the still. That's called "reflux," and it's part of keeping some flavors out and letting others through, because it can be tuned and tweaked—and that's a lot of the effects of having the pot stills in different shapes and having cooling jackets at the top of stills.

When the vapors do escape, they go to a condenser. From there the liquid will go either to a second (or third) pot still or to the doubler (or thumper)—or whatever is being used for this spirit—and be distilled again. This run cleans things up a lot more. Then it's another run to the condenser, and we're done. That's new make, ready to be proofed and poured into a barrel.

Pretty simple. Heat beer to boiling, extract the alcohol and aromatic compounds you want from the water and grain bits and leave the others behind, run the vapors past a lot of copper (to pull off more nasty stuff), and condense them to liquid. Then boil it again, lose more undesirable components, condense this good vapor, and you're done. Different distillers do different things with the leftovers: They may become sour mash, they may become animal feed, or they may be burned off. And that's it.

FEW Spirits (Evanston, IL) went from a hybrid still to the beer still shown here.

WHAT MAKES A MASTER DISTILLER?

The master distiller runs the distillery. Or do they? The master distiller has the certificate. Or do they? The master distiller's been there the longest. Or have they?

Master distiller is a term we outsiders throw around pretty loosely. They're the person in charge, right under the owner, or CEO, or president, or founder, or maybe the owner is the master distiller?

Master distiller is a relatively new term, only in use since the later 1800s. Its definition is not precise or widely agreed upon. You can earn it by rising to the top in an established distillery. You can simply become it by applying and getting the job of master distiller at a company; that assumes you have some kind of qualifications, like pertinent experience or a degree, usually in something like chemical engineering. But there's no certificate or diploma that makes you a recognized "master distiller."

You can become a master distiller by starting up a new distillery and putting "master distiller" on your business cards. No one can tell you that you can't, and you don't have to do even a little bit of distilling.

Because of that looseness, some distillers shun the term. I was at Laws Whiskey House in Denver not long ago, for instance, and there is no master distiller. There's a "lead distiller," Sam Poirier, but he told me that they consider the staff of distillers to be the "master," and they're all still learning and haven't mastered distilling. That reminded me of something my father told me once. "If you think you're the master of your car, that you know everything about it," he said, "it's time to sell the car. No one's that much of a master."

I'm not quite sure I agree with that about distilling. There are some people I've met who have amassed a huge amount of knowledge and experience in distilling. The late Parker Beam comes to mind, mainly because even though he was every inch a master distiller, and a good human being, he did not back down from challenges or opportunities to learn.

That's one of the best parts about whiskey. I've been learning and writing about whiskey for almost thirty years, and I learned new things writing this book (and yes, passed them along to you). A good master distiller is always learning, and knows that.

Old Fitzgerald Bottled in Bond 13 Years Old (2024 release)

Warm corn, carefully polished oak furniture, hints of citrus, pastry dough. Full, soft on the tongue, repeats the nose. Slides into a mellow, warming finish, glowing with oak and cooked cereal. Comfortable. Parker Beam (opposite), late in his career, learned to make wheated bourbon and made this batch in 1999. Well-done, Parker.

Evan Williams
SINGLE BARREL
Barrel
FINISHED
Bourbon
WHISKEY

Making It Work

If this is distilling, what does the master distiller do? That's the term used at some places, but others have a distillery manager, a distiller, an operations manager, a brewer, and a stillman. But someone makes the decisions about when to make the cuts, how much sour mash to put in the newly set mash for fermentation, when to add more cooling water in the summer, and when to turn up the steam.

A lot of that job gets done by rote. You turn things on because it's time to turn them on; you do it because the saccharometer indicates that fermentation is complete. But other things get done because the still just sounds right, because the liquid coming out of the pipe is clear and doesn't smell cheesy, or because it feels slick between your fingertips. Distillation is a science with numbers and energy and temperature changes, but distillation is also an art, which is why there are always people on the job.

There's a saying in the Scotch whisky industry: "You can't sneak up on a stillman." That's because as they get more experienced and used to their job, they know what the machinery is going to sound like at every stage, and any sound that's out of place will trigger their alertness.

The same thing will happen with strange smells in the brewery, the fermentation hall, or the warehouse. The very first time I met Wild Turkey's legendary master distiller Jimmy Russell, back in 1997, he told me that he doesn't smell the whiskey at all anymore—which seems mad, because to the casual visitor it's a wonderful rich bath of vanilla, oak, and fruit—but if something's off, he smells it immediately.

People get the job done in distillation. Stills are tools, but people run them. Let's move on to the next chapter and see how pot stills perform in the hands of the masters.

"Distillation is also an art, which is why there are always people on the job."

Maker's
Mark
KENTUCKY STRAIGHT BOURBON
WHISKY
Handmade since 1953
Made by the Maker's Mark Distillery Inc., Star Hill Farm,
Loretto, KY., under the personal supervision of ROB SAMUELS
750 mL · 45% ALC./VOL.

THE STILL MAKERS

Most of the large stills (and some smaller ones) in America are made by Vendome, a family-owned company that has been located in Louisville, Kentucky's Butchertown neighborhood for more than one hundred years.

Vendome Copper & Brass Works makes both column and pot stills, mash cookers, doublers and thumpers—I've even seen their black-and-brass nameplate on brewing equipment occasionally.

A good number of the craft distillers in America use hybrid pot-and-column stills made by the German manufacturer CARL (formerly Christian Carl). They've been making stills in Eislingen for more than 150 years. Quite a few eau de vie distillers in Europe use their stills.

The big name in Scotch whisky stills is Forsyths. The Forsyths works in Rothes, Scotland, makes and maintains pot stills, column stills, fermenters, condensers, tanks, and all the copperwork you require for making whiskey. They mainly sell to distillers in Scotland, but I've seen their stills in America as well. They also make heavy equipment and fittings for the oil and gas industry in the North Sea.

Heat exchanger and pot still being built at Vendome

Huge sheets of copper fill the sheds at each of these plants, and the pounding sound of hammering, the hiss of welding torches, and the whine of drills fill the air. There are few standard configurations at Forsyths because every change in a pot still changes the flavor. No one wants to be the same. The column stills change in size at Vendome, depending on how much whiskey you think you'll need to make. Designs change at CARL, depending on how flexible you want your still to be; they make stills for eau de vie distillers, which are very tight on the cuts. But a distiller may want to be able to make a fat, funky rum as well.

The still is the heart of a whiskey-making operation. Without it, you've got a brewery and a bunch of empty warehouses. It's worth the money to get the best.

VAPOR TEMP
H2O OUT
VAPOR TEMP
H2O OUT
LOW WINE CONDENSER
12.7 GAL.
HIGH WINE CONDENSER
9.7 GAL.
MICHTER'S

8

Pot Still Romance

When the discussion of distillation turns to the difference between making whiskey with pot stills and column stills, there is always the temptation to come up with a neat analogy that will make everything clear. They tend to be a bit subjective. Following are some fresh ones I made up for you:

Using a pot still is like doing crochet by hand; a column still is like using a sewing machine.

Using a pot still is like driving a sports car; a column still is like driving a truck.

Using a pot still is like cooking a meal from scratch; a column still is like cooking with a microwave.

Get the picture? The general idea seems to be that making whiskey with a pot still is the real thing, the way it's supposed to be done. There are definitely people in Kentucky who disagree with that (and some folks making good grain whiskey in other places), but pot stills are linked indelibly with the idea of hand-making good whiskey.

If you look at whiskey history, as we did in the previous chapter, that connection is easy to understand. The pot still is how things started hundreds of years ago, after all, and in an industry that practically shrink-wraps and sells *tradition* by the portion, that goes a long way.

All I'm selling are thoughts and ideas, though, so let's take a closer look at just what a pot still can do in terms of creating and refining whiskey flavor.

The two vintage pot stills at Michter's Fort Nelson Distillery (Louisville, KY)

Like a Pot

That's why a pot still is called that, after all. It's because that's what it looks like, and that's how it works, like a pot on the fire. Do this: Go to your kitchen and fill a pot about one-third full of water. Put the lid on the pot and then put it on the heat to boil. After the water boils, lift the lid—carefully!—and take a look at the underside. It's covered in water. That's condensed steam, and that's exactly how a pot still works.

Well, almost exactly. For one thing, you'd have wash in the pot (again, "wash" is the strained beer from fermentation) instead of water, and that would be condensed water and alcohol on the lid. As we discussed in the previous chapter, the difference in boiling points of these liquids (and the other flavors in the wash) is what makes distillation possible.

But the other difference is just as important: You need an outlet, an exit for those alcohol vapors to get out of the pot. Otherwise, they'll just keep condensing and falling back in (remember that reflux thing?) and escaping around the very loose seal of your pot lid until you have nothing left but a scorched, stinking pot.

So a pot still is built with a rounded bottom and a tapered neck on top. The vapors go up and exit at the top of the still, usually a 90-degree or so bend into the "lyne arm," the tube that leads the vapors away to the condenser. This is where all resemblance to boiling water in a pot ends, but it was useful to our initial envisioning of the process.

In the first distillation in pot stills, the "wash run," the wash is going from the low alcohol concentration of beer, between 7 percent and 15 percent, roughly, and leaving the water behind to bring the concentration of alcohol to between 20 percent and 25 percent.

This is pretty straightforward, leaving a lot of water (plus any small grain bits that made it through the lauter, some proteins, and a tiny, unrecoverable amount of alcohol) behind as alcohol and flavor are captured. The liquid left behind, the "pot ale," is disposed of or may be sold as a cattle-feed additive.

Once the vapors from the wash run have condensed (they're now called "low wines"), they'll be sent to the spirit still, combined with leftovers from previous spirit runs, and distilled again. This time the distillation will be carefully monitored, and the first rush of liquid from the condensers—called the "heads" or "foreshots"—will be diverted and captured for redistillation in the next run. There is alcohol in here, and the distiller wants to capture it. But there are undesirable compounds as well, and they'll have to be further transformed through distillation or disposed of.

Once these undesirables have run out and the spirit runs clean (almost all alcohol), a "cut" is made and the liquid is now sent to a holding tank reserved for new make spirit. There will be a lengthy run to capture as much of this "heart cut" as possible. A tighter, shorter heart cut leaves out more of the sharper and heavier flavors. A broader, longer cut

Woodford Reserve's spirit safe, where the output from a still run is directed to the proper reservoir

WOODFORD RESERVE

will leave in more of the nonalcohol elements, called "congeners," giving the spirit a deeper, somewhat oily character. Again, not better or worse: a choice, a difference.

The next change in the character of the liquid is the cut that redirects the "tails" or "feints." The feints are saved like the heads and blended back into the next set of low wines, the next "charge," for redistillation. Once there is no alcohol coming over in the feints, the remainder of the liquid in the spirit still, called the "spent lees," is disposed of.

That's how a full whiskey run on pot stills works. But that's similar to telling you how to drive a car by telling you to turn the key, shift into Drive, move the wheel to steer, and press the brakes to stop. We've said nothing about manual transmissions, trucks, sports cars, SUVs, or off-road vehicles; we've said nothing about turbochargers, all-wheel drive, snow tires, or changing the factory-standard computer chip. Or, for that matter, directions, speed limits, and the other cars on the road.

Pot stills are almost insanely adjustable. We're going to take a look at that and, of course, how it affects flavor.

Tweaking the Pot

The first thing you notice about pot stills, once you've seen a few, is that you don't often see ones that look alike. There are easily explained differences: Wash stills are bigger than spirit stills because they have to contain a much larger volume of liquid. But we've got bulging balls and skinny necks and all kinds of things going on.

Is this just decorative? Of course not; it's about flavor. The stand-out observations are about relative sizes and ratios, the "still geometry" as I like to call it. Some stills are broad and squat, while some are tall and lean. Some distillers have one fairly large wash still, whereas others may have a few smaller ones. You may see a distiller that has increased capacity by copying the existing stills in painstakingly exact larger ratios.

Why does still geometry matter? It's about reflux and copper. Reflux occurs as the wash boils and vapor rises in the pot. When the boil has just begun, the neck is not fully heated and the vapor will condense on the cooler metal of the neck and run back into the base of the still; it's looking like our cooking pot again.

As the still becomes fully heated, the vapors reach higher and higher before condensing. Eventually they make it to the exit and into the lyne arm.

What's the point of reflux? Think of it as heavy and light balls in a pit. We want the lighter balls to go into another pit while leaving the heaviest ones behind. So we start vibrating the floor of the pit rapidly up and down, bouncing the balls, adding energy to their flight—the equivalent of adding heat to the spirit still.

The lighter balls bounce higher. The lightest ones—the compounds with the lower boiling temperatures—will escape the pit first, while the heavier ones are still bouncing off the walls and falling back into the pit. Some of the heavier balls may bounce pretty high, but as long as we keep an eye on things and dial back the energy when they start getting too close, they'll stay in there. Eventually the lighter balls will all bounce out, and some of the medium-weight balls will come out as well, leaving the heaviest ones inside. This is a middle-run spirit, fairly standard.

Now say we decide we want a lighter spirit: only the lighter balls. We raise the walls of the pit, making it less likely for the heavier balls to escape. That's the equivalent of a taller still making a more floral, "elegant" spirit.

Balcones Texas Pot Still Bourbon

At least two years old. Apple, warm corn bread, and hints of oak on the fairly gentle nose. Clings to the palate, bringing that corn bread and oak up to a higher pitch. Oak dries things out on a finish that feels like a bright-skied Texas summer.

(Continued on page 127)

PARTIALLY POTTED

You may think you need to buy from a small-run craft distillery or Woodford Reserve to get pot still–made bourbon. All the big-distiller bourbon is made on a column still, right?

Well, yes—and no—because almost all of the big distillers use pot stills for a second run after the column. You may have heard of them as the *doubler.*

The doubler isn't generally batch fed like a regular spirit pot still, although that can be done. The stream of rough spirit off the column's condenser dumps into the pot, which is steam heated. The alcohol-rich vapor passes out through a lyne arm, and water and impurities are left behind in the pot. The alcohol level of the spirit doesn't rise that much; it's mainly a purification run.

A couple distillers use a simplified version of a pot still, called a thumper. It's a simple chamber about two-thirds full of water. The hot vapors off the column are fed directly into the water, coming out below the surface. The compression of the vapor as it hits the water causes a thumping sound, hence the name. The constant addition of heat from the vapor boils the liquid. The vapor that comes out the top has left impurities and water behind, leaving it cleaner and a bit higher in alcohol. It passes on to a condenser and becomes the new make.

No one who does this calls their spirit "pot stilled." They're proud to be distilling on a column. But they use the pot to put the finishing touches on the spirit.

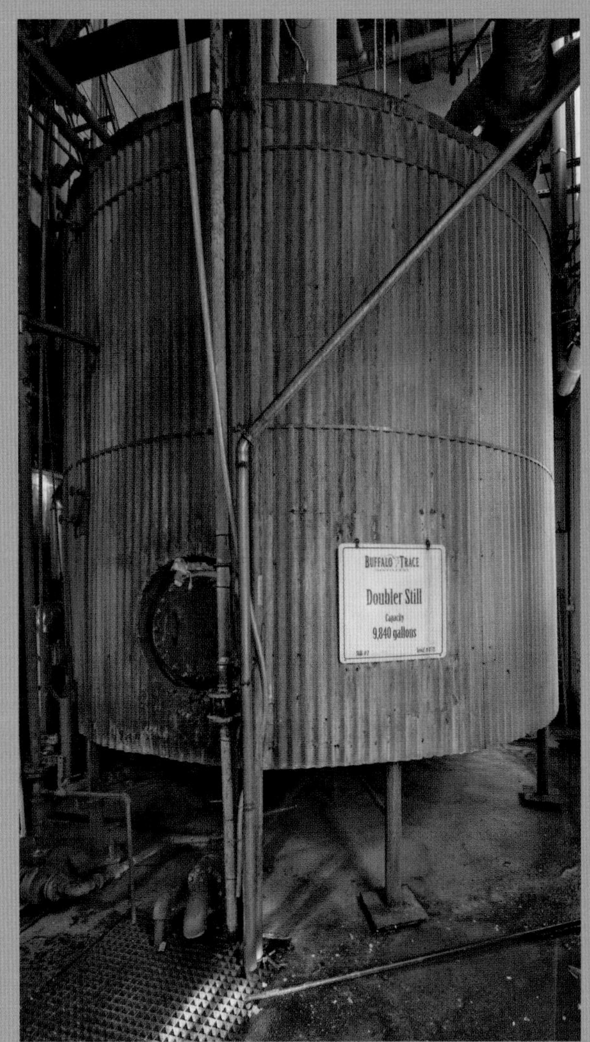

The doubler at Buffalo Trace; not pretty, but it gets the job done.

Conversely, a squat, short-necked still allows more of the heavy components into the spirit: a bit sulfury, some of the flavors we call "meaty," a spirit with some chew to it. We've lowered the walls of the pit, making it easier for more of the balls to bounce out.

In our ball-pit analogy, the first, lightest balls out are the heads, and we'll scoop them up and keep them for next time because there are a few good medium-weight balls in there that "got lucky" and escaped. When the balls are coming out the fastest, in the middle, that's the hearts. The last balls out are the tails, and we'll put them back in the next time to recapture the few slow-moving medium-weight balls.

The height of the still changes the reflux, but that's not the only way to do it. Tall and slim causes even more reflux, as the vapor is more likely to hit the copper; tall and wide, there's less contact and the vapor keeps moving. A still may have a kind of wasp-waisted constriction at the base of the neck (called a "lamp-glass" still); that gives some separation between the vapor and the active surface of the wash. It gives a smoother flow that pushes against the copper walls. A bulge at the bottom of the neck—a boil ball—also slows down the vapor flow to create more reflux.

It doesn't even have to be about the body of the still itself. Running the spirit still at a barely boiling temperature will give a longer distillation and also lead to greater reflux.

Some lyne arms have a slight upward tilt to them, and condensing vapor will run back down into the pot again; a sharper downward tilt, and you make it a bit easier for the vapor to get away (i.e., less reflux).

The easiest way to increase reflux, of course, is to add another run through the spirit still. Triple distillation is most famously done at the big Irish distilleries: Midleton, Bushmills, and Tullamore. But it's also done in America. Triple distillation makes for a lighter spirit because of that increased reflux.

To reinforce, more reflux means a cleaner, more elegant spirit, a lighter spirit with more floral and fruit and citrus aromas. Less reflux means a heavier, more gutsy spirit, with a bit of chew to it, that "meaty" character that some of us prize. Both of those can come through aging in interesting ways, delicious ways. Reflux is terrifically important to the flavor, body, and aging profile of whiskey.

Reflux also increases the amount of contact with copper, and as we've mentioned before, copper cleans up the whiskey. Everywhere hot spirit touches hot, clean copper, the whiskey gets cleaner. That's the main reason that stills (and pipes, worm tubs, and shell-and-tube condensers) are made of copper. Steel would last much longer and be cheaper in the long run. It's just that copper makes whiskey better than any metal we've yet found.

STRANGE STUFF

Some distilleries using pot stills are simply straight-up normal. Wash still, spirit still, boil the wash, run the low wines, redistill the heads and tails, send the new make to the spirit receiver—done. There are a standard repertoire of shapes, tall and short stills, but all pretty similar.

Then there are the other distilleries, with other ideas.

For example, a small handful of Scottish distillers put a cooling water jacket on the necks of their spirit stills, keeping them cooler to increase reflux. The hot vapors never get a chance to heat the copper of the neck, resulting in greater fallback and a lighter spirit. I don't know of any small distillers in America doing this, but I suspect it's only a matter of time.

Almost all pot stills run on wash, but there are some that distill "on grain," like the column stills in Kentucky. The best-known exception is probably Woodford Reserve, where they run their bourbon mash right into the wash still, unstrained. They have to pump it out and clean it after every run, but it gives an authentic bourbon character.

And then there's Mary, at the A. Smith Bowman Distillery in Virginia. Though run as a batch-process spirit still, Mary is really a doubler, designed to do the second distillation on column-distilled bourbon.

Mary is a wide, straight-sided copper cylinder, topped with a constricted boil ball that leads straight up to a spiral lyne arm that goes through about three and a half turns before finally leading to the condenser. I've never seen anything like Mary in almost thirty years of writing about whiskey.

John J. Bowman Virginia Single Barrel Bourbon

Triple distilled bourbon. Big corn, big oak on the nose, honey, flowers, bright notes; is that the Mary Effect? Light, bright, and warm on the tongue with a high sweet ceiling, long light oaky finish.

"Mary" at A. Smith Bowman Distillery (Fredericksburg, VA)

Heating and Cooling

How the still is heated makes a difference. Back in the early days, every still was heated the same direct way—with fire.

It may have been in a brick firebox or a simple wood fire around a secret still back in the woods, but fire was on the copper. This is called "direct fire." It started as charcoal or wood, then coal and fuel oil, and now the few distillers still doing direct fire use natural gas.

Direct fire had disadvantages. It is harder on the copper, inside and out. On the outside, there are deposits from the fire, so the fire had to be carefully tended. On the inside, sugars would caramelize on the copper and grain might stick and scorch in hot spots. But that caramelization also adds flavors to the spirit.

Almost every distiller these days uses steam heat or some other "indirect" method. A few distillers stick to direct fire, though, because of the flavor it adds to their whiskey.

Pot stills represent perhaps the most tradition-bound part of the industry. When a distiller has a certain shape (or shapes) of still, and a particular way of running it, they will want to stick with that forever. Some of that is because of the effect it has on their spirit, and some of it is because they don't want to change anything that *might* have an effect on their spirit. I won't say distillers are superstitious, but because of the years-long aging process that precedes finding out everything a change in process or equipment might mean . . . they are *cautious*.

Now about that idea that pot stills make better whiskey: The next chapter is the column still's rebuttal. I'll see you there.

COPPER CHEMISTRY

Copper pot stills and copper column stills are gorgeous when they're gleaming and polished.

But they're prone to dents, they wear out quickly and have to be repaired, and even when they're working, they get tarnished. And you know some low-tenure stillman is going to wind up polishing them by hand. Yet distillers are in love with copper.

What's the story? I talked to a Scotch whisky blender about it; they've been doing pot stills forever. Dr. Bill Lumsden is the long-time master blender at Glenmorangie and Ardbeg.

"Originally copper was used because it was available," he told me. "It was malleable, you could shape it fairly easily into the shape of a still, and it had good heat transfer capability. It was by chance that it was discovered that the copper chemically reacts with the condensing vapors." It happened *after* fabricators learned how to make affordable stainless-steel stills—then learned a few years later that they made awful whiskey.

You may see steel column stills, because steel does hold up much better and is cheaper in the long run. Rest assured: Somewhere in the vapor path, where the hot vapors off the still are rushing toward the condenser, there is copper. Maybe copper parts, maybe spun copper "wool," maybe something as simple as some sliced-up chunks of copper pipe that gets replaced every so often, but distillers know there must be copper in the still.

It comes down to chemistry. Freshly cleaned copper reacts with sulfur compounds in the vapor—the sulfur comes naturally from the grains—to create copper sulfate. The black noxious-smelling compound stays behind and the spirit flows clean.

Without copper? "[The whiskey] would be very pungently sulfury, meaty, almost a cabbagey smell," said Lumsden. "Not really what you would want. Not only would there be too much of the sulfur itself; it would mask a lot of the fruitiness and subtlety of the whiskey."

Chemistry can be wonderfully serendipitous like that. It's also somewhat romantic in this case. When copper binds to the sulfur, it uses up the metal, thinning the stills, the condensers, the lyne arm; everything copper eventually has to be replaced, all because it literally gives itself away to make our whiskey taste better. We say the best people have hearts of gold; the best whiskeys have shiny souls of copper.

Beautifully gleaming pot still at Balcones Distilling in Waco, TX

FORSYTHS

9

Columns Crank It Out

I told you that I think people have the idea that pot stills somehow naturally make better whiskey than column stills. Pot stills are more aesthetically pleasing; they have shapely curves, the copper is often polished, or at least softly burnished, and the stills are often the highlight of a tour, standing in a well-lit hall, tended by staff in white coats. Pot stills are also easier to understand; they're simpler. Maybe it's my own prejudices speaking, but I also think that pot stills are romanticized because Scotch whisky dominates the world markets, and until quite recently, had been successfully marketed as the superior choice in whiskies.

Let's take that apart.

Let me make a confession right now: I'm an American, and I cut my whiskey-drinking *and* whiskey-writing teeth on bourbon. American-style distilling tends to color the way I think about distilling in some cases, and I have to keep that in mind when I'm writing.

The reason I bring this up is because when I hear the words "column still," I tend to automatically picture the classic Kentucky beer still. But a Scottish or Irish distiller will have a different image.

The column still used in Scottish grain distilleries is some kind of variation on the "Coffey" still, with multiple columns and a pretty complex distillation path. In America, you'll usually find a single column "beer still," sometimes called a "stripper" still.

Column stills used to hide in the depths of distilleries. No longer.

The Coffey still, patented in the United Kingdom in 1831 by Aeneas Coffey (a former exciseman, ironically), revolutionized the distillation of beverage alcohol. It turned the batch process of pot stills—load, heat, distill, clean, repeat—into a much more efficient continuous process. Fermented beer (wash) could be pumped into the still and distilled for as long as you kept the beer running and the steam heating. The resulting grain whiskey comes off the still around 95 percent ABV, or 190° proof. It's aged in wood and used in blended Scotch or in single grain whiskies that become absolutely delicious after twenty-plus years in the barrel. At least, they are in my opinion. The Kentucky beer still, though, takes a single column of Coffey's original two-column still and runs it by itself, with a condenser to cool the vapors and a second pot still–like device, the doubler, to clean the distillate. Still continuous, still efficient, but it's not designed to run at the higher alcohol levels that Scottish continuous stills are. Remember: Top alcohol level for final distillation in most American whiskeys is 80 percent, 160° proof, no more.

To understand how the American column still works, we'll have to get into some details (and illustration). You may have heard that a column still works like a series of stacked pot stills. I don't believe that image is sufficiently correct to be useful. I find it easier to do a very simple walk-through of the column, following the path of the beer.

Here's how things work in a beer still. The column can be of variable diameter; I've seen them as small as 12 inches (30.5 cm), and Buffalo Trace Distillery runs an 84-inch (2 m) monster, the biggest in the bourbon business. (The one at the J.P. Wiser distillery in Windsor, Ontario, is even larger and puts out distillate at an amazing 240 gallons (908.5 liters) a minute, more than a full-size fire hose.) They run from about 30 feet (9.1 m) tall to more than 60 feet (18.3 m), but they're all straight columns—no balls, no bends, not even any squat, fat columns. These aren't pot stills; they're pretty uniform in shape.

In columns, it's about what's *inside*. You have plates, or trays, each one the same diameter as the still. Depending on what the still is for, and how big it is, they may have anywhere from fifteen to more than seventy of these trays. The trays are perforated with holes; the size varies, but the largest would pass through a large man's finger. Then to one side of the tray, alternating sides as you go down through the column, is a wider pipe, with a low dyke around it. This is called the "down-comer."

How it works is pretty simple: The unfiltered beer, mash and all, may start with a run through a beer preheater above the still; it's a kind of protocondenser that uses the hot vapor coming off the still to heat the beer, which in turn cools the vapor. Heated or not, the beer enters the column about three-quarters of the way up and flows downward. As it descends, it fills each tray up to the level of the dyke around the down-comer opening.

Meanwhile, pressurized steam is fed into the bottom of the column. The hot steam rises through the holes in the plates, bubbling through the beer, heating it, "stripping" the alcohol out of it, and carrying it up the column (and that's why some folks call them "stripper" stills). As the beer falls, it gets hotter; as the steam rises, it gets cooler. The whole column is pretty hot, though, and the alcohol and congeners continue to rise.

(Continued on page 137)

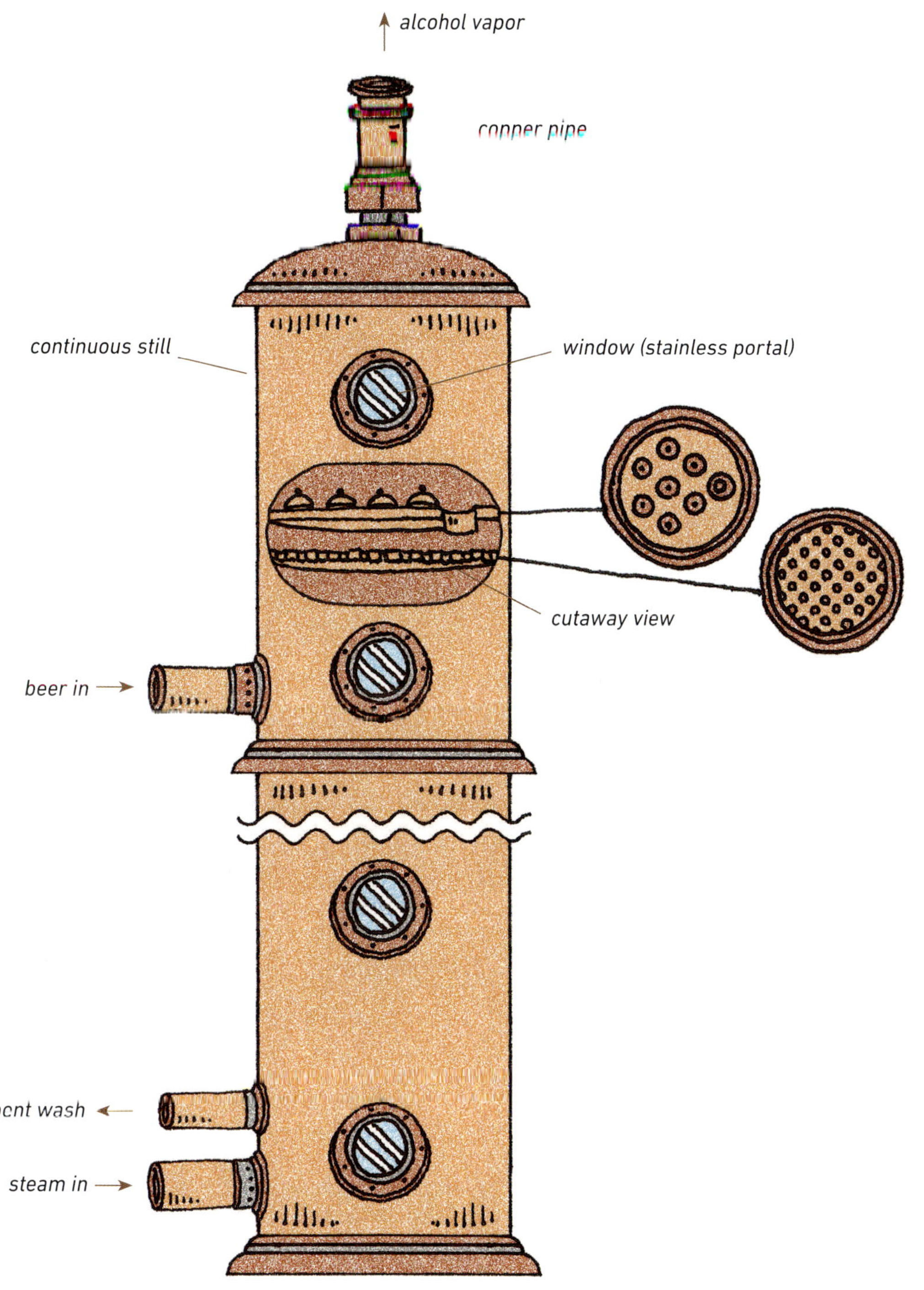

Column Still

OTHER, OLDER STILLS

There may be a lot of new distillers using hybrid pot stills with a column and straight-up pot stills to make American-style whiskeys like rye and bourbon (there are a small number using column stills, too). The bulk of bourbon and rye (and corn and wheat) whiskey in America is still made on beer stills, with doublers or thumpers.

The column still didn't always rule American whiskey making. There were other options, not limited to pot stills, though there were some pretty large pot stills making whiskey even post-Prohibition.

Back in the 1800s, there were stills made of wood, and there were reflux columns filled with smooth river rocks. As long as there was copper somewhere in the system—and there always was, usually in the condenser—the design of the still could take various forms, and often, in this time, large wooden beams were cheap and plentiful. They were effective and cheap to repair. When copper became cheaper and rail transport made shipping easier, the wooden stills and the "box of rocks" would fade in favor of more efficient equipment.

There's another older still type that was used widely in American rye whiskey making in the 1800s and early 1900s that fell so far out of favor that no one in the twenty-first century, not the oldest legacy distillers, even remembered it existed. That's the three-chamber still, but it's actually having a renaissance, so we'll talk about it a bit further on.

The revived three-chamber still at Leopold Bros.

New Riff Bourbon

New Riff does bourbon old school on a beer still. Stone-cold classic bourbon nose: cinnamon, hot corn, and slab-cut oak. Amp it up and lay it on the tongue: focused, in the groove, nothing that isn't needed for bourbon.

Jay Erisman, the guy who runs the pot still (and handles strategic development) at New Riff Distilling in Newport, Kentucky, is, perhaps surprisingly, a column still chauvinist. He pointed out that it's not just "beer" that is falling through the column.

"What goes in a Kentucky beer still is all the grains—everything—and those grains get pounded by live steam," he said. "They enter about three-quarters of the way up the still, and on the way down, they're giving up flavor. The beer still allows for that, and that's important for making the biggest, fattest whiskey possible." That grain also becomes "stillage," the future sour mash we talked about in Chapter 5.

Once the beer's fallen and the vapors rise above the level of the beer entrance, the upper trays often have something called "bubble caps." That's a copper cap, looking something like a straight-sided mushroom cap or umbrella with slits cut in the lower sides, that fits over each hole in the tray.

As reflux causes the vapor to condense in the upper spaces of the column, the liquid falls through the down-comers and fills the trays. The bubble cap is covered by the liquid, and as vapor comes up through the hole, it bubbles through the slits. The bubble cap keeps distillation going at a steady rate, despite levels of liquid on the trays; it also increases contact with copper, with the resulting cleaning effect on the spirit.

The vapor experiences reflux in the top of the column, falling back, encountering the copper (in the bubble caps and often the entire shell of the column), and eventually escaping. At this point, it either goes to a condenser, and then to the doubler, or it goes directly to the thumper.

The doubler, as explained in the previous chapter, is essentially a continuous pot still. The vapors off the beer still go through a condenser (where they encounter more copper), then, as low wines, go to a reservoir to be fed into the doubler. They are heated in the doubler, and more water and undesirable elements are left behind as the vapors come off and go to a second condenser for the high wines.

A thumper does roughly the same thing, only the vapors don't go through the condenser first; they go directly into the thumper and exit under the liquid in the thumper. This condenses the vapors, heats the liquid, and causes a secondary distillation that cleans and concentrates the alcohol in the distillate.

An upper still tray, resting on the downcomer; note the slits on the side of the bubble caps for vapor to escape.

By the way, in doing the research for this book, I finally got an answer to a question that's been bothering me for years and something you may be wondering, as well. In a pot still, you cut off the heads and tails, and while you redistill them, eventually there's stuff you get rid of. With the way a beer still runs continuously, without diversions, where does that happen?

Dr. Pat Heist, cofounder of Wilderness Trail Distillery in Danville, Kentucky, had the simple answer: "The heads come off [before] the condenser as vapor," he said. "The tails either go into the stillage or they stay in the doubler." The doubler gets emptied and cleaned whenever the column still is shut down for cleaning. There's that question answered.

The distillate is pumped to a spirit well (a simple holding tank) and then to a barrel-filling station; next stop, the warehouse.

TUNING THE STILL

You get different distillate from a pot still by design, or by how hard you boil the wash, even by how much wash or low wines you put in, leaving more or less bare copper to interact with the spirit vapors.

How do you "tune" a beer still? Jimmy Russell at Wild Turkey told me how stillmen used to prop a chair up so they could sit, balanced on the chair's back two legs, with their feet up against the column. "You run the still by the sound, the whistle," he said.

The stillman would have one hand on the steam valve and one hand on the beer flow regulator. Some of them, he told me, would doze over the night shift yet be so attuned to the rumble and slosh of the still and the whistle of the steam that they'd be adjusting it, practically in their sleep—a bit more cold beer to bring the temperature down, a bit more steam to bring it up.

Do I believe him? Russell told the story with a straight face, and he's certainly been around long enough to have seen something like that in a pre-safety-conscious industry. But I don't know that I'd want to play poker with the man.

That is how you fiddle with a Kentucky beer still. Adjust the heat with the hot steam or cool beer flow, and you get a slightly different distillation, a bit more or less congeners of different types. Stay awake, though.

The endearingly toy-like spirit safe at Wilderness Trail

Column Complexity

Now that I've explained how column stills work, we need to talk about the role they play in flavor development. It's been my experience that there's very little agreement on this.

Distillers who run pot stills take it as given that pot stills conserve more of the flavor of the wash, the delicate aromas of fermentation, the cereal flavors of the grain. Distillers who run American-type column stills dispute this vehemently, pointing to the relatively low exit proofs as evidence that there's plenty of "room" for flavor in their distillate. Distillers who are making grain whiskey on column stills in Scotland or Canada don't generally get involved in these arguments; they just keep their still running, filling barrels, and keeping it all consistent.

When I set out to write this book, I had a grand theory of whiskey making that I'd been working on for a few years, based on conversations with distillers in Scotland, Ireland, and America. It went like this: Single malt whiskeys all use roughly the same yeast, malt, and variety of barrels; and the warehouses in Scotland and Ireland fell into two general categories: the old dunnage warehouses and modern racked ones. The variety in single malts, therefore, came largely from the casks that were used, the amount of peating that was done to the malt, and the type of pot stills and how they were run. The image I had was of a narrow set of choices at the beginning and end of the process, with a broad variance in the distillation step.

For column-distilled American whiskeys, on the other hand, the image was reversed. My theory was that while the mash bill, yeast, and fermentation regimens were quite varied, and the new barrels could be charred and toasted in different ways and placed in wildly different spots in the warehouses, the beer stills were almost all the same, varying only in diameter. They were a consistent uniformity in the process, with everyone's whiskey coming through there the same. It was not so much flavor creation as uniform flavor conservation.

I was generalizing, of course; but I realized that and accepted that there would be exceptions. But the first time I took the theory out and showed it to someone—Brown-Forman master distiller Chris Morris—the beer still side got shredded! Morris would be the right man for the job. He's one of the few people who has run several large beer stills (at their Louisville, Kentucky, plants) and big pot stills (at Woodford Reserve) for making whiskey.

"They're uniform in their concept," he said about the beer stills. "But in the world of Brown-Forman, you have diameter as a difference, height, number of plates, copper versus steel versus a combination, steam pressure, heat (they run at different ranges of temperatures), how many trays at the top without beer, how much reflux, and the beer itself: flow rate, water/grain ratio. At the Old Forester distillery, you have the Old Forester recipe and Early Times recipe, and [along] with all the [other] differences, you also have a difference in distillation proof. You have to make adjustments to how you run that still to get that difference."

Woodford Reserve

A mix of pot and column still whiskeys, all aged in cycling warehouses. Woodford is rich with vanilla, roasted nuts, baking spice, and toffee, with brighter notes and firm oak on the palate. What comes from the column; what comes from the pot: Who knows?

He then pointed out that with Woodford Reserve, they *do* have differences going into the pot still. They don't just make bourbon there but are constantly experimenting with different mashes: rye, malt, and oats, for instance. The wash still is run differently for each of those. "You have to run the spirit safe differently because the cuts are different, because the grain bill is different, and flavor is different," he said, "and off we go again."

There are a lot of differences, a lot of options in building and running a beer still, maybe more than most pot still distillers realize. It's not as simple as turning a few valves and reading a book till your shift's over.

Columns look very industrial, especially to the uninformed eye. That's why I'm thrilled to see the gleaming copper beer still at the exhibition distillery Brown-Forman has built on Main Street in Louisville, Kentucky. It looks, as I've remarked on social media, like some machine god from *Metropolis*, brilliantly central, posed for pictures.

Maybe now beer stills, column stills, will gain some well-deserved respect. Instead of being hidden away, the beer still has taken center stage, wreathed in steam and roaring with power.

The Hybrid

There's another type of "column" still that's become quite numerous in craft distilling, and I should explain it. If you've been to a new, small distillery in America or Europe, chances are very good that you've seen one and you may have thought, "Hey, that's a column... is that a column still?" You almost certainly didn't see a column still. As far as I know, no one new is running a straight-up Coffey still, and while the number of craft distillers using beer stills has increased, it's still not many.

But it's quite likely that you saw a hybrid still, or what some call a "pot and column" still. It had something that looked like a column, either sitting right on top of a pot still or maybe off to the side of a pot still, connected to it by piping of various sizes. It probably didn't look big enough to be a column still; not enough ports, not enough plates, and lots of extra levers on it.

The hybrid stills grew out of the stills used for making eau de vie and schnapps in Europe, and the biggest maker is the CARL company (we talked about them back in Chapter 7). It's not quite a pot still, but it certainly isn't a column still, either.

Mountain Laurel Spirits, the folks in Bristol, Pennsylvania, who make Dad's Hat rye whiskey, are very close to where I lived until recently; I used

A beer still at Wilderness Trail Distillery (Danville, KY)

to stop in fairly often. They have a hybrid still, and cofounder Herman Mihalich was good enough to take me through how it works when I was there.

It is a batch process, like a pot still. You fill it with wash (or beer; the stripping run for Dad's Hat is done with the grains in) or low wines, and throw the steam to it. As the boil begins and the vapors rise, you'll start a heads cut, then switch over to collecting the hearts when it reaches the right point, the clean point. You'll run that as long as you can, getting clean spirit, then do a tails cut. Just like a pot still. Mihalich did note that when he's distilling for aging in their smaller 15-gallon (56.8 liters) barrels, he'll take a sharper, tighter set of cuts. He goes less tight on the distillate destined for the full-size 53-gallon (200.6 liters) barrels. "We let some of the funk in," as he put it, noting that "the funk becomes flavor in the big barrels."

So what about the column? The column's there to create reflux opportunities. The viewports and levers on the side are to operate the rectifying plates in the column. The plates start out open. As the operator moves them closed—sort of like a damper on a fireplace, not actually closing the vapor path but restricting it—it slows down the vapor's upward progress, creating reflux.

The column may also have what's called a dephlegmator, which is a kind of internal version of the water jackets on some pot stills, or maybe more like an in-still partial condenser. The dephlegmator sits at the top of the column. It is a series of tubes with water of varying temperature running through them. The temperature varies with how much reflux the operator wants to create. As the vapor hits it, the cool surface of the dephlegmator causes condensation, and presto! Reflux: Liquid drops back down.

The hybrid is designed to give the distiller more options to control the distillate. To some extent, it allows the distiller to make more than one pot still out of their pot still. An operator can control the distillation—what regional style it is, how clean it is, how much *flavor* is in it—by a few methods that can vary different processes in the pot and in the column.

For example, the distiller can increase the steam heat on the pot. More heat means a more energetic separation of vapors and liquid, and an increased carryover of congeners to the distillate, which gives a fatter, heavier spirit with some funk in it, like Mihalich said. Shut down the dephlegmator and open the plates and you increase the effect; everyone's going to the party in the barrel! Increase the flow of cool water to the dephlegmator to lower its temperature and you'll make it rain in there: lots of reflux, a much cleaner spirit making it out of the still, and more of the lighter flavors becoming evident. The question is, What kind of whiskey do you want to make today? With the hybrid still, you have options.

That's the whole idea of a hybrid still: to give the operator more options, to put several stills into one. You can open everything wide and make a fat, wobbly whiskey, or screw it down and chill it and make a lighter whiskey. You can add a rectifying column and really crank it down to make vodka. You can even put a gin head on it, with built-in baskets for botanicals, pour grain-neutral spirits (more about these in Chapter 13) into the pot, and let the vapors pass through the juniper and orris root and such as they rise to the condenser.

That's one reason small distilleries buy the hybrid still: more options, more ways to make spirits, because a lot of small distilleries have to make

A hybrid still and distillers John Cooper and Herman Mihalich making Dad's Hat Pennsylvania Rye Whiskey

vodka and gin (and aquavit!) to generate cash flow. They want to be able to experiment with different types of distillate for whiskey because they need to find the right setup for the whiskey that becomes theirs.

The other reason for a hybrid still is because running a column still, a beer still, is an undertaking. The idea of a continuous still is to reach efficiencies by making a lot of spirit. If you aren't selling a lot of spirit, if you don't have the capital to buy enough barrels and storage space to take up the output of a column still, then you probably don't want to take that on until you're ready.

Dad's Hat Bonded

Dad's Hat is rye made in a hybrid still. That's righteous rye, dry grain with a hint of dill and mint. Flavors roll around: that rye grain, sweet malt, wood-spice, just a rim of dill, and a long finish. Plenty going on.

Genuine
Small Batch
Dad's Hat
PENNSYLVANIA
RYE WHISKEY
CRAFT
WHISKEY
OF THE YEAR
Whisky
ADVOCATE
90
PROOF
45% ALC/VOL
750 MILLILITERS
DISTILLED AND BOTTLED BY
MOUNTAIN LAUREL SPIRITS, LLC IN BRISTOL, PA USA

Three-Chambered Throwback

There's one more type of still that's recently gained some new attention: the three-chamber still I mentioned previously. It was widely used in rye whiskey distillation even after Prohibition. Booze historian David Wondrich describes it as "a sort of bolt-action rifle to the pot still's muzzle loader and the column still's machine gun." But by the early 2000s, they had been gone so long, no one in the industry remembered they even existed or knew how to run one.

What does it look like? Well, back in the late 1800s, it was about as likely to be made from wood as from copper. With steam heat, not direct heat, wood is a cheap, easily shaped material for stills and provides a level of insulation not present in copper. Older illustrations of the stills, for patent applications and distillery documents, are actually more likely to show wood.

It would be a relatively tall cylinder, though not as tall as a beer still, divided into three chambers by internal barriers. The beer was poured in the top, and low-pressure steam came in from the bottom. The steam rose slowly through the beer in each chamber to the top through copper heat exchangers. The beer would be "cooked" in each chamber for twenty to thirty minutes, at least an hour for the full process, compared with the ninety seconds it takes for beer to drop through a Kentucky beer still.

As the beer got hotter, it would slowly give up its alcohol, which would rise to the top through valves and pipes and be directed to a doubler, while the spent beer was released through the bottom at the end of a run. The middle chamber charge, now mostly water, would flow into the bottom chamber, the top chamber charge into the middle, and fresh beer would flow into the top chamber.

Distillers seem to have moved to column stills in the late 1800s, but then rye whiskey distillers mostly changed back to the three-chamber still after ten or fifteen years. There were reports that the flavor of the distillate was not the same; it was missing a depth, a richness, a character some referred to as a "darkness."

In 2023, my friend Sam Komlenic, a rye whiskey historian, took me to the ruins of the Old Overholt distillery, where Abe Overholt and his descendants made rye whiskey in Broadford, Pennsylvania. A lot of rye whiskey. Even in ruins, the place is enormous. And we saw the concrete base that used to support the three-chamber still there, about 20 feet (6.1 m) across. Massive. Very few three-chamber stills continued post-Prohibition, and like pot stills, they disappeared in the 1950s. Old Overholt shut down the stills at Broadford in 1951.

Then, more than sixty years later, Todd Leopold, of Leopold Bros. distillery in Denver, was reading old technical papers—"for fun," he told me; it's what he does when he gets home from work. He came across a mention of a "three-chambered still" and was curious, especially when he found that almost all the rye distillers had one.

Indeed, it was always there, right in front of our eyes. I know I saw at least one of the Sanborn Map Company's historic fire insurance maps of distilleries that showed a "three-chamber still" on it, and either never noticed it or passed over it. I wasn't alone; many people didn't ask that question.

But Todd Leopold did, and eventually convinced his brother, who manages the business side of the distillery, that they should spend the money to have one built. The Vendome Copper & Brass Works in Louisville, Kentucky, where they make almost all the big stills in America, agreed to make it, and they worked out the design.

I finally made it to Denver in late 2023, after the still had been in operation for about six years, and Todd showed me his baby. It looks like a piece taken out of an oddly built column still; cylindrical, pieces bolted together, but taller sections than a column still. It's chunky, and even a bit squat, despite being 20 feet (6.1 m) tall. It does gleam in shiny copper, but there are external pipes bolted on and the black trim typical of a Vendome-made still.

Leopold Bros Holiday Edition Three-Chamber Rye

Bottled in bond. Unstoppable rye grain nose, sweet grain, floral notes. Rich grain, sweet dough, bitter oil, more floral notes rolling directly into an echoing finish. Huge complexity. Best three-chamber bottling I've had.

From back in the days of wooden stills, a three-chambered still in cutaway

Also, there are visually *four* chambers to the still, which is a bit confusing, but there's only distillation taking place in three of them. The top chamber is a beer preheater; the fermented beer—with grains and all in it—flows into there and is heated by the waste steam and heat coming off the still so that it's warm and ready to go when it drops into the first chamber.

Leopold lets each chamber cook about 30 minutes, and each chamber brings off different components to the condenser. Top chamber: alcohol and lighter aromatics. Middle chamber: still some alcohol, heavier alcohol-soluble aromatics. Bottom chamber: The alcohol's gone, and it's water-soluble oils and aromatics . . . that you rarely if ever get in a column still. There's the "darkness."

As Todd will point out, that's a total of 90 minutes that the beer and grain are in contact with live steam, compared with a typical run through a column still of about 90 seconds. You would expect that to have an effect, and as I can tell you from tasting, it surely does. It is richly floral, with deep chocolate and fruit notes. A taste of the old days, and that taste has enticed other distillers to commission their own three-chamber stills. It's going to be fun when they all start hitting the market with three-chamber whiskeys.

No matter what still you have and use, it's only spirit at this point. To make whiskey out of the distillate you just made, you have to put it in barrels. That's next.

A peek inside the still

Building the Barrel

I find it fascinating to recall that when I first became seriously interested in whiskey, more than twenty years ago, the majority of whiskey drinkers didn't give the barrel a second thought. They were blissfully unaware of the enormous contributions of the barrel to the whiskey and often didn't even realize that every bit of color in whiskey comes from the barrel.

It seems hard to believe now, twenty-odd years further on. Almost every drinker can quote you the rule of thumb that 50 percent (or 60 percent, or 70 percent, even 80 percent, depending on whose thumb it is) of whiskey's flavor comes from the barrel. They may even know that there's a difference in the contribution of new, charred barrels, toasted barrels, or used sherry casks, and they'll be quick to tell you that the color comes from the barrel.

That's the main reason I decided to write this book, or rather, the obverse of that is the reason why. I remembered a chat I had with Scotch whisky blender Dr. Bill Lumsden back in 2017. "If the barrel gives a whisky 50 percent of its flavor," he said, "that just means that the other 50 percent *doesn't* come from the barrel." Finding that other 50, or 40, or whatever percent is what this book is about . . . but in this chapter, we're going to talk about that huge amount that *does* come from the barrel.

When we do, though, keep in mind that not all of that comes directly from the barrel, from flavors pulled from the wood. Some of it comes from processes that occur during barrel aging that need all the flavors that come from the processes and ingredients we just talked about, all that stuff that happens *before* the whiskey goes in the barrel.

If you run your distillation too tight, you've wasted your efforts with mash and fermentation, and you'll get what folks derisively refer to as "brown vodka," whiskey that's been stripped down too far before entering the wood so that all it comes out with is color and the taste of a lumberyard. The flavor of a good whiskey is the synergy of combining the flavors of the new make and the flavors of the barrel, along with the physical changes of maturation, developing something that's much more than any of them alone.

King Oak

Whenever we talk about whiskey barrels, assume that they are made of oak unless they are specifically identified as being made of another wood.

The regulations for making American whiskey are clear: It must be aged in oak. Almost every other whiskey is also aged in oak for a few very good reasons. First, by those regulations, almost all American whiskeys are aged in brand-new oak barrels, used only once. That makes used American whiskey barrels plentiful and relatively cheap, so they're popular with other whiskey makers, who largely age their spirit in used barrels. Sherry casks are also made from oak, as are the other wine barrels most commonly used for flavor-finishing whiskey: port, Madeira, and various reds.

But the main reason oak is used, and the reason the regulations require it, is because it works really well. Oak has a lot to recommend it, several species in particular.

First of all, oak is just waterproof enough. There are structures at the cellular level in oak that are called *tyloses*, which are essentially small plugs that develop in the channels that pass liquid, sugar, and nutrients through the living wood, the sapwood. As the tree grows and gains more of the woody outer layers, tyloses will block the channels, protecting the live wood of the tree from losses in times of drought or if the tree is infected.

The tyloses will not pass liquids. But they will pass air and other gases, like alcohol and water in vapor form, as the liquids more slowly seep through the interstitial spaces in the wood. This is the source of the slow evaporative loss that's known as the "angel's share," a loss that can run as high as 10 percent a year or more in hot, dry climates like Texas, or much lower in New England or coastal Washington.

More importantly for flavor development, oak is simply stuffed full of delicious flavors. The processes involved in making barrels out of trees don't just make barrels; they create even more flavor compounds.

Is it all a happy accident, much like the ideal nature of copper for stills? Or did whiskey makers evolve to using oak, to charring it, to toasting it? I think we can put the use of oak down largely to its waterproof nature. But charring was used for its effects on color and flavor, and toasting was discovered by wine-makers and adapted to use in aging whiskey. Oak is a gifted wood, and the various species used for whiskey all contribute different flavors to the process.

THE OTHER SIDE OF THE OAK

For a long time, almost all the American white oak used in making American whiskey came from Arkansas and Missouri. There's a lot of oak there, and consequently a lot of sawyers who know what they're looking for in oak, and the coopers' stave mills are there. There was white oak in other places, but moving an oak log worth cutting into barrels to those mills is expensive over distances like that; they're heavy, long, and awkwardly irregular.

When the whiskey boom hit, and craft distillers started buying barrels, conference room lights went on at cooperages across the U.S. and in Europe. They took a careful look at what was going on, decided it was a long-term trend, and took measures. Those included building stave mills in the eastern range of the Appalachian Mountains, West Virginia, Ohio, Pennsylvania, Virginia, and Tennessee. Now the mills were where the trees were.

These eastern white oaks were different from the ones that grew in Missouri and Arkansas. They grew on steeper slopes in more marginal soil. That meant harvesting was a bit more difficult (or a lot more difficult on some truly steep slopes, requiring special equipment), and it also meant that the trees grew more slowly, which meant they had a tighter grain. That meant less leakage, less loss, and that changes how whiskey ages. Again, not better or worse: different.

I've also heard from a couple of distillers that barrels made from white oak harvested in Minnesota may impart a minty note. It's the same species of tree, but a different climate, different amount of sunlight, and different soil all have the potential to change the flavors and aromas the barrel can give the whiskey. Every little thing can make a difference.

"Every little thing can make a difference."

***Quercus alba:* White Oak**

White oak from the forests of Missouri and Arkansas makes up the lion's share of American whiskey barrels. It grows relatively straight and clean, with few branches in the first 20 feet (6.1 m). The cellular structure is fairly loose, but with the effect of the tyloses and the quarter-sawing technique that cuts across the growth rings to take the most advantage of that effect, white oak will make a watertight barrel.

White oak, once air-dried, toasted, and charred, will yield a distinct set of flavors to a whiskey. This species has more vanilla, citrus, and coconut sources than in the other species favored for barrels. The barrels are charred for use in aging bourbon, and that char will also act as a filter for the sulfur compounds found in corn.

Some folks believe that American whiskey must be aged in white oak, but it's merely the most common species used. Here are some others that are used in small amounts, either new or used (usually as a finishing wood, after the main maturation in white oak).

***Quercus petraea:* Sessile Oak**

Q. petraea is what most people are thinking of when they talk about Hungarian oak, for the same reason that *Q. robur* is thought of as Limousin oak; there are extensive forests in Hungary of almost all *Q. petraea*. It is just beginning to be used for whiskey making and has lower levels of tannins than *Q. robur* but is described as "quite aromatic" by winemakers.

***Quercus garryana:* Oregon White Oak**

Q. garryana grows on the West Coast of the United States in an area much smaller than it used to be. It is largely protected now, so coopers are making barrels from trees that are either newly harvested from private lands or had already been cut or fallen. The high level of tannins requires extra-long air-drying to leach the astringency out of the wood. Once that's done, *Q. garryana* will give aromas of dark fruit and tangy smoke, almost like a sweet Kansas City barbecue sauce. Westland Distillery in Seattle has been doing some groundbreaking work with *Q. garryana* aging.

Westland Garryana

American single malt, aged in Garryana oak. A big sweet/acid edge, like a Kansas City barbecue sauce. Roars on the palate but doesn't blow out the sweet malt or the cocoa notes. Dynamic balance of two huge influences.

***Quercus robur:* Pedunculate Oak**

Q. robur is also known as Limousin, or French oak, because of the large forests of *Q. robur* that grow in the Limousin area of France. It also grows in Eastern Europe, often mingled with *Q. petraea*. The largest part of the harvest of *Q. robur* goes to the wine industry, but it is also used in barrels for cognac and Armagnac, and for sherry, port, and Madeira, the fortified wines whose *Q. robur* casks are prized for whiskey aging. *Q. robur* is less dense than white oak but has a tighter grain and higher levels of tannins. The grain makes it necessary to split the oak rather than sawing it to get a watertight barrel.

Whiskey will get flavors of dried fruits, spice, leather, and chocolate from *Q. robur.*

***Quercus mongolica*: Mizunara Oak**
Japanese-grown mizunara represents a tiny portion of whiskey barrels overall, but the interest in the whiskey aged in them has been intense. These trees take two to five times as long to reach barrel-making maturity. Not only do they have to be tall enough, but their porous wood requires a larger-diameter trunk to be cut in a way that prevents too much leakage.

Mizunara gives aromas of sandalwood and spice. Like *Q. garryana*, it is used in only a small handful of whiskeys.

Yama Mizunara
Bainbridge Organic Distillers paid dearly for some mizunara barrels to age their unmalted barley spirit. It yields aromas of sandalwood, tropical fruit (ripe firm mango), putty, and spicy oak, and bright flavors of ripe fruit, busy woodshop, vanilla, and allspice. Money well spent.

Putting head hoops on a new barrel

MAKING IT HARDER

We put white oak flooring in our house when we remodeled and stained it with a color called "Antique Bourbon." Our contractor, who'd been working with me for a while by this time, laughed when he saw the choices. "I knew you'd pick that!" he said, and he was probably right. But the thing that sealed the deal was that the flooring was quarter-sawn. I mean . . . bourbon stain, bourbon wood, and bourbon cut!

What does "quarter-sawn" mean? It's pretty literal. The oak log is cut in quarters, lengthwise, four equal pieces, like a carrot sliced up for a relish tray. Then the pieces are sawn into staves sequentially, one off the first flat side, then the other, and so on until the piece becomes too small to cut more staves (see illustration).

Why do they do this? It's not to save money; quarter-sawing is more labor-intensive and wastes more wood than plain-sawing, straight through the log. But quarter-sawing cuts perpendicular to the growth rings, which makes the plank stronger, resistant to warping and "cupping" (where the long edges on one side curl upward, cupping the surface), and, most importantly for barrels, more water-resistant.

Quarter Cut

Making Barrels Creates Flavor

Oak is an aromatic wood. If you've ever been at a cutting site and smelled the tangy wetness of fresh-cut oak, you know there's a lot to work with.

Flavor is already *in* the oak when it's about to be cut to make barrels. But the full process of bringing oak from the forest to the point of filling a finished barrel with new make spirit refines those flavors and aromas and creates new ones. Here's how it works:

Sawyers are the first folks in the chain, the people who go out in the woods with chainsaws. They're usually cutting for general lumber, but they are always looking for oaks that are the right size for making barrels, because those trees are worth more money. The diameter will vary with the type of oak, but it's somewhere between 14 inches (35.6 cm) and 27 inches (68.6 cm). They need to be able to get at least one 4-foot (1.2 m)-tall set of staves out of the log, preferably two, before hitting the first branch. Branches mean knots; knots mean leaks.

Human-led flavor creation begins when the logs arrive at the stave mill yard. They will be kept wet until they're ready to be cut into staves. As the logs sit wet, constantly hosed down by water guns, tannins begin to leach out of the wood. You can see the darkness in the runoff. Beneficial fungus has begun growing on the wood that's doing similar things: breaking down tannins and also making sugars out of cellulose.

When it's their turn, the logs will be cut into staves, which are still flat at this point; the curving comes later. Then they'll be stacked in a drying yard for seasoning. It seems counterintuitive to see open-air-drying yards where the wood gets soaked by every passing shower, but it's not the wood's surface that's being dried. Water is coming out of the wood's dead cells, and as it does, it brings more tannins with it.

The wood is seasoned to the liking of the individual distilleries: some as short as three months, some as long as twenty-four months or even longer. Some bourbon aficionados have developed a mythology around the length of this open-air seasoning and feel that the longer, the better (and that the only reason to season for less than three years is to save money).

I wanted to know if there's anything to that, because I tend to be a skeptic, so I asked Andrew Wiehebrink. He's the director of spirit research and innovation at Independent Stave Company; they make a huge number of new, charred oak barrels for American whiskey every year. Andrew is the go-to guy in American whiskey for oak research.

"It's a great story, seven-year-old wood, but I don't know how much difference it really makes," he told me. "Seasoning does nothing a proper toast or char can't do. They're both breaking down cellulose and such. An aged stave will give you more extractants, but a toast will give you a lot more. We'll season American oak up to twenty-four months, for the tannin extraction."

That's not to say that's always best. Just that maybe air-seasoned to seven years isn't necessarily always best either. In any case, the staves are often put in a moist kiln after seasoning to get the moisture level uniform, so every stave behaves the same when being shaped.

The staves go from there to the cooperage to be made into barrels. The moisture level may be uniform, but by this time—unless something notably unusual has been going on—the staves cut from a given tree are scattered throughout the yard, and it's unlikely that they'll wind up in the same barrel. Call it uniformity through chaos, as each barrel has a random assortment of trees represented in its staves.

The staves are cut to uniform lengths and shaped with one side (the outer side) slightly wider so they will fit together in circular barrel form. Widths are inevitably *not* similar, due to the pattern of quarter-sawn logs.

The coopers pull staves from bins and place them in a circular guide, "raising" the barrels and achieving remarkably similar dimensions, working only by eye to judge the size of the staves that will go together. It takes them about a minute for each barrel, and it's fascinating to watch.

The workers putting the heads together perform a similar puzzle-piece assembly with shorter staves and pin the staves together with dowels. They then put the head in a jig that holds it in place as a saw cuts away everything that isn't a circular barrelhead. The edge of the head gets cut in a double bevel, called a croze, that will fit into a corresponding croze groove that will be cut into the inside of the staves in the raised barrel.

Now the staves are briefly steamed to make the wood pliable, and the two ends are drawn together by tightening a cable around them, creating a tight seal. This also begins flavor creation again, incredibly. The lignin in the oak, the "woody" part that gives it strength and structure, has been breaking down into sugars and vanillin (which tastes exactly the way you'd think it does—it's used in artificial vanilla flavoring) during the seasoning, and this physical stress of bending continues that process. The next step will accelerate it.

Heat comes next, either a slow, radiant heat for what's called "toasting" or a roaring direct flame that will actually char the wood to a varying degree, depending on the distiller's specifications. The heat changes the oak, physically and chemically, making a wooden container into a chemical-reaction chamber, a filter, and an infusion vessel.

Depending on whom the cooperage is making the barrel for, the first step may be to toast the wood. This involves heating it with an electric element like an infrared quartz heater or, more traditionally, by placing the still open-ended barrel over a small fire of wood chips. Toasting changes the sugar makeup of the wood surfaces and caramelizes other sugars. Not every distiller requests toasting.

Toasted or not, a barrel that's going to be used to age American whiskey is required to be charred. This high-intensity treatment with an open gas flame literally chars the inside of the barrel, creating caramels, breaking down more lignin to create more vanillin and flavor compounds and precursors to flavor compounds, like 4-Ethylguaiacol (smoky), furfural (biscuit/grain), and esters (fruits). These are concentrated in a layer just below the char, a reddish layer that's called, simply, the "red layer."

The char itself is a highly effective filter that will pull undesirable flavors out of the spirit, particularly sulfur compounds. Organic charcoal, known for thousands of years and very low-tech, is still one of the most effective chemical filters known, and it works well in barrels. Char level is measured on a 1 to 7 scale that rises with the depth of char; most whiskey barrels are between a 3 and a 4.5.

The heads of the barrels are now fitted into the croze grooves in the barrel. The heads have also been either toasted or charred; some distillers choose to only toast the heads without charring them, exposing the spirit to a greater amount of the toasted sugars and caramels.

Michter's US*1 Toasted Barrel Finish Bourbon 2024

Finished in toasted (not charred) barrels. Vanilla and horchata with spikes of oak fill the rich nose. Some heat on the palate, but gentle waves of vanilla and light spice soothe it sweetly. Lovely stuff.

Once the steel hoops are placed and hammered into place, the barrel is done, at least as far as flavor-creating work is concerned. A bunghole is drilled and a bung fitted, either in the large bung stave for a barrel headed for a rickhouse or in one of the heads if the barrel is destined for a palletized warehouse, where it will sit up on end.

(Continued on page 162)

Sending barrelheads through char treatment

SOMETHING UNUSUAL: BUFFALO TRACE'S SINGLE OAK PROJECT

Back in 1999, the folks at Buffalo Trace Distillery in Frankfort, Kentucky, started an ambitious project that had something quite unusual at its core. Working with barrel maker Independent Stave Company (ISC, the world's largest maker of whiskey and wine barrels), they arranged for ninety-six oaks to be cut and carefully kept track of each stave cut from the top and bottom of each log.

After seasoning, the staves from each top and each bottom were put together by ISC's coopers; each top making one barrel, each bottom making one barrel, 192 barrels in all.

Seven different factors were varied: mash bill (wheat or rye bourbon), entry proof (105° or 125° proof), stave seasoning (six or twelve months), wood grain size (tight, average, or coarse), warehouse type (concrete or wooden floor), barrel char level (three or four), and the big one: tree cut, whether the wood for the barrel came from the top or bottom half of the harvested log. The "top" is just the top of that bottom log of the tree, what they call the "money log." Anything above that is usually cut for railroad ties or pallets, at a much lower rate paid to the sawyer.

The filled barrels were aged for eight years, then bottled with numbers that were tagged to the different variables, known only to the distillery at that time. They were released on the market, and customers were encouraged to enter their opinions of the various bottles online.

Buffalo Trace gathered this crowd-sourced data and threw it into a huge spreadsheet. There were about a dozen that rose to the top, but the ultimate favorite was a rye recipe bourbon, entered at 125° proof into a barrel charred to a number four depth, made from staves cut from the bottom half of a tree with average grain and air-seasoned for twelve months, and aged for eight years in a concrete-floored warehouse.

But the real lesson of the exercise, according to Buffalo Trace master distiller Harlen Wheatley, was that making good whiskey actually depended on mixing things up—that "uniformity through chaos" I mentioned earlier. "We realized that our regular bourbons need to have barrels made from randomly sourced logs," Wheatley said, "not all bottoms or tops, not all from one place. They all have something to offer." Besides, as Buffalo Trace president Mark Brown pointed out, it's not like they could go through the forest only cutting down the bottom of trees.

"We realized that our regular bourbons need to have barrels made from randomly sourced logs."

Time to see if it's ready for whiskey. The barrel is filled with water, a rubber bung is hammered home in the bunghole, and the barrel is pressurized to check for leaks. Any leaks are quickly repaired with a fascinating selection of special tools, small wedges and plugs of wood, and reeds (which are thin enough to slip into a crack, and then swell to seal it). Once it's watertight, the barrel is shipped.

That's how more than 95 percent of the barrels used for American whiskey are made. Wine barrels destined for refill as whiskey barrels are built in largely the same manner, though in different sizes and shapes, and the European oak is not quarter-sawn, but split. These barrels are usually toasted but will not be charred.

ENTRY PROOF

"Entry proof" is the alcohol proof at which the new make goes into the barrel. The legal maximum for American whiskey is 125° proof, or 62.5 percent ABV.

A distillery would be tempted to put the whiskey in at higher proof because it's cheaper. You can fit more higher-proof whiskey into fewer barrels, and barrels cost money, as does warehouse space to age them. A higher entry proof isn't traditional, and some distillers have decided that lower entry proof makes their whiskey taste better, even though it's more expensive to do so.

But is it better? Or is it different? A few years ago I talked to Jane Bowie about this when she was still director of innovation at Maker's Mark (she's since opened the new Potter Jane distillery in Springfield, Kentucky, with former Maker's distiller Denny Potter). She told me they'd done some trials with different entry proofs, tasting them over seven years.

"We did different entry proofs from 110 up to 125," she said. "Changing it just a little made it something you wouldn't recognize. The tannins in the 110 are much higher. It wouldn't be Maker's. You knew entry proof matters; you just never knew how much."

Some drinkers think a lower entry proof means better whiskey, and I wonder if they think that because they've tasted it or because they feel that if it's more expensive, and traditional, and harder, it must be better. But recall the results of the blind crowd-sourced tasting for the Buffalo Trace Single Oak Project we just talked about. When they tasted it blind, overall people preferred a whiskey that had a high entry proof. Like a lot of things with whiskey, low entry proof isn't better or worse; it's another choice.

Barrelheads getting charred

BUNGS: THE OTHER WOOD

Whiskey barrels are filled through a bunghole, which is plugged with a wooden bung. The bung is often made of poplar, not oak. Some distillers do use oak; Maker's Mark uses walnut. But the great majority use poplar. (Silicon bungs may be used on a finishing barrel to facilitate the more frequent sampling.)

Why poplar? It's cheap and plentiful, it's soft (but not too soft), and it expands well to make a tight seal. The important question is whether it has any influence on the flavor of the whiskey. It doesn't, but not because it's poplar. If the warehouse workers have done their jobs right, the bung is in the topmost stave as the barrel rests through the years. They're placed that way to minimize leaks. The bung isn't actually touching the whiskey, so no flavor. Simple.

BROWN FORMAN

PALLETIZED BARRELS

A barrel has traditionally had the filling hole in the side in one of the wider staves so that the wood could be drilled for the hole and still be strong. Since this hole, no matter how tightly bunged (the plug is known as a "bung," and the hole therefore is a "bunghole," making the stave the "bung stave"), is the spot most likely to leak, it is part of the warehouse crew's job to "clock" the barrels as they roll them into the racks. That means they're placing them so that when the barrel comes to rest, the bung is on the top stave and won't leak.

Through experience, they know where to place the bung stave as they roll each barrel in; that position changes as each barrel rolls into the rack and shortens the run.

Some distillers have begun to place their barrels on end, on pallets. The bung is in one of the heads. Once the barrels are filled, they're strapped together—usually four to a pallet—and the pallet is then put in place in the warehouse by forklift. A very expensive, sparkless forklift.

These palletized warehouses can hold a much greater density of barrels, as they can be stacked with only the strength of the barrel and the pallet to hold them up. The barrels are easier to move and place than with muscle power. The downside is that they are harder to pull apart to get at particular barrels, and there isn't as much air circulation. There also is not as much contact with the wood on the heads of the barrels—exactly half as much. If you want to toast your heads rather than char them, this is an issue.

Palletization remains the choice of the individual distiller. It also can make for good whiskey.

"The pallet is then put in place in the warehouse by forklift. A very expensive, sparkless forklift."

Filling the Barrels

We'll cover more of this in the chapter on aging, but let's talk about what's going to be delivered (and taken away) from the whiskey pretty quickly in the first few years of interaction with the barrel. As has been said several times, the barrel delivers the largest part of the flavor to a whiskey. But it's relatively easy to explain because it is so concentrated and so direct. There are flavors in the oak; alcohol and water pull them out.

The strong flavors a new barrel will impart are generally considered overpowering to other types of whiskey (Scotch, Irish, Canadian). American whiskeys are designed for it, fermented for it, distilled for it.

Whenever I think about what goes on in a new, charred oak barrel as new make becomes whiskey, a Winston Churchill quote comes to mind. The politician, author, and adventurer was noted as having said, "I have taken more out of alcohol than alcohol has taken out of me." Whatever he meant by that, aging in a new barrel is partly a question of absorption running in two ways.

It's more about the water than the alcohol. Some of the flavor components in the oak are more soluble in water than alcohol, and they tend to give whiskey a dry, astringent character. When the water pulls them out of the wood, they will oxidize as the slow air exchange takes place in the barrel. More water means more oxidization of those astringent compounds, and that means smoother whiskey.

Alcohol and water are both solvents. As they penetrate the char and the red layer, they absorb the color, which becomes the color of the whiskey.

They also start pulling out the sugars, vanillin, and other flavors. There are two isomers of oak lactones: cis-lactone gives the whiskey a sweet vanilla-coconut character; trans-lactone yields a spicier blend of cloves and coconut but is weaker. Methyl salicylate is present in low levels in some white oak; it gives a minty aroma to young whiskeys.

Meanwhile, the alcohol is continuing the work of lignin breakdown begun during the air-drying phase (it's a long, multistep process), adding more sugars and aldehydes, which will break down into esters, yielding varying levels of fig, tobacco, cinnamon/spice, and smoke aromas. As the alcohol continues to break down other parts of the wood, melanoidins are produced that deepen the flavors and add more color, and other compounds can add aromas of butterscotch, lighter caramels, and nuts.

On the other side of the absorption balance, the char is at work. Charcoal is one of the most effective filters known and has a simply amazing internal structure. Consider this: A single gram of charcoal has about 2152.8 square feet (200 m2) of effective surface area that can grab and sequester unwanted aromatic compounds. Any sulfur compounds in the corn that got past the copper in the stills will be grabbed by the char.

The char layer may only be subtracting flavor, not creating it, but that subtractive effect allows additional flavor to be added. Because of the char, distillers don't have to run as tight a cut on distillation, leaving some good flavor behind in the still in the effort of cutting out all the bad. Instead more of both can come over and be left to the char to sort out.

Jack Daniel's Single Barrel

Jack Daniel's Single Barrel filters through a bed of charcoal before barreling. Deeply sweet smoky corn on the nose, with a bit of barrel oak. Big sweet cooked corn flavor, smooth and mellow, with oak heat on the finish.

If that seems like a very brief description of what's going on in the barrel, which we've said several times is the source of 50 percent of the flavor of the whiskey, remember: We've got two more chapters on the flavor creation that takes place in the warehouse and during aging. Here we're only looking at potential.

Now that we've filled the barrels with whiskey, let's take a look at why the Scotch, Irish, Canadian, and Japanese distillers like to work with used American whiskey barrels. (And remember: Corn whiskey is mostly aged in used American whiskey barrels, and some American single malt and "distilled from XX mash" whiskeys, so the same thoughts apply.)

The folks in the respective industries joke about this. American distillers say that once they've used the barrels once, there's no flavor left in them and the other distillers are welcome to them. The other distillers joke about using bourbon to soak the harsh woodiness out of the barrels to get them to the point where they're good for making "real" whiskey. All in

CASK? BARREL?

You'll see the words *barrel* and *cask* used almost interchangeably. Are they actually different? Not really.

Unlike the particular word *hogshead*, which means a barrel of between 225 liters (59.4 gallons) and 250 liters (66 gallons), or the "American standard barrel," which in the bourbon industry is a 53-gallon (200.6 liters) barrel, simply saying barrel or cask means the familiar round container made of oak staves bound by steel hoops. "Cask strength" and "barrel proof" mean the same thing: bottled at the strength the whiskey was when dumped from the cask or from the barrel. (Almost: See the note in Chapter 14.)

Scots tend to say "cask," and Americans and Canadians tend to say "barrel." But no one's really hard-nosed about it—not the way they are about the "correct" way to spell "whiskey" or "whisky." And that's about the same difference.

good fun, but at the core, that is exactly what's going on. That first aging does take a lot out of the barrel, and the flavors imparted to the next occupant are more restrained.

How much is "a lot"? I went back to Andrew Wiehebrink at ISC again. He told me about a study that had been done in the 1980s, filling both a new barrel and a two-year-old used barrel with new spirit. After two years of aging, the amount of solids extracted into the spirit from the used barrel was about 15 percent of what it got from the new barrel. I think that qualifies as what we'd call "a *lot* a lot." That's why the new charred barrel makes such a difference on aging times with American whiskey.

(By the way, Andrew also told me about some barrel innovations that were so wild—flash charring, pre-aging, and something he called "pre-Prohibition" barrels—that I wasn't sure if he was talking about stuff that was actually happening or just pipe dreams. And then I saw that Heaven Hill's Elijah Craig Toasted Barrel is finished in a heavily toasted barrel that is then "flash-charred," exactly as he described it; long, intense toasting, followed by a quick ignition to char that's immediately put out. Wonder when the pre-Prohibition barrels come out?)

Refill a freshly used bourbon cask with new make—Scotch, Irish, Canadian, Japanese, corn whiskey—and you'll be getting an echo of what the bourbon took from the oak: caramel, vanilla, coconut, and smoke, with some light citrus touches. Are those whiskies getting those flavors from the leftover bourbon, or rye, still in the wood?

That's what we used to think. According to the latest research, the flavor comes from the wood. Which makes sense; that's where the American whiskey [illegible]

I want to talk a bit more about the way other distillers use American whiskey barrels. Because they don't just use them once. There are what are called "second-fill" barrels that have been used to age American whiskey, and then to age, say, single malt Scotch. The distiller may then use them again to age another barrel-full of single malt.

Why would they do that? Isn't the flavor soaked out of the wood by now? Largely, yes. But the barrel is still capable of holding the spirit in without leaking—too much—and it can still do the transformative work of filtering and more importantly, the work of oxygen and spirit vapor exchange. That's what a blender wants when they want to taste more of the character of the spirit, and not so much of the barrel.

I bring this up not because we need to talk about making Scotch; not in this book. I bring it up to emphasize how much a source of flavor these processes are. Aging in a barrel, like so many things in the making of whiskey, doesn't just do one thing. It does a number of things, all at once, and it's up to the distiller and the blender (who may be the same person, or not), and the warehouse manager, to some extent, to decide how to balance those processes to get the aromas, the flavors, the whiskeys that they want.

That's where the first part of the story of barrels ends. In the next chapter, we'll talk about where the barrels go and what happens to build flavor there. Then we'll return to the barrels for the long, long haul and talk about what happens during the aging process.

Most barrels go to a warehouse; O.H. Ingram's warehouse is a specially fitted barge on the Mississippi.

11

Welcome to the Warehouse

Barrels do a huge job in giving whiskeys the flavor we cherish. As I told you in the previous chapter, the oak holds a great amount of sugars, vanillin, and other flavors, as well as the important char layer that acts to filter the spirit's less desirable flavors. The influence of the barrel cannot be overstated when it comes to the whiskey in your glass: every bit of color, the lion's share of the flavor.

The barrel can't do all that on its own. It has two necessary allies. The first, which we'll take on in the next chapter, is time. The barrel needs time to create the flavors, to transfer and enrich and transmute the compounds in the wood into the whiskey; time to give up that small percentage of spirit to the air, the so-called angel's share, that is so important to maturity; time for oxygen to slowly creep through the wood to replace that missing liquid.

But the barrel also needs a place to live. That's the warehouse, and like other whiskey components that influence flavor, they come in a bewildering variety. There are low, one-story warehouses and towering nine-story behemoths that can hold more than 50,000 barrels each. The brick warehouse at Castle & Key in Kentucky, the world's longest whiskey warehouse, is 534 feet (162.7 m) long and can hold about 33,000 barrels.

Warehouses can be made out of brick and are also made of stone, concrete, steel, or wood frames skinned in sheet metal. Small distillers may use garages, truck trailers, or shipping containers as warehouses. Some warehouses are heated; most are not and rely on the climate to change the temperatures inside. Barrels may be stacked on dirt floors, they may sit on end atop pallets, and they may be rolled into racks.

Barrels will sit in warehouses for months, years, decades. Very few distillers move the barrels about inside the warehouses, but mostly, when a barrel has been placed in a warehouse, it's there till it's time to harvest it. Let's talk about how that affects the flavor of the whiskey.

DISASTER

On a really bad day, storing whiskey in warehouses can cause complete flavor destruction. Anytime you get thousands of barrels of whiskey together, there's the potential for disaster, if only because huge amounts of whiskey can be affected—or ruined—at one time.

Warehouse-destroying disasters are why warehouses are filled piecemeal, a few days in one, then a week in another, so that, for instance, all the five-year-old whiskey won't be lost in one night.

Warehouses are vulnerable to structural failure from the sustained weight of the barrels. A full 53-gallon (200.6 liters) bourbon barrel weighs about 500 pounds (about 226.8 kg); thousands of them add up to a huge amount. Loading or unloading the wrong way can stress the racks and lead to collapse, or a warehouse may simply get too old to support the weight. One of the older Barton 1792 distillery warehouses in Bardstown, Kentucky, collapsed in two stages in 2018, spilling thousands of barrels and crushing some.

In 2010, Glenfiddich suffered a warehouse collapse in Scotland. This one was caused by heavy snows, and the weight of the white stuff eventually staved in the roofs on several warehouses, allowing tons of snow and subzero cold to pour in on the barrels. The distillery manager saw this as opportunity, though, and pulled the barrels exposed to the extreme cold together to make a blended malt named Snow Phoenix.

Similarly, in 2006, a tornado ripped off part of the roof and the brick walls of Warehouse C at Buffalo Trace Distillery in Frankfort, Kentucky. Reconstruction began fairly quickly, but the delicacy of repairing an older building meant that many of the barrels were exposed to the open air for most of the summer. The barrels were blended to create what was known as E. H. Taylor Jr. Warehouse C "Tornado Surviving" bourbon (more about that in a later sidebar).

A few bourbon warehouses have been hit by tornadoes—they're fairly common in Kentucky—and *twisted*. The buildings themselves will be skewed by the power of the cyclonic winds. That seems like an aesthetic problem until you consider that the racks inside are all twisted as well, and now you literally cannot get the barrels out of them. Jim Beam's Fred Noe told me that they tried untwisting one of their tornado-hit warehouses, setting up huge bollards and attaching cables to the warehouses from powerful winches. "But we couldn't get it straight," he said. "You wind up just breaking it up and getting out as many barrels as you can."

The worst disaster that can befall a warehouse is fire. There have been several warehouse fires in

Kentucky over the past few decades, and they are roaring. Imagine 5,000-odd tons (4,500-ish metric tons) of seasoned oak and 60-plus percent alcohol catching fire. Barrels explode and fly through the air; the heat is felt hundreds of feet away.

The worst in living memory was the 1996 fire at Heaven Hill in Bardstown, Kentucky. About 90,000 barrels were lost, as well as the distillery itself. The flames could be seen 30 miles (48.3 km) away, and a river of fire more than a foot (0.3 m) deep rolled down the hill at one point. When it was all over, the distillery was a concrete slab with melted metal drooped all over it. The warehouses . . . well, they were just heaps of steel hoops. Everything else burned or melted. Heaven Hill rebuilt, and the industry learned a new set of rules that included sprinklers to stop fires and berms around warehouses to contain burning liquid.

Then there's creeling. I saw a plumb bob in a Heaven Hill warehouse once, just inside the door. There was a chalked circle about 4 feet (1.2 m) across, and the bob hung in the center. I leaned in and looked up. The bob hung down through a hole from the top of the warehouse.

"What's that?" I asked. "Well, you see that circle?" my guide answered. "If you ever see the bob hanging outside that circle, run for the door. It's *creeling*." That's a word I've never heard anywhere else, and Heaven Hill master distiller Conor O'Driscoll confirmed it when I asked him about it. Creeling is when a warehouse leans past the recovery point and the weight of the barrels continues to pull it over. Time to head for the door and hope you picked the right one.

"The flames could be seen 30 miles away, and a river of fire more than a foot deep rolled down the hill at one point."

Rackhouses and Rickhouses

The most common warehouse type for American whiskey at the larger end of the industry is what's known as an ironclad or a rackhouse. These are large wood-framed warehouses, open structures that are covered, "skinned" with thin metal sheathing, and usually painted gray or white.

If you go back a hundred years or more, whiskey warehouses were built of masonry or brick. You'll still see stone warehouses at Woodford Reserve and Buffalo Trace, and Brown-Forman and Heaven Hill have brick warehouses in and around Louisville, Kentucky. It was proven technology, used for warehouses and distillery buildings alike. There was a bonus for aging whiskey. The thick stone or brick walls held heat for a long time after the sun went down and slowed the change in temperature as the sun came up, a phenomenon known as "thermal lag."

The thermal mass of the stone, coupled to the ground, combined with damp dirt floors to moderate the temperature swings that affected the aging whiskey. Imagine if every whiskey barrel was slammed by hot days the way the barrels on the top floor of a seven-story rackhouse are. Bourbon would taste quite different.

The masonry warehouses worked well and were aesthetically pleasing as well, but they were expensive. Distillers must have asked, "Can we get similar results for less money?"

Ironclad rackhouses were the answer. The thin, light-colored metal walls have low emissivity and actually reduce heat loss in the winter; they're so thin that the air can act as insulation. The barrels of whiskey themselves, the huge thermal mass of tens of thousands of barrels in the now much-larger warehouse, fill in for the thermal mass of the stone walls. It is a rough equivalent of the masonry warehouse—not exact, but reasonably close—for much less money and overall a smaller footprint.

It was pretty common over the past fifteen years or so to see rackhouses being built in Kentucky. An oak frame goes up with the racks built in as the structure is raised, three to nine stories high. Then the finished frame is covered in relatively thin sheets of corrugated metal. The 53-gallon (200.6 liters) American standard barrels are then rolled into the wooden racks on each floor, usually ten deep and three rows high. The fill is staggered, both to spread the weight out as the warehouse fills and to spread out the influence of the different floors over the full batch of new barrels.

You'll hear them called rackhouses or rickhouses. They're not *quite* the same thing. "Rickhouse" is a warehouse built using a patented system of Buzick Construction, the family-owned company that builds almost all of the ironclads in Kentucky. So while not every whiskey warehouse is a "rickhouse" (some of them predate the company's founding), there are so many that it's become a common name for it. But you'll hear "rackhouse" as well, and "warehouse," of course. The "almost" similarity of the words is as confusing as the use of either "setback" or "backset" for sour mash added to fermentation.

(Continued on page 179)

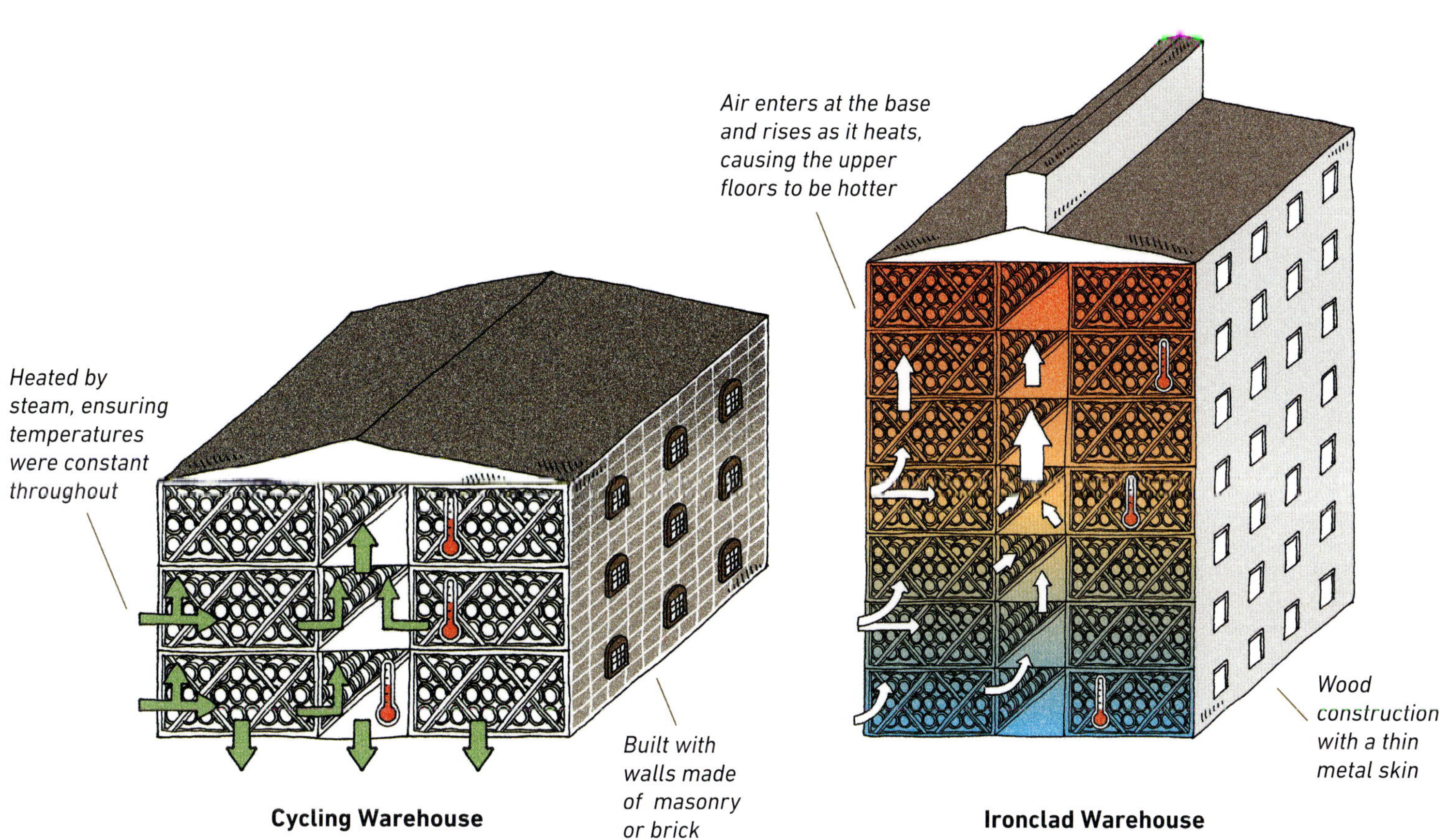

Note: See "Cycling Warehouses," on page 181, to learn more.

THE WAREHOUSE ZOO

Buffalo Trace Distillery sometimes resembles a living history exhibit more than a distillery. They're currently making whiskey in a copper-lined brick fermenter built in the 1870s that, until recently, was buried under a concrete floor in a building used for storage.

Their warehouses are a combination of old, new, and experimental. The old ones are a variety of brick, masonry, and concrete dating from the 1800s and the mid-1900s. Two of the latter were recently reclaimed from a past conversion to office space and are now holding barrels again. The different types of warehouses give master distiller Harlen Wheatley more flavor options when it comes to creating whiskeys.

But they have some novel, if not completely unique, warehouses as well. For example, Warehouse V is a tiny, one-barrel-capacity warehouse that has traditionally housed the distillery's milestone barrels. The seven-millionth barrel was placed there with great fanfare in September 2018.

Warehouse P is a new idea in warehousing—a truly extreme project. Warehouse P is refrigerated and kept at a constant temperature of 45°F (7.2°C). The plan is to age bourbon (and other whiskeys; Sazerac has distilleries and joint ventures all over the place) at this temperature for up to fifty years. This is a completely new idea, and no one really knows what to expect in terms of flavor creation.

They're also building regular ironclad warehouses—a hilltop covered with them, behemoths that will hold just under 69,000 barrels each—in an attempt to finally get ahead of the demand for their whiskeys. It's a major undertaking, but proper planning makes it possible.

Finally, do you remember the "Tornado Surviving" bourbon I mentioned earlier, the one they made at Buffalo Trace, from those barrels that were exposed to the elements after their warehouse was hit by a tornado in 2006? That got the folks at Buffalo Trace thinking: Do rackhouses really keep whiskey in optimum conditions?

So they built a small warehouse—Warehouse X, and be careful how you say that aloud—with five bays and a hugely expensive air-handling system. Experiments are done using barrels filled with their regular Buffalo Trace new make, a rye bourbon mash bill.

Each of four bays holds a maximum of thirty barrels and is subjected to different conditions: constant light, no light, constant temperature, high-volume airflow, no airflow, and so on. The fifth bay is essentially a breezeway with a roof and locked gates on either end, used as a control, similar to what the Tornado Surviving whiskey experienced.

Distillery president Mark Brown is excited about the idea of finding new ways to age whiskey. But at the same time he wryly notes the possibility of the control bay producing the best whiskey. "If we've been building warehouses all this time when we should have been just piling barrels in an open field with a tent overhead and a fence around them," he said, "we'll look like a bunch of proper monkeys." Monkeys in a warehouse zoo—brilliant, innovative proper monkeys.

These tall, broad warehouses can hold more than 50,000 barrels of aging whiskey, every one of them singing a slightly different song of aging, from the cool, mellow bass of the lower floors to the searing soprano soar of the top level. Much of that is driven by convection heating. As the summer sun beats down on that metal skin, the warehouse heats up; and *up* is the operative word. The heat, the hot air, will rise, and the top floor of a big warehouse can hit 135°F (57.2°C) in the summer. I know; I've been there. And although it's relatively dry, it will make the sweat pop right off your brow.

The heat expands the whiskey, drives it hard and deep into the red layer, picking up more than just the regular load of sugars and vanillin, getting into more tannins. In the industry, these barrels, these top floors produce whiskey that is known as "high and dry," referring to the bracing, lean character. This is where you get the leather, heat, and fiery oak spice. It's happening faster, too, and the barrels are giving up a much higher percentage to evaporation. You can almost get buzzed taking a deep breath.

Evan Williams 23 Year Old

Hard-to-find bottling of a classically "high & dry" bourbon. Sharply oaked nose, hot, and a bit sweet. Flashing hot on the tongue, oak and dry corn, some acidity. Long dry finish. Water smooths and sweetens it significantly.

Warehouse V, the unique single barrel warehouse

The lower floors stay cooler, both because of the heat rising and because of the intake of fresh air to replace the rising hot air that's fueling the top-floor furnace. Some blenders will skip over these barrels; some use these floors (or rent them) for aging spirits other than whiskey. If you're drinking a bourbon or rye that's more than twenty years old, chances are good that it spent those years down here, cruising along on a slower course to maturity.

Are they forgotten? No, but while they will develop deeper wood notes, without the dry brightness of the hotter barrels, the chances of over-aging into heavy acetone notes are less. These barrels are not particularly sweet, either, because of the lower extraction.

Meanwhile, in the middle floors, as you'd expect, the barrels are hitting a balance. Oak tones are strong but not burly or piercing. Sweetness is bigger here, where the extraction is active without digging deep enough to mine additional tannins. This is where a lot of the distillers will find their favorite "honey barrels."

Top to bottom in the warehouse, you'll find plenty of difference in the same distillate in the same type of barrels. This makes the biggest difference, but there are more. Barrels will age differently by how close they are to the southern-facing wall, which gets more sun. The prevailing winds will make a difference in an ironclad. There are brick warehouses with closed floors, where the airflow is all horizontal and the differences between the floors are less. Everything makes a difference in how long a barrel is hot, how swiftly it cools, and how much airflow it gets, all of which impact evaporative loss and wood extraction.

(Continued on page 185)

Airing out a warehouse

CYCLING WAREHOUSES

Brown-Forman has a number of masonry and brick warehouses at their Shively and Versailles (Woodford Reserve) sites that they call "cycling" warehouses.

In a process that dates back to the 1800s, they use steam heat during the cold weather to slowly bring the warehouses up to about 80°F (26.7°C) over a period of roughly ten days, and then allow it to sink back to the mid-50s Fahrenheit (low teens Celsius) over the next ten days, and then start the cycle again. Buffalo Trace Distillery has been steam-heating their brick warehouses in a similar fashion since 1886.

This is something that's not done with the typical ironclad warehouse, and for good reason. The uninsulated metal walls would make it an exercise in heating the outdoors. The old-style, solid-wall warehouses hold the heat and allow for an economy of energy use.

Interesting, but do they affect the flavor? The assumption most drinkers jump to is that cycling warehouses are an attempt to speed up aging by continuing the in-out extraction of flavor from the wood that happens during the warmer months, even in the depths of winter. Such as those depths are in Kentucky, that is.

Brown-Forman master distiller Chris Morris and I were in one of the cycling warehouses a while back, and I asked him about that. He said that it's not about aging the whiskey faster, or better, but differently. "It does make a difference," I remember him saying. Maybe I could taste it in the Woodford Reserve I sampled back in Chapter 9.

Brown-Forman and Morris have these warehouses right there in Louisville, Kentucky. The Brown family has always felt free to take chances with innovation through the years, Morris and his team have both the opportunity and the will to play around with wood-aging tricks, and they take that chance often with things like various wine finishes on Woodford and the Coopers' Craft bourbon aged in grooved barrels.

Heating warehouses full of barrels of whiskey by as much as 30°F (16.7°C) takes a lot of steam and that's not cheap. If they weren't getting an impact on flavor from it, I doubt they'd be doing it.

CAVE OF WONDER

I hate the phrase "the most unique." Unique means "singular." Either there's one of something and it's unique, or there's more than one and it's not.

But I'm going to use it because the aging cave at Maker's Mark is the most unique whisky warehouse I've ever seen. The concrete half-pipe at Kilbeggan in Ireland is weird, and the big steel-railed whisky box at the showpiece Old Forester distillery in downtown Louisville, Kentucky, is downright cinematic. But both must give way to The Cellar.

Maker's Mark produces their Maker's 46, a collaboration with Independent Stave Company that transforms their bourbon by aging it for six weeks post-maturity with the addition of ten toasted oak staves hung in the whisky on a food-grade plastic-and-steel insert in the barrel. It's great stuff, but they soon realized that the barrels they'd "extra-aged" over the winter months tasted a lot better. The warmer months led to over-extraction. As distillery president emeritus Bill Samuels Jr. put it, it didn't "taste yummy" anymore.

The decision was made to continue production of Maker's 46 and to keep it cool, so they dynamited a big hole in the hill on the distillery grounds. It was fitted with impressively huge doors, racks, and glass interior walls. Maker's Mark runs their Private Selection tasting sessions in the cave, where groups buying a barrel can pick their own special blend of staves to hang in a barrel of Maker's. (I've done it, with three other whiskey writers. We called it the Curmudgeon's Blend, and it was delicious—and a lot of fun to do.)

The Whisky Cave of Wonder: Amazing what a warehouse can do and be.

Maker's 46

Maker's 46 adds toasted staves as a finish. Rich sweet corn and leather with oak heat on the nose. Flavors of vanilla, caramel, toasted corn with an oak frame, sliding into a sweet, warm finish.

Entrance to the Maker's Mark cellar (Loretto, KY)

> "They soon realized that the barrels they'd 'extra-aged' over the winter months tasted a lot better."

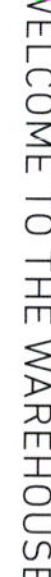

ROCKY MOUNTAIN HIGH

One of the great things about the proliferation of craft distillers is that the wide distribution of them means that we get to find out what effects very different climates have on aging. The one that interests me the most is high-altitude whiskey making, in places like Colorado and Wyoming.

Think about that. There are several big factors here. These distillers are mostly working on the eastern side of the Rockies, in the rain shadows that massive range creates. That means low humidity, as you've probably noticed if you live there or have traveled there. Low humidity means greater angel's share, which means less yield per barrel. Perhaps more importantly to the drinker, low humidity generally means that the barrel will proportionally lose more water to evaporation than alcohol, and that means a change in flavor. These low-humidity barrels may be more intense in flavor, and more dry in character.

You're also working with a lower atmospheric pressure. Denver's average air pressure, for instance, is almost 3 psi less than at sea level. That affects boiling points in distillation—though that's pretty much a wash, it's just a matter of adjusting timing—and also affects the angel's share. There's less pressure keeping the liquid and vapor in the barrel; more evaporation again.

But when I talked to lead distiller Sam Poirier at the Laws Whiskey House distillery in Denver and asked him about the tricks of high-altitude whiskey making, it wasn't the humidity or the atmospheric pressure that he thought had the biggest effect.

"It's the pressure drops," he said. The sudden movement of large air masses off the Rocky Mountain front directly to the west of Denver can change their weather in a matter of minutes, and with that comes sudden, sharp changes in barometric pressure. Sam feels that the way those drops and rises slam the whiskey in and out of the staves in the barrels has an effect on how it ages.

And that's what I love about all this. You can think about it and conjecture about what might be . . . but there's no substitute for going ahead and doing it, and then seeing what happens. That's how we learn.

Laws Whiskey House Four Grain Bourbon

Colorado-grown corn, rye, wheat, and barley (6/1/2/1 ratio). A mighty nose of black tea, orange peel, rye spice. Corn on the tongue, with pepper and vanilla. Finish is sharply delineated, with a return to rye spice.

There's a variety in how the rickhouses are sited that I find intriguing. Warehouses may be high on a hill to catch the prevailing wind or lower down to avoid tornadoes. They may be aligned north-south to maximize the amount of sunlight on the broad sidewalls or east-west so the prevailing winds blow through the doors. Some have windows; some do not. A warehouse may be built by a stream or river to get the cool air or well away from a river to avoid the damp.

All of these decisions are the result of a distiller's experience with previous warehouses and whiskey. I think of it as "Kentucky feng shui," similar to the Chinese ideas of how to orient a building auspiciously. Some make sense, like the one about keeping the trees and bushes clear around the warehouses. It keeps the light regular, and no tree is going to get high enough to fall on the warehouse.

Most of them, though, come down to something the late Parker Beam, longtime Heaven Hill master distiller, told me about the idea. "That's just one guy saying, 'This worked for me, that's why I do it,' and another guy saying, 'Oh hell, that don't work at all.'" Sounds familiar, doesn't it? Siting your warehouse is another choice about whiskey flavor.

I saved my favorite influence on American whiskey warehouses for last. The late Ronnie Eddins, the longtime warehouse manager at Buffalo Trace Distillery, told me that he was sure the regular fog off the Kentucky River beside the warehouses—and the way it would wetly come right in the windows—gave his whiskey a "sweeter, more mellow taste." Well, why not? It's not like we can explain everything about whiskey.

Warehouses can provide a wide range of character to bourbon and rye. We'll talk more about this in the blending chapter. This is how different bourbons are made from the same mash bill, fermentation, distillation, and barrel choice. They say that 70 percent of whiskey flavor comes from the barrel, but it's really the combination of the barrel and the time it spends in the warehouse.

Mother of Invention

Craft distillers are often working on a shoestring, and it shows. The distillery may be in a sketchy part of town or way out in the country because the rents are lower there. There may be a great address but a tasting bar made of repurposed pallets to save money. The fermenters are often food-grade plastic totes, the ubiquitous intermediate-sized shipping containers used for syrups, grains, and other free-flowing cargo.

The "warehouse" is often just a room, or a corner of a larger room, stacked with barrels on steel racks. As mentioned at the start of the chapter, some distillers use shipping containers, some use steel-skinned pole barns, and some use truck trailers. The aim is to get all your barrels somewhere that's lockable, safe from sparks, and subject to temperature swings.

LOW HOUSES

While other bourbon distillers are building five- and seven-story rackhouses and blending great, yet different, bourbons from the variety created by those temperature and airflow differences, Four Roses ages every bit of their whiskey in single-story, steel-walled warehouses that some old-timers call "flat houses." They're relatively small and are clustered fairly tightly in a few areas down in Bourbon Country.

What's the story? Four Roses, like Maker's Mark, is trying to keep the aging process from affecting barrels differently. Maker's does this because they only have one brand that's coming straight from the barrel. The other Maker's Mark bottlings, like 46 and the Private Select line, vary by the use of an additional process.

But Four Roses relies on their unique system of blending ten different straight bourbon barrelings that derive from their two mash bills and five yeast strains. They want the whiskey from each of these ten varieties to be as uniform as possible, so they limit the differences created by larger warehouses by keeping their whiskey in single-floor, smaller warehouses. This keeps the heat and air circulation the same for each barrel, as much as is possible. It's another flavor choice.

As inventory grows, or if these distillers transition fully to 53-gallon (200.6 liters) American standard barrels, expansion is necessary. Some distillers lease space; some build it. The hard part is keeping things consistent: If you were aging in a shipping container in the sun, you don't want to suddenly go to a concrete building in a shaded valley. It will change the flavor of your whiskey.

One of the more interesting quirks to warehousing was an old technique revived by the Jefferson's Ocean brand. They put some of their barrels on a ship, so they went through the rocking and temperature changes that happened on the voyage. Different ships and different routes seemed to make for different bourbons.

Warehouses can be on hills or by rivers—or on them! They may be in wooded glades, wide-open fields, or city streets. They can be made of wood, brick, or stone; short or toweringly tall. And all of that can affect the whiskey inside. In the next chapter, we'll put the whiskey that's in the barrel into the warehouse and see what happens when you add the critical ingredient: time.

Buffalo Trace Distillery's Warehouse X

EXPERIMENTAL
X
WAREHOUSE

ROCK ME ON THE WATER

Bourbon, more than other American whiskeys, is a category that is aware of its heritage. Rye's trying to reclaim its past, but with bourbon, every day is a callback to what came before. The American roots of the whiskey are in corn and link to the Whiskey Rebellion, to the frontier, to the Civil War and Prohibition. Even the name "bourbon" is freighted with age: Bourbon County, Bourbon Street in New Orleans, the narrow but unbreakable link to the history of French colonialism.

And what's the common thread literally flowing through bourbon's history, linking the rebellious distillers of southwestern Pennsylvania to the rich cornfields of Kentucky and the bustling access to international markets in New Orleans? Why, the rivers: the Monongahela, Ohio, and Mississippi rivers that carried the whiskey down to the Delta, and that slow, wave-rocked trip on flatboats that gave the wood and the char a little time to work its magic on the whiskey.

Hank Ingram (opposite) looked at that history and brought it into the twenty-first century by building floating rickhouses and putting them on the Mississippi River in Columbus, Kentucky, way down in the far western nub of the state, less than 20 miles (32.2 km) downstream from the confluence with the Ohio River. That's what makes O.H. Ingram River Aged bourbon special.

"The history of bourbon in America cannot be told without talking about the river," Ingram said, and I agree. "My family has been in the river transportation business for more than 150 years, and I grew up familiar with this heritage. My idea with O.H. Ingram was to recreate the origins of bourbon while combining them with the innovations of the modern river era. It's that mixture of art and science that makes what we do unique."

The rickhouses are built on former grain barges, two stories high, made of steel with removable fiberglass roofs. Windows, ducts, and sparkless fans create ventilation. The barrels are ricked six or seven high, and the barge holds roughly three thousand barrels. They recently filled their second barge.

What does the river location do for the whiskey? "The constant motion and changing water levels of the river means our barrels are always rocking," Ingram said. "That drives a more intense interaction between our whiskey and the barrel. We also see massive daily heat cycles. On a sunny day in the summer, our rickhouses will easily get up to 130°F [54°C]. At night, the river acts as a giant heatsink, pulling the heat off and dropping the temperature inside down dramatically. Finally, the higher humidity helps keep our barrels from drying out and provides osmotic pressure, which helps reduce angel share evaporation.

"These factors all drive complexity into the finished product," he concluded. "The result is more spice on the mid palate while knocking out much of the burn on the finish. These factors have created more variety in our whiskey profiles. For example, some barrels had much higher concentrations in furfural (darker notes like coffee, molasses, etc.) where others were guaiacol heavy (think more smoked vanilla and spice). This variety in our barrel profiles has given us the ability to create more depth and complexity in our products."

It's not going to end there, either. Hank told me that after six years of aging on the river, they have enough data to start expanding the experiment with different barrel treatments and char levels. The whiskey is being distilled at Green River Distilling in Owensboro, Kentucky, and they're able to try several different mash bills.

I have to be honest . . . when I first heard of this, I thought it was a pointless gimmick. I got hold of a sample and invited my friend Sam Komlenic (the guy who's edited my whiskey books) over to try it. The first sip put looks of pleased surprise on both our faces. Rocking on the face of the Father of Waters had certainly done this whiskey no harm, and was not a gimmick. It's a piece of bourbon history and lore.

O.H. Ingram 2024 Flagship

Full-bore 117.7°; six years old. Bright, grassy nose backed with sweet cornmeal. Even-tempered palate; more cornmeal, vanilla, baking spices, cool for the high proof. Gentle, lasting finish recaps everything. Well-integrated.

WOODFORD RESERVE DISTILLERY
DSP-KY-15018
BOURBON WHISKEY 1
RC 53 G
FILL DATE
LOT NO
WOODFORD RESERVE DISTILLERY
DSP-KY-15018
BOURBON WHISKEY 1
RC 53 G
FILL DATE 04-17-17
LOT NO 17-D-17
WOODFORD RESERVE DISTILLERY
DSP-KY-15018
BOURBON WHISKEY 1
RC 53 G
04-13-17
FILL DATE 17-D-13A
LOT NO
WOODFORD RESERVE DISTILLERY
DSP-KY-15018
BOURBON WHISKEY 1
RC 53 G
FILL DATE
LOT NO
WOODFORD RESERVE DISTILLERY
DSP-KY-52
RYE WHISKEY
RC 52.8 G
FILL DATE 07-02-14
LOT NO 14-G-02

Invisible, Indispensable: Time

We've made the whiskey, which took less than a week from milling to mashing to the completion of fermentation. We distilled it, which took maybe two days at most. We put it in barrels, which even at a small distillery doesn't take more than a couple minutes per barrel, including hammering in the bung. Then we loaded it on a truck (or rolled it by hand or used a forklift), took it to the warehouse, and put it in place, deciding the right place for this particular barrel, and recording where it was put. Ten days, tops.

And then we wait. It might be for months at a start-up craft distillery; it might be for twenty years or more at one of the established legacy distilleries. However long it is, in almost every warehouse, the only thing that's going to disturb that barrel's slumber is the occasional sampling.

It certainly looks like nothing's happening on a day-to-day basis. The barrel sits there, a big lump of steel-bound wood in a long line of big lumps of steel-bound wood, not moving.

There are obvious clues that something is going on. The biggest one is the smell: the rich, ripe roll of aroma that says "whiskey warehouse." If nothing was going on, there would be no smell at all. The smell proves that the oak is "breathing." The slightly permeable wood is doing its job, allowing a slow exchange of air from the outside with water and alcohol (and wood aromatics) from the inside. That's an essential part of whiskey maturation, another amazing thing that happens naturally—like the reaction of copper with sulfur-bearing compounds in distillation—to make whiskey better, to make whiskey even possible.

Another clue is the presence on some barrels of slow, sticky leaks from between the staves. I call that "barrel drool" or "barrel candy." The whiskey will leak at a slow enough pace that very little additional loss is taking place compared with the "angel's share" losses of evaporation exchange, but it does make for a sweet, sweet smell in the warehouse. I remember being in the warehouse at A. Smith Bowman Distillery one time with the late Truman Cox, who'd recently become master distiller there. We came across a barrel that was leaking pretty heavily, and he licked his finger, ran it slowly along one of the leaks, and licked it again. "Go on," he urged me, "it's good!" I did, and you know, it was sticky and a little dusty, but it was good: caramel, maple syrup, vanilla, a bit of burnt sugar.

We know the barrels are doing something because we can smell and see bits of evidence on the outside. What's really happening inside while the whiskey slumbers? The actual magnitude of the number of chemical interactions going on inside a barrel of whiskey is dizzying and far beyond the scope of a work such as this. Research continues, and the fullness of what happens as a whiskey ages may never fully be known.

The thing to avoid is focusing on one set of reactions over another, the type of tunnel vision we're specifically trying to move beyond. In this case, when the number of possibilities is almost literally endless, the best we can do is acknowledge that and touch on the major classes of actions that are going on.

First Things First

The first and fastest thing that happens is color extraction. Unless a barrel is a second or third refill, the new make whiskey is going to pull a lot of color out of the wood in the first few months.

The extraction rate is even faster in the smaller barrels favored by some craft distillers due to the higher ratio of wood surface to volume of spirit.

The color comes partly from the color already in the wood. You can see that in lakes that are fed by streams or bogs that have tannin-bearing vegetation in them which are often fallen trees: willows, pines, and oak. The lake waters will be dark with the tannins, almost like strong tea.

The color is also coming from the heat-treated part of the barrel: the red layer. The caramelized sugars are leaching out of the wood into the spirit, and the color comes with them. This is the same kind of caramel used to add color to whiskies, but those sugars come from malt, not wood.

As explained in the previous chapter on the barrel, flavor and aroma are also coming directly out of the wood. Simple chemical extraction from the solvent effect of the alcohol and water is pulling flavor out of the wood itself and also the red layer.

Not a lot of American whiskeys are aged in used barrels—yet, though I expect more American single malts will be going to used barrels—but they accumulate flavors in another way: directly. Used barrels are giving up the flavor that's left in the wood, and any flavor from the liquid they may have held previously—whiskey, wine, rum, whatever—is mixing in as well. That would seem to be added flavor, but the standards of identity are largely silent about it.

Ranger Creek .36 Texas Bourbon

This bottling from my collection was aged in a low-ceilinged small warehouse in 5- and 10-gallon (18.9 and 37.9 liter) barrels (they use 53s in larger warehouses now). Texas heat and small barrels put a lot in here quickly; this was only nine months old. Very dark, and an oaky-sweet nose. Oak and corn sweetness dialed up to twelve, but the head-to-head battle is a prize fight, engrossing and brutally delicious.

Besides simple extraction, flavor is being created in the barrel over time by chemical interactions among the alcohol, the various polymers in the wood (hemicellulose and lignin chief among them), acids and esters in the wood and the distillate, higher alcohols (generally called "fusel oils"), and more than two hundred different compounds that are reacting in this oaken crucible. Aging whiskey in containers other than wood simply wouldn't result in whiskey, not just because of regulations but because of the amazing array of flavors that are either already in the wood or are created by air-drying, toasting, and charring, as well as the flavors created by the interaction among components of the wood and the distillate.

Flavor is also created by the slow interaction with the outside environment. That's the evaporation of alcohol and water that slowly moves out of the barrel, almost like an extreme slow-motion distillation, that we romantically call the "angel's share."

The Angel's Share

You've all heard the term; I've used it already in earlier chapters. It's a fanciful imagining of where the evaporating whiskey goes when it escapes the barrel.

If you've ever been in a whiskey warehouse, it's pretty obvious where the whiskey goes; it's all around you, so heavy in the air you might catch a buzz walking around. That's no exaggeration; I toured one particularly boozy warehouse with two other writers, and afterward we decided we'd best walk to lunch rather than drive.

The longer whiskey is in a barrel, the more it will evaporate. A reused barrel will lose whiskey faster; a smaller barrel will lose it faster. The loss will be slower in cool or wet climates; it will be frighteningly fast in tropical climates—but it never stops. It is the true end point of aging a whiskey. Eventually the angels take so much of their "share" that either the whiskey goes below legal proof limits (more likely in cold climates) or it slowly disappears in an oaky cloud of astringent vapor.

(Continued on page 195)

REFILLS ARE SLOW

It's well known that American whiskeys are, for the most part, aged in new, charred oak barrels. Bourbon and rye whiskey must be, by regulation. But corn whiskey, and a growing amount of American single malt, is aged in used barrels, and most of those are ex-bourbon barrels.

The first filling of the new barrel for bourbon usually pulls a generous amount of flavor—vanilla, coconut, caramel—and some color from the wood.

Clearly, the second filling has less to work with after the barrel has already had spirit in it. The color is quite a bit slower to accumulate, and if the whiskey is left uncolored, with no added caramel, even a 20 year old aged in a second-fill cask can be quite pale. The flavor is also harder to come by, and the whiskey will have less of the identifying tastes of the cask—being more about the flavors of oxygenation—and may well taste a lot more like the new make spirit, with a lot of distillery character.

We talked about the oxidation in the chapter on barrels, but there's more to it; it works better in the right used, tired barrels. I learned this from Matt Hoffmann, former head distiller at Westland Distillery in Seattle: Air-dried wood works better in refill barrels than kiln-dried wood.

"It's one of the most important things but one that no one really knows about," he told me. "After a point, the oxidation doesn't take place unless you have a catalyst. Oxygen occurs naturally as O2, but oxidation takes place with only a single oxygen atom. Without a catalyst [to split the molecule], you won't get the effect.

"That's one of the benefits of air-drying," he continued. "It creates phenolic acids that drive that oxidation. When you have every other variable equal, you'll have more development in whiskey in air-dried wood, whereas kiln-dried wood doesn't drive that."

It's complicated. You don't know what's going to affect what, and it all drives the flavor.

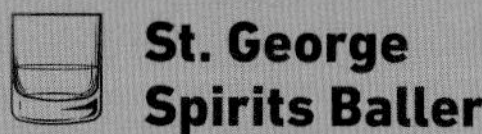

St. George Spirits Baller

Baller is unique: a Japanese-inspired American Single Malt, pot stilled and aged in a combination of used bourbon barrels and French oak wine casks, finished in plum *umeshu* casks. Lightly malty with a wisp of smokiness, wreathed in fruit. Delightfully singular.

Horrible as that is, it is necessary for whiskey maturation. Without this exchange, the whiskey simply will not mature properly. The oxygen and heat that come into the barrel drive chemical change (which is why accelerated aging schemes often center on these two factors). Oxygenation reduces astringency, creates new flavors from tannins, and also increases color.

This oxygenation through the wooden walls of the barrel is a big reason why distillers can't properly "age" whiskey by simply pumping it into a huge stainless-steel tank with a bunch of charred wood chips or spirals. A tank is much cheaper than using wooden barrels, but it's not permeable. And an oak barrel, as I said elsewhere, is just waterproof enough.

There are so many flavors and aromas that come from aging whiskey in oak barrels, and the paths that create those flavors and aromas are so complex that they have not all been recorded. Like so many other things to do with whiskey, there comes a point in aging where science still has to step aside and give way to art and empirical knowledge. "If we do it this way, it smells like this" is still the way to make whiskey.

Size Matters

The size of a barrel will affect the aging rate. It also has an effect on the economics, so you have to be somewhat careful when making judgments about barrel sizes.

The larger the barrel, the longer the aging process takes, and the lower the evaporation rate.

That's a trade-off, with longer time costing more and lower evaporation saving money. Counter-intuitively, larger barrels actually take up less room in a warehouse, because the volume is a square of the radius of the barrel. Larger barrels cost less per unit of volume, so there are substantial savings to be had by using larger barrels.

It's not only about economics, though. Past a point, larger barrels don't lose enough whiskey through evaporation for the maturation process to work at an optimal rate, and the surface-to-volume ratio is too low for effective wood extraction. They also become prohibitively heavy and harder to move and concentrate valuable whiskey into a container that's more likely to tip and shatter when being moved. The largest casks regularly used in aging whiskey are port pipes (550 liters [145.3 gallons]) and Madeira drums (up to 650 liters [171.7 gallons]), but most whiskey is aged in casks of 200 to 250 liters (52.8 to 66 gallons) in size.

At the other end of the scale are the small barrels craft distillers use, which may be as small as 2 gallons (7.6 liters). There are quite a few 10- and 15-gallon (37.9 and 56.8 liters) barrels in use by small distillers. The idea is to age the whiskey more quickly. With the much higher surface-to-volume ratio, the spirit gains color and flavor rapidly, but the question is whether the flavors are all desirable. Tasters talk about "small-barrel character," an excessively tannic note that can overwhelm the spirit flavor.

The smaller barrels also have cost issues. The price is almost as high as full-size barrels—the labor is the same or greater—and the evaporative loss is quite a bit faster. I've heard of 10-gallon (37.9 liters) barrels being almost empty at five years old. That's not all bad, as small-barrel whiskeys are mostly American and spending that time in new, charred oak, so two years' aging is usually about as much as you want to subject them to. More than that and the barrel can get overwhelming.

There's a more subtle issue with the flavor and character of the small barrels. I've got a buddy who's a whiskey chemist, Scott Spolverino, who describes the difference as aged versus matured. "Aging is what you put on the bottle: How old is it?" he said. "It has more to do with wood compounds, wood-based flavors, more extraction, and literally the time it's in there. Maturation is the culmination of chemical reactions and evaporation."

There's also a physical process that takes time, and the size of the barrel has nothing to do with it. It's called "ethanol clustering," a structural integration of ethanol and water that makes the ethanol sensation on the palate smoother. "A small barrel can't force the hand here," he said. No matter what your whiskey snob friends tell you, *smooth* really is a word to describe a mature whiskey!

All that said, I've had some small-barrel American whiskeys that are quite good. Distillers have learned to use what the small barrels have to offer and adjust their spirit accordingly. Some distillers use the small barrels only when they're getting started, to have something to bottle and sell quickly and get some cash in the door, then transition to larger 30-gallon (113.6 liters) or standard 53-gallon (200.6 liters) barrels. But some stick with at least some smaller barrels to add to the blend, maintaining the flavor that their fans first gravitated toward.

Kings County Peated Bourbon

Kings County has stuck with small barrels for some of their whiskey. Peat, green corn, and shiny oak. Hot, peaty, fresh corn finish slides into sweetness and gentle smoke.

How Old?

We're taught that asking someone's age directly is rude. Whiskey can make it easy by putting the age right on the label. It's a little bit complicated in that if there is an age on the label, say, fifteen years old, that means that the youngest whiskey that's in the mix that went into that bottling is fifteen years old.

There may be older whiskeys in there as well, though to be honest, in current times, that's nowhere near as likely as it was twenty years ago, when there was a bit of a glut of aged whiskeys. They allow the blender to bring a touch of complex depth to a bottling by adding some more mature whiskey to it.

What if there isn't an age statement? There are quite a few No Age Statement (NAS) whiskeys these days, more than there used to be. That's more than likely due to the shortage of whiskey stocks, a direct result of people like you and me talking more people into trying good whiskey—because then they go out and buy more whiskey, which means less for us!

The smug and cynical believe that there are more NAS bottlings because we're being sold younger whiskey as a way for the distillers to save money. I've seen drinkers opine that age statements are important as gauges of whiskey value: How much a whiskey is truly worth.

(Continued on page 200)

TEMPUS FUGIT

Barrels aren't cheap, warehouses are big money, and taxes never go down. But the biggest expense in making whiskey is time.

It takes time to make good whiskey, most definitely, but while that time passes—months, years, decades—the whiskey makes you no money at all. It *costs* you money: warehouse maintenance, security, warehouse staff, and taxes, taxes, and more taxes. What's worse, it's not just sitting there losing you money. It's literally evaporating, disappearing at a rate of 1 to 10 percent a year! Sure, that's necessary to the development of mature whiskey, but it's also necessary to have mature whiskey to sell.

Is it any wonder that distillers have constantly been tempted to cheat time by speeding up the aging process for whiskey?

Distillers in the past tried heating the barrels (not cycling, *heating*), bubbling oxygen through the whiskey, ultrasonic agitation—and those are only the schemes I've heard of. None of them worked well. How do I know that? Because everyone is still putting whiskey in barrels and stacking them in warehouses.

Almost everyone. There's a new wave of accelerated-aging experimentation going on. Distillers are trying sonic agitation: vibrating the whiskey to accelerate the progress of aging. There are elaborate plans for removing certain chemicals, adjusting levels of others, smashing the whiskey with high-intensity lights, and so on. And yes, they're still bubbling oxygen through the whiskey.

Does it work? That depends on what you want the processes to do. If you expect to get the equivalent of a $200 bottle of fifteen-year-old bourbon in six months, well, currently, that's not going to happen. (It's interesting that almost all the accelerated aging schemes I know of are about making bourbon or single malt whiskey, usually peated single malt.) I've tasted a variety of accelerated-age whiskeys—some blind, some open label—and I've been unimpressed. I picked out the quickie whiskeys four times out of five in a blind tasting.

If, on the other hand, you're fed up with paying $50 for a good blended Scotch, or you want a bottle of bourbon for making highballs over the weekend and don't want to pay a lot for it, then there might be a market for this stuff. Some distillers are aiming higher than that, and they've got a ways to go, in my opinion. But some distillers are looking to make commodity whiskey, and that's within reach.

One guy stuck to a pretty simple method. Rick Wasmund, at Copper Fox Distillery in Sperryville, in the mountains of Virginia, wanted to get more wood character into his 100 percent malt whiskey. When he put it in the barrel, he added a mesh sack of wood chips: oak and fruitwood, like apple or peach. The sack stayed in twelve months, and the whiskey was in the barrel for an additional two months or so. It came out surprisingly smooth and tasty for a malt whiskey under two years old.

As is true with any bottle you buy, you need to know what's in it. Who made it, and what are you paying for? Does that work for you? Like I keep saying, it's all about making choices.

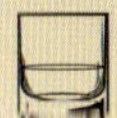

Copper Fox Peachwood Malt

Finished with a "tea bag" of peachwood chips. Nose is sweet, doughy, and shot with green wood. Dry malt on the tongue, hints of the peachwood coming through, and a fruity finish, tapering off to oak dryness.

"Is it any wonder that distillers have constantly been tempted to cheat time by speeding up the aging process for whiskey?"

Distillers counter that NAS whiskeys are not blended by the clock; they're blended when the flavors are ready. They also point out that there are some NAS bottlings that draw plenty of critical acclaim and mad love from their drinkers.

In the next chapter, on blending, we'll take a look at how blenders choose the whiskeys that go into a bottling. For our purposes here, if it says fifteen years old, it's at least that old, period.

What about those thirty-year-old, forty-year-old, and even fifty-year-old Scotch whiskies? I had a forty-one-year-old Canadian not long ago that was pretty darned special, too. Why aren't bourbons aged that long? Are they just not as good?

American whiskeys have a whole different *gestalt*. I've said this so many times about different whiskeys. Whiskey drinkers who stick to one type either want to measure all other whiskeys by those standards or simply not try them at all. It shouldn't work that way; it *doesn't* work that way.

Consider American whiskey's life cycle. American whiskeys ferment and distill on the grain, making for a more beefy distillate. They are aged in new charred-oak barrels, which put a lot of huge flavor into the whiskey pretty quickly. Then consider the American climate, particularly in Kentucky—or Texas!—when compared to Scotland, Canada, Ireland, or Japan. It's not only a new barrel; the whiskey's getting slammed into it by raging hot summers, concentrated at the top of a seven-story ironclad warehouse, or in a metal building.

If you tried to keep that up for forty years, you'd wind up with a barrel with maybe a pint of whiskey left, dark as tar and tasting like burnt wood. It simply doesn't work. We've seen some very old bottlings in the past fifteen years or so: twenty-three-, twenty-five-, even a twenty-seven-year-old bourbon in Heaven Hill's Parker's Heritage Collection. These are super-rare for several reasons: So many barrels evaporate out, most barrels are used up in younger bottlings, and some barrels just go bad when they get too old, all harsh and hot. The idea that older must be better is something Heaven Hill's Larry Kass called "the Methuselah Myth."

The ones that *do* last are almost always in the lower floors, where it's cooler. Buffalo Trace's Warehouse P, the chilled aging we talked about in Chapter 11, takes that to extremes, but it's also changing the whole concept of warehouse aging.

As for me, I'd just as soon have a six- or ten-year-old bourbon—or a two-year-old rye!—because that's more in the sweet spot for that spirit; at least, that's where it is for my tastes.

The more you know about how a whiskey is made and how it fits into its own category, the more you'll understand how it tastes and how good a job the distiller and blender did in creating it.

Michter's 25 Year Old 2020 Release

116.2°. Nose: dry oak, dark dried cherry, fine furniture. More dried cherry on the tongue; oaky heat, sweet vanilla, baking spices galore. Finish is hot, spiky with oak. Water opens it beautifully: sweet corn, more spice, less hot oak, the finish becomes inviting. I'm not a fan of super-aged bourbon, but this is exceptional.

MICHTER'S
LIMITED RELEASE
1753
25 YRS. OLD
KENTUCKY STRAIGHT
BOURBON
WHISKEY
MICHTER'S DISTILLERY
BOTTLE 132 OF 415
BATCH No. 2313017
MICHTER'S
LIMITED RELEASE
1753
25 YRS. OLD
KENTUCKY STRAIGHT
BOURBON
WHISKEY

FINISHING

Back in the late 1980s and early 1990s, in a surprising display of synchronicity, a few Scottish master blenders came up with the same idea at about the same time. After aging a whisky to maturity in one type of cask—an ex-bourbon barrel, for example—they would transfer the whisky to a different type of cask, maybe an ex-sherry or ex-port, for a few more years. The whisky developed the flavors and aromas of the bourbon barrel, then had a layer of fruit and nuts laid on top of it.

It was a success, and more "finishing"—as it came to be called generally—spread throughout the industry, eventually crossing over to the other whiskey-making regions. American makers and regulators took a while to figure out how to handle it, but now we do have finished American whiskeys too. Angel's Envy based their entire business on it, and it's been a well-deserved success.

Some worked better than others. I recall a young rye finished in some pretty raw red wine barrels; honestly, not drinkable. On the other hand, I loved the Woodford Reserve that was finished in Sonoma-Cutrer chardonnay barrels, one of the very early ones. Not many people agreed with me on that one, but I thought it was a great sunny afternoon sipper. There was a St. George malt whiskey finished in pear eau de vie casks that was stunning, and I wish I still had a bottle.

Don't be scared off by my young rye story, either. Some of the best finished American whiskeys I've had have been young rye whiskeys finished in port barrels; it seems to work wonderfully well. Old Elk, in Fort Collins, Colorado, finished a bourbon in cognac casks recently, and that was superb; I'm quite taken by cognac-finished whiskey.

I wish I'd had a chance to get more than a sip of the original Beam's Distiller's Masterpiece, an eighteen-year-old cognac-finished bourbon released in 1999, created by Booker Noe. It was possibly the first finished American whiskey, and way ahead of its time, with a very fancy bottle, a previously unimagined flavor profile, and a very non-1999 bourbon price tag of $250. I remember it as shocking and delicious.

American distillers in particular have expanded finishing to more than used barrels from different wines and spirits. For instance, they're doing collaborative projects with breweries, a kind of "barrel exchange." These are usually dark, rich beers, though a big barleywine or Belgian-type tripel also works. The whiskey gets a nice extra layer of flavor: maybe chocolate, coffee, treacle, or orange.

I facilitated one of those recently. My local brewpub, Elk Creek Café + Aleworks in Millheim, Pennsylvania, wanted to age some of their beer in two whiskey barrels. I reached out to Stoll & Wolfe distillery in Lititz, Pennsylvania, and made a deal: The barrels were free if they got them back after the aging was done. I drove down, we put two recently emptied rye whiskey barrels in my Subaru, and I brought them back to Elk Creek. A few months later, they extracted the beer, and I drove the freshly emptied (and bunged) barrels to Stoll & Wolfe. (I also picked up two used barrels from a brewer friend at Iron Hill Brewery on that trip to install as rain barrels in my garage.) I've tried the beer; it's delicious. I'm looking forward to trying the whiskey.

But it's not just used barrels. American whiskey makers have been trying a number of ways to get more varied wood character into whiskey. The best known might be Woodford Reserve Double Oaked. The whiskey is matured in a standard new, charred oak barrel, then transferred for additional aging in an oak barrel that has been deeply toasted, then subjected to a light charring. The heavy toasting brings more vanilla and nut character to the whiskey. Some distillers will simply transfer the whiskey to another new, charred oak barrel to stuff it full of that character.

I told you earlier about the Maker's Mark 46 and their Private Selection program, where they hang additional oak staves of different types inside the barrel after initial aging to add new wood flavors. The staves may be toasted, roasted (toasted in a convection oven), seared (hotter infrared heating; this stave is also cut with ridges), or baked (slower toasting) and may be cut from American or French oak. The differences that using ten staves of these woods in varied proportions are striking and unique.

It's not just oak anymore, either. Distillers have gone to other woods, and one that has exploded in popularity for finishing is amburana *(Amburana cearensis)*. This South American hardwood gives an immediately recognizable, delicious aroma of fresh cinnamon bun to whiskey. People clamor for it, which brings up a problem: Amburana is considered an endangered species because of over-harvesting and habitat loss, as central South American forests continue to be cut down.

Are there alternatives? I tried a whiskey finished in wood from a jackfruit tree *(Artocarpus heterophyllus)*; it was sweet, with rich fruit notes. I've had whiskey finished with chestnut wood, a more mild flavor, nutty-sweet. A distiller can source all kinds of wood and barrels these days: acacia, palo santo, cherry, mulberry, ash, and more.

Toasted or charred, new or used (and infused), finished whiskeys have become part of the landscape, another way of adding interesting flavor to the glass. The wild exuberance of the blenders for different finishes has subsided a bit, but experiments continue, and the future undoubtedly holds more surprises.

Angel's Envy Bourbon

Finished in port wine barrels. Dried fruit, berry pastilles, light dried flowers, a gentle nose. A lot more red fruit on the tongue, with more subdued vanilla and oak spice. Gentle finish.

13

Putting It Together

It's time to talk about one of the final steps: blending. I can see some of you making a face. You don't like blended whiskey? You think it's some kind of lesser whiskey, good only for mixing with soda and ice?

It's time to let you in on a little secret: Almost all American whiskey is blended. Unless it's a single barrel bottling, more than one barrel is going in the vat—tank, tub, vessel, whatever—and being blended together to create the consistent whiskey you count on finding. But it's *blended*, not "blended whiskey." It's a clear difference.

Well, kind of. Part of understanding "blending" is understanding "blended." Let's take that on first.

One of the saddest things I hear otherwise sophisticated and well-informed whiskey drinkers say, particularly in America, is that a blended whiskey someone else might be talking about, might be enjoying, maybe a blended Scotch or a Canadian whisky, is just "brown vodka." The implication is that the whiskey is cheaply made by adding a small amount of whiskey to a large amount of neutral spirits that were run off a column still at vodka strength.

A bottle being filled from a bourbon barrel using a whiskey thief

What's truly sad is that in American whiskey terminology, and more importantly, American whiskey regulations, that's pretty much what a blended whiskey is. I explained that back in Chapter 2 if you want to go back and check in; just to recap, American blended whiskey has to be only at least 20 percent straight whiskey, and the rest can be grain neutral spirits (GNS). "Brown vodka" is almost charitable.

Assuming that "blended whiskey" means the same thing everywhere is an easy error. But you're smarter than that. America is the only one of the major whiskey regions where blends can be such debased mixtures. Don't tar Canadian or blended Scotch, or the beautiful Japanese Hibiki blends with that same brush.

Seagram's 7

25 percent whiskey, 75 percent GNS. Aromas are mostly alcohol sweetness, with some vanilla and brown sugar. Light mouthfeel and, again, sweet with some heat. Best as a mixer.

In the rest of the whiskey world, blended whiskey is a respected drink, made from all whiskey. Scotch blended whisky, the most popular whisky in the world, is made from blends of malt whisky and grain whisky. Malt whisky is distilled to a lower proof in pot stills, full of flavor; grain whisky is distilled to a higher proof in column stills, with less flavor. Both are aged for at least three years, the malt whisky usually significantly longer. The blend leans on malt whisky for flavor, for smoke and cereal and fruit notes, and on the grain whisky more for mouthfeel, sweetness, and—not to put too fine a point on it—volume.

That's the pattern for blended whiskey outside of America: full-flavored whiskey plus lighter-flavored whiskey to produce a whiskey suitable for cocktails, highballs, and steady unreflective drinking. We could do that here, if we wanted to, the standards of identity only set 20 percent straight whiskey as a minimum for blended whiskey.

But the demand is met by the whiskeys already heavily in the market: Scotch, Irish, Canadian. Fighting them for that market would be an uphill battle, and not one most whiskey makers would want to take on.

It's kind of funny that there *are* whiskeys like that on the market, in a way. The Canadians make a lot of whisky, and some of the "flavoring whisky" winds up here in the U.S. in blends, or just bottled as is. WhistlePig started out that way, when the late Dave Pickerell sourced a large amount of aged 100 percent rye from Alberta Distillers Ltd., and surprised everyone.

7&7 AND BOILO

I took a slap at American blended whiskey there. I did. I called it a "debased mixture."

I maybe spoke too soon. There are uses for American blends—fun and tasty ones. The best known is the iconic 7&7, a highball mix of Seagram's 7 Crown and 7UP, with a lemon slice if you want. I remember drinking a lot of those in college. We were young sophisticates, drinking cocktails! The drink is pale gold in color, fizzy, and sweet with citrus notes from the soda. There's just enough whiskey in there to let you know you're drinking, while the GNS provides the power.

There's also Boilo, a traditional holiday punch from the coal regions of northeast Pennsylvania. I have a family recipe I got from a friend. Boilo is served hot to guests arriving in the winter's chill. The punch base is water, honey (a LOT of honey), caraway, cloves, cinnamon sticks, cut whole oranges and lemons, and a handle (59.2 ounces [1.75 liters]) of "cheap whiskey, the cheaper the better." The traditional add is Four Queens 101, a blended whiskey made by Laird & Co. (the Applejack people). You can easily track Boilo season by Four Queens sales at Pennsylvania's state-owned liquor stores.

I've made Boilo, too, and I've gotten pretty good at it. I like the 7&7, it's a fun drink—juicy and pleasant. And here's the thing that makes these drinks special and worth your attention: They are very social drinks. Hand arriving guests a coffee mug full of steaming Boilo at a wintertime get-together, or a dewy-cold tumbler of 7&7 at a rocking house party, and I guarantee that no one's going to be stopping the party to ask you what whiskey you put in it. They'll sip, smile, and keep on talking. Whiskey's really good at that, too: blended, straight, or any other way you choose it.

> "There are uses for American blends—fun and tasty ones."

I TOOK IT BACK TO MY ROOM

Until I started prying into it, I assumed that blending a new whiskey was work completed in a couple weeks.

Surely the blenders knew what the whiskeys tasted like going in; it was just a matter of finding the right proportions and carefully noting how much of which whiskeys went in. Of course, you'd have to consider sustainability and blend with whiskeys you'd have available in the future, but still, we've all mixed beers, mixed cocktails, and mixed whiskeys on the tabletop. How hard could this be?

Then I was talking to the late Dave Pickerell about a bottling of WhistlePig he'd done. I think it was the Old World Rye Madeira Finish. He described trying different ratios of the Madeira finish, Sauternes finish, and port finish—0.3 fluid ounces (10 ml) more or less of one or the other—and I realized that he had taken samples along with him on the road and was blending in his hotel room after a long day of meetings. That's involved. Maybe this takes longer than I thought.

I've been involved in a couple whiskey blending projects since then, and it is absolutely not something you approach and complete in an afternoon, or even a week of afternoons. It's a huge job for the blenders to create a new whiskey, a new interpretation of what the distillery and the warehouses can produce. Keep in mind, the work has to be done on top of making their regular bottlings—the flagships, the second-rankers, the bottom-shelfers, the store picks—every week, sourcing oak and maybe interesting barrels for finishes. Well, and talking to ignorant journalists, too.

Blending isn't throwing things together, tasting it, and calling it good. It's hard work, a life's work that you must practice for years in order to get to the point where you can recognize what's needed to achieve something great.

WhistlePig

100°, ten years old, 100 percent rye Canadian "flavoring" whiskey; additionally aged and bottled in Vermont. Dried fruit, spice lozenge (horehound, clove), donut nose. Fireworks on the palate: spice, bitter rye, oak vibrancy that funnels into a warm, tingly finish. Tour de force.

Finding the Right Blend

Everything that goes out the door, over the road to the store and the bar, every drop of whiskey that eventually makes its way to sitting in front of you and me, has probably been selected, in at least some way, by the blender.

Bourbon and rye, wheat, corn, and every other odd little whiskey have to be made, and they're all going to take the blender's skill, as well. Even the whiskey that's "blended" has to be blended. Unless a whiskey is a single barrel, it's been blended, which can be confusing in American whiskey, given the intentionally lesser nature of "blended whiskey."

It might help if we had a bigger vocabulary for this topic. No one wants to put the word *blend* on a whiskey that's not of the type we traditionally refer to as "blended." Some distillers try to make the distinction by saying they "mingle" or "marry" the different barrels used to make a whiskey. But in the end, blending is what's being done.

Why is this so? Why can't you just pull barrels of the same age and type and just combine them? Unless you skipped directly to this chapter without reading the rest of the book first, you shouldn't have to ask that.

There are so many factors combining to make barrels different that despite everything the

TASTING THE WAREHOUSE

A blender often works alone, backed up by a tasting panel that will trial the blends to reach a consensus.

Blenders also rely on the warehouse staff, who have a strong sense for where the best barrels are. In years gone by, that was often because they'd be smelling the barrels and illicitly dipping samples. It's blender's lore that the best barrels in the warehouse are the shiny ones because they're the ones that the warehousemen's coveralls and leather aprons are always rubbing against as they lean in to steal a sip.

Sampling used to involve rolling out barrels, lowering them to have the bungs knocked out, and having a sample dipped out with a siphon-like device known as a "thief." Then the whole thing would be reversed to put the barrel back. These days it's a matter of a quick buzz with a sparkless electric drill into the head of the barrel, catching the spout of whiskey in a sample tube, and tapping a small wooden plug into the hole—a minute's work. The speed allows more samples, and the use of bar codes on every barrel means more accuracy.

The blender (or the distiller in some operations; titles and responsibilities vary) doesn't really sample every barrel, certainly not in large companies. The blender will nose and taste representative samples, and two or three barrels will stand for entire areas of the warehouses. As they develop, the blender will go back and taste them. Over years, the blender will get to know the distinctive areas of the houses and will probably develop favorites.

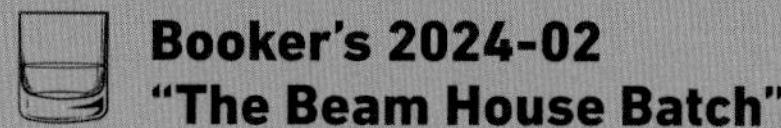

Booker's 2024-02 "The Beam House Batch"

124.6°, seven years old. Taste it like a blender: unfiltered, uncut, untouched. Whiskey-soaked oak, cinnamon (I get that in almost all Beam whiskeys), heat, and a fruit bowl. Vanilla, oak, hot corn bread, cinnamon, and some honey on the tongue. Finish is hot, oaky, and long. A little water really sweetens things up. Broad-shouldered bourbon.

It reminds me of something the late Ronnie Eddins, longtime Buffalo Trace Distillery warehouse manager, told me about three years before he died. "You know, in your life, you only get about two chances to learn from a fifteen-year-old bourbon," he said. "There's your first one, and you learn from it all along the way, and you put all that into the second one. By the time the second one's done . . . you're usually about done, too."

That's why a blender should always be working on another important part of the job: training a successor.

distillery manager does to make the whiskey uniform. The blender is still faced with the task of smoothing things out to make the whiskey consistent before it goes in the bottle. That's why at most distilleries, the person or people who do the blending are considered the most important people on the site.

Blending seems simple, but it's fiendishly difficult when it's done right. It can be a bit opaque to the general drinker. There are some things about whiskey that seem naturally resistant to being understood. Blending is at the heart of a few of them.

For instance, I still hear people passing along that "this whiskey is from the same mash bill and the same distillery as that one, but you're paying twice as much. It's the same whiskey!" Except they're not.

Bourbons from the same distiller, of the same mash bill, are different because of how long they're aged and where they are aged (except for Four Roses; more on that in a bit). Blanton's bourbon always comes from Warehouse H at Buffalo Trace Distillery, for instance, because it's an ironclad (their other warehouses are stone and brick), which pushes the bourbon into the wood on faster cycles. It makes for a notably different bourbon from Elmer T. Lee, which comes from the middle floors of Warehouses I and K, but they're both made from the same "recipe."

Four Roses flipped that on its head by employing two mash bills and five yeasts to make ten different bourbons that they take great pains to age separately and consistently in single-story warehouses. They then blend from among those ten whiskeys to make their different bourbons.

Blenders Make the Whiskey

It's no secret that the vast majority of the bottles of whiskey sold every day are branded, regular bottlings that you'll see on the shelf week after week: Jack Daniel's Old No. 7, Jim Beam, Evan Williams, Old Forester, and many others that are standard expressions that distillers and blenders produce year-round. They are not the one-off limited releases that might generate wild excitement, but they are the bottles that drinkers and bars buy again and again, without hesitation.

There are "recipes" for blending these flagship and regular offerings. So many barrels from this floor on that warehouse, so many from that floor on this warehouse, dump and mingle them. Some distillers may allow the whiskeys to "marry" together for as long as a month; some may have them together only long enough to fill the tank that feeds the bottling line.

But before it goes in the bottle, the blending team will sample to make sure the batch meets the guidelines for that expression. If it does, the buttons are pressed and levers are pulled, and the bottles fill. If it's not quite right, it's back to the master and time for a tweak; a few more barrels of

WHAT HAPPENED TO MY WHISKEY?

Older drinkers have seen several whiskeys disappear from the shelves, usually old bourbon or rye labels that were around for years, maybe value brands that were great whiskeys for the price. They never got any ads, or new labels, but those of us who knew reached for them over and over, and enjoyed them.

Then one day, they were gone, often without warning, or maybe with a tragically brief announcement. Elijah Craig 12 year old was one; Heaven Hill 6 year old bonded was another. Even Knob Creek disappeared for some months a while back. Where did they go?

Sometimes they simply ran out. Knob Creek reached a point where there wasn't enough nine-year-old Beam bourbon to properly stock it. Happily, that was a temporary situation, and there's plenty on the shelves now.

But when companies realize that the whiskey in that bottle could be going into the blend of another label, one that's running low on stocks, one that maybe sells for a much better price, that's going to be an attractive option. Or that six-year-old value brand that the drinkers in the know love and buy by the case and tell their friends about, the value brand that sells like crazy without any promotion, might get a branding facelift and maybe another year or two of age, and return as a premium bottle.

I'll be honest: That's why I don't tell anyone about my favorite bargain brands anymore. No, not even you, my friend. Instead, I would tell you to do what I did. Buy some bottom shelf bottles—they're not that much—try them, and find your own favorites. (But don't tell anyone!)

Heaven Hill Bottled in Bond 6 Years Old

Extinct bottling, but I've still got some. Oak, fiery cinnamon, cornmeal. Mellow, pleasantly sweet corn and cinnamon on the palate, lingering gentle finish framed with oak. Delightful; the "Bonded 6" was a great value at the time.

one parcel or another. It doesn't happen often, but the blend will always come out right. That's the blender's job.

Blending makes the whiskey, really. The blender takes what the farmer, the brewer, the yeast, the barrel, and the warehouse yield and makes whiskey, consistently, with art and individuality.

As the Scots say, it's horses for courses. You need different whiskeys to do different jobs. The everyday flagship bottle of four-year-old bourbon: cocktails, a carefree splash in an iced glass of ginger ale. The carefully selected twenty-year-old rye: a quiet, contemplative sip at the end of the day, a shared drink with a friend or relative in recognition of accomplishment. The deftly resurrected interpretation of a Prohibition-era recipe: maybe a hearty discussion at a whiskey club, or a signature cocktail at a speakeasy-style nightclub.

Blenders make sense of what is given them, whatever the charge from the head office may be. Even when you're talking about a single-cask bottling, chances are very good that it's the blender picking that cask. Who better?

LOST LANTERN: AMERICAN INDEPENDENTS

Scotch whisky has a long tradition of the independent bottler. These entrepreneurs will, like a *négociant* in the wine world, buy whisky in bulk from distillers, sometimes new make, sometimes aged whisky, in lots ranging from a single barrel to hundreds, to blend a whisky, bottle it, and sell it under their own label. Some, like Gordon & MacPhail and Cadenhead's, have been doing it for well over one hundred years, and have their own warehouses; some, like Blackadder, are relatively new to the business.

The intriguing aspect of independent bottlers for the whiskey drinker is that they often try to present less familiar aspects of a distillery's character; a less peaty Islay, a lighter Highland, a single malt expression from a distillery that largely produces for blended Scotch. They'll also blend casks of malts from different distilleries, often of the same general character, to create a unique "flavor package" that drinkers can't find anywhere else.

That idea intrigued Nora Ganley-Roper and Adam Polonski, two Americans who were deeply entwined in the whiskey business. (I worked with Adam at *Whisky Advocate* magazine; Nora worked at Astor Wines & Spirits, a top American spirits retailer.) Both loved the whiskies from these indy bottlers, and they thought it could work for American whiskeys.

"Our decision to start Lost Lantern started from our perspective as whiskey consumers who really wanted something like this to exist," Nora told me. "We spent a couple of years discussing how we wished that someone was applying this historic model to American whiskey. This eventually evolved into a conversation about doing it ourselves."

That turned into an eight-month road trip to visit the small American distillers that interested them the most, and a business launched to create bottlings and blends from those whiskeys. "Our hypothesis was that we couldn't be the only people excited about this type of curation," she said, "And, now that we're a few years in, it's safe to say we were right."

They've been sending me samples on and off since they started, and the whiskeys have never been less than good, while some are stellar. They have three series of bottlings. The Single Cask series is exactly that: one mature cask, some chosen from "a distillery that people likely wouldn't discover otherwise," Nora said, "or an unusual barrel from a more well-known distillery. Recent examples: Union Horse Kansas Straight Bourbon and a Wollersheim Wisconsin Straight Rye."

The Single Distillery series blends casks from one distiller. In independent bottler tradition, these often highlight a less known side of a distillery. "Our Gentle Giant Balcones Texas single malt shows off the light and elegant side of Balcones, which is best known for big and bold whiskeys." I'll note that "big and bold" with Balcones is an understatement.

The Blend series is just that; multi-distillery blends of whiskeys. The Far-Flung bottlings "blend bourbon or rye from states and distilleries that have never been blended before," Nora said. The Flame and Shadow blends bring together, respectively, mesquite-smoked and peat-smoked American single malts.

All the whiskeys are unfiltered (including no chill filtering), and almost all are bottled at cask strength. "Our attitude is that every whiskey drinker should be able to decide what proof they want to drink their whiskey at," Adam said, "whether it's cask strength, on the rocks, diluted with water, or whatever else."

I've always wondered why distilleries sell to independent bottlers (and I'll ask Proof & Wood's Dave Schmier the same question in the next chapter). Adam said it was largely about one thing: It's another way for these smaller distillers to drive people to sample their whiskey, to learn about them.

"For smaller distilleries, we are often helping to introduce them to a national whiskey audience," he said. "Some of our partners, like Corbin Cash in California or Boulder Spirits in Colorado, are only really available in their home market or region."

That kind of transparency about their distillery partners is a hallmark at Lost Lantern. "Every whiskey we've ever released, including multi-distillery blends, has proudly displayed right on the front label the distillery or distilleries it came from," Adam told me.

That's true even of the ones that are no longer open. In 2023, Nora and Adam bought the entire remaining stock of bourbon made by Rich Grain Distilling, a Mississippi distillery that had closed in 2020. They blended it to create Mississippi Memory, which turned out to be their most popular release in 2024.

Adam pointed out that this is something independent bottlers in Scotland have done for years. "Now-legendary distilleries like Port Ellen and Brora were not famous when they closed," he said. "It was only in their afterlife, driven by independent bottlers, that they became famous.

"We, as an independent bottler, have the opportunity to take up the legacy of a ghost distillery and continue to share what made them special, even though the distillery itself is gone," he said.

That's the kind of thing that reminds me that whiskey is, and always can be, more than just a drink. By virtue of the long, long aging process, whiskey becomes generational, a drink with a history. I remember writing about how an acorn planted one hundred years ago is cut down, air-dried another two to three years, made into a barrel and filled with new make spirit, aged for two to twenty years, and then may be used again for corn whiskey or American single malt for another two to twenty years; when we pour it into a glass, it's the end of a trip that may have taken 150 years. Whiskey is a time machine, an epic, a saga that can't help but become romantic and exciting.

Nora and Adam get that. Lost Lantern represents the challenge and promise of the independent blender, and a generous helping of the romance of whiskey as well.

Lost Lantern Whiskey Tom's Foolery 10-Year-Old Bourbon

Barrel proof: 119.4°. Fresh, delicate aromas of oak spice, toasted nuts, meadow herbs. Delightful recap on the palate with a happy sweetness. Finish framed with oak. Great intro to the distillery.

Nora Ganley-Roper and Adam Polonski with some of the Lost Lantern whiskey stash

Eagle
KENTUCKY
STRAIGHT
WHISKEY

Proof, Package, Bottle

If you've read much about whiskey, you've probably read that whiskey doesn't change once it's bottled. If you *haven't* read that before, I'll tell you now: Whiskey doesn't change once it's bottled—until you open it.

It's not exactly true, because if the whiskey's mistreated—set in the sun, subjected to extreme heat or cold, or tilted so the whiskey touches the cork, or if the cork is tainted—it will change the flavor. But under pretty simple optimal conditions (out of direct light, at room temperature or a bit cooler), the flavor of whiskey doesn't change between being bottled and being opened for consumption.

If that's true, then why does a book about how flavor is created in whiskey have a chapter on bottling? That's because even after a whiskey is dumped from the barrel and mingled, blended, or married, there are still some things that can add or change or take away flavor before the whiskey is put in the bottle—and then before the whiskey hits your glass.

Filtering, proofing, coloring, packaging, and transportation may have an effect. Because of the subjective nature of taste, even the shape of the bottle, the name of the whiskey, or the price can affect the flavor of whiskey for individuals. We'll talk about this more in the final chapters, but we're going to touch on it here, when we talk about the sensual experience of opening a bottle of whiskey. First let's get the whiskey in the bottle to begin its trip to your glass.

Filtering

There are a couple different layers of filtering that take place with whiskey once it's aged (remember: the charcoal filtering of Tennessee whiskey, the Lincoln County Process, takes place before aging). There is the coarse filtering that takes place when barrels of whiskey are dumped after aging, which is a simple physical screen to catch bits of char from the inside of the barrel. There may be a more restrictive filtration through layered pads to remove more material.

There is another step that can be taken, called chill filtration. There are proteins in whiskey that are in solution. Extreme cold can cause these proteins to denature, to change at a molecular level as some of the weaker molecular bonds break. This will bring them out of solution and cause cloudiness in the whiskey. This chill haze isn't harmful, but it can look like a flaw and can cause consumers to reject the whiskey as a potential purchase.

To avoid this issue, distillers may chill filter their whiskey. This requires chilling the whiskey to 32°F (0°C) or lower, which will cause the haze to form. Then the whiskey is filtered through pads or sheets, and the haze particles are left behind. Potential problem solved, but what about the potential flavor that's just been stripped out?

That's a matter of some debate. While there is definitely *something* being filtered out, judging by the smell and somewhat greasy feel of the pads, I understand that blind tasting of filtered and unfiltered whiskeys has often been inconclusive.

On the basis of that possibility, though, some distillers have made the decision to avoid chill filtration. That's easy to do, it turns out. If a whiskey is bottled at 46 percent ABV or higher, it prevents the haze from forming. Problem solved, if that's a proof where the whiskey tastes best to you.

Michter's has made an art out of filtering. Their former master distiller, the late Willie Pratt, dove deep into the different methods of filtering and determined that using different filters had an effect on whiskey aroma and flavor. It wasn't just "filtering"; it was what kind of filtering.

I visited their distillery outside of Louisville, Kentucky, back in 2017. (By the way, that makes me one of a *very* small number of people who've seen that Michter's distillery, their Fort Nelson distillery on Main Street in Louisville, and the original Michter's distillery in Pennsylvania [which closed in 1989], in operation. I cherish that distinction.) Founding partner Joe Magliocco was excited to have me try four different samples of the same whiskey, so I did.

They were clearly different, and when I asked, he told me that the only difference was how they'd been filtered. Michter's will use different filtering methods to achieve the desired flavor for their whiskeys. Which ones do they use? *I don't know.* The filtering/bottling room was the only area in the entire distillery where we were asked not to take pictures, and at the time, I didn't know that was what was going on and didn't ask the right questions. Guess I'll just drink the whiskey.

Filtering is, by its nature, a subtractive rather than an additive process. That would seem to mean that it can only make the whiskey smell or taste lesser, but that's not how it always works. As Michter's demonstrated, a different filter removes different things, and ideally what happens is that by taking away or diminishing one or some elements, others will come to the fore. Those flavors and aromas were always there. Filtering doesn't add them; it *reveals* them.

We're going to see that again in the next process in this chapter.

Proofing

What does proof have to do with flavor? It's all about water: colorless, odorless, tasteless water. Yuck!

To hear some people, you might think water is the very worst thing that could happen to whiskey. Whiskey snobs, who will suck the fun out of this fantastic liquid by telling you everything you must or mustn't do to enjoy whiskey, will tell you that the only "right" way to drink whiskey is neat, with no added water and no ice, ever. They may allow a scant few drops of spring water "to open it up," but they'll want to use water from the same source as the distillery and add it with an eyedropper.

I love to watch their heads explode when I point out that during the bottling process, significant amounts of water are added to almost every whiskey (except the cask-strength ones) in the process called "proofing."

The whiskey comes out of the cask at, say, 55 percent ABV, but the bottled product is at 40 percent. The only way that happens is by adding water. It's highly purified water, put through processes like deioniza-tion, distillation (how's that for irony?), or reverse osmosis to pull any possible flavor out of the water so it doesn't affect the flavor of the whiskey. Only, it does. That's part of the reason you see so many different proofs on whiskeys.

Proof is an old word for the alcohol strength of a spirit. The story goes that the British Royal Navy needed a way to "prove" to sailors that no one had fiddled with their spirit ration, watering it down to make more money per barrel. It's amazing to me that they feared mutiny about this enough to come up with a test and yet regularly served the sailors hardtack full of weevils and salt beef that would be rinsed in ocean water to make it *less salty*.

The test they came up with was arcane, but it worked. A spirit would be tested ("proofed") for strength by soaking a small charge of gunpowder with the spirit. If the wet gunpowder could be lit, the liquor was deemed to be a "proof spirit." Unlike a lot of "the story goes" tales, this one has evidence to back it up, although it may have originated in taxa-tion law rather than keeping sailors happy . . . but the navy's use of it came quickly afterward if it did, and the sailors make a better story.

There were, however, obvious problems with this test. Gunpowder from different mills had slightly different compositions, and the test was affected by temperature; warmer spirits would light more readily. The test was done away with when analyt-ical methods caught up with requirements in 1816. If the specific gravity of the spirit—its rela-tive weight compared with an equal volume of water—corresponded to an alcohol content of at least 57 percent ABV, it was a "proof spirit."

The determination of proof is now a relatively straightforward analytical test of alcohol content, usually by volume. Determining what proof a bottling *should* be is a different matter. There are economic reasons, to be sure. Many cynical drinkers have pointed out that lowering the proof results in more whiskey to sell, just by adding water, and if we're being honest, at times that might be the main reason.

There are flavor reasons as well, because proof can directly affect flavor. Distillers consider the use of the whiskey (there's that "horses for courses" thing again) and the market for the whiskey. Is this a whiskey for highballs? For more involved cocktails? Or for neat sipping? Each one may require a different proof.

Look at a shelf of whiskeys. You'll see a lot of whiskeys bottled at 40 percent ABV, mainly because that's the legal low end for whiskey in most countries (and in all of the Big Five whiskey producers). But it's also where you find almost all Canadian whisky, almost all blended Scotch whisky, and where you'll find (since 2004) Jack Daniel's Old No. 7.

It's a popular proof for many whiskey drinkers because many whiskey drinkers like their whiskey as "whiskey and." That's whiskey and water, whiskey and ginger ale, whiskey and cola, whiskey and juice, even the humble whiskey on the rocks. They want the flavor of whiskey in a refreshing drink, nothing more. I enjoy a highball myself and usually reach for something in the low–40 percent range to make it. Much more and the whiskey is going to overwhelm the drink.

You can also enjoy a good whiskey at 40 percent all by itself for the same reason; the standard Four Roses bottling comes to mind, what we used to call the "yellow label." It's a good whiskey for drinking with a splash of water, or a single cube, and you still get good flavor without getting banged up too quickly. Too much alcohol can punch away the flavors of the whiskey, heat up the aromas, light up the finish with a blaze of perceived heat. The lower-proof blends make a great everyday whiskey because of this.

Elijah Craig Barrel Proof Batch C924

129.0°. Big oak nose from this 11 year old, with smoky corn. Hot and sweet, but not crazy: corn, spicy oak, vanilla, wifts of smoke. Long spicy finish. Quite drinkable for the proof.

Forty percent isn't the only proof, of course. It goes up incrementally starting at a simple 40.5 percent and running up to the low–70 percent region for a couple exceptionally strong bottlings for a variety of reasons.

The high-proof bottlings embody a simply understood desire to deliver the whiskey right from the barrel. As the late Booker Noe said of his eponymous Booker's bottling, the whiskey is uncut—no proofing water added—and unfiltered, the way the distillers and blenders (and warehouse workers, on the sly) taste them. These cask strength/barrel proof whiskeys have every bit of flavor that's in the barrel. They also have every bit of alcohol fire, but drinkers can tame that by adding water to just the right level for their own individual tastes.

In between the low and high end of the range is where proofing gets interesting. Think about the reasons for adding water to your glass of whiskey and you'll get a peek into the thinking of the blenders and distillers who add water to their bottles. The neat freaks are right; you add water to a whiskey to open it up. But how does that work?

Adding water changes the alcohol level, which changes the aromas that come forward. More alcohol will carry oak tones; lower the alcohol and the oak backs down, allowing the richer vanilla notes to come out. Distillers will proof whiskeys to different levels to find the optimum aroma profile or to find the level that brings out the particular flavor they're looking for.

Adding water doesn't change what flavor components are in a whiskey, nor does it take them away or add them. Adding water changes how whiskey presents itself to your senses, shifts what you sense first or more intensely. It's like a person changing their wardrobe. The person is the same, but your perception of them is different.

Old Overholt 11 Years Old

92.6°; that's the story. Beam's blenders very carefully proofed this one for maximum effect. Floral (violets, daisy), rye grain, licorice on the nose. Gentle entry widens suddenly across the palate into rye oils and oak. Finish is the palate, tenaciously lingering.

STAY BONDED

I've made some good friends in the whiskey business, I won't deny it. One of them is Bernie Lubbers, the national brand ambassador for Heaven Hill. Bernie has a big tattoo on his right arm that says, "Bonded Kentucky Straight Bourbon Whiskey 100 Proof." His business card proclaims, "Stay Bonded."

Early on in his days with Heaven Hill, Bernie (opposite) noticed that they made the lion's share of the old bottled-in-bond whiskeys that were still on the market. He took that up as a cause, as a hook, and loved to point out this corner of the market.

Let me recap what we covered back in Chapter 2 about the Bottled-in-Bond Act of 1897. It set regulatory parameters for what was deemed authentic whiskey. That meant bourbon, primarily, but the other whiskeys are able to be bottled-in-bond as well, and Laird's makes a delicious bottled-in-bond apple brandy.

(One of the strangest quirks of the bottled-in-bond regulations is that you *can* make bottled-in-bond vodka. It has to be aged in barrels for at least four years, but the barrels have to be lined with paraffin "or other substance" to keep the vodka from coming in contact with the wood. *Why?*)

Historically, though, it was all about bourbon. To be labeled as "bottled in bond," the whiskey in a bottle of bourbon had to be the product of only one distillery, distilled in a single six-month distilling season ("spring" runs from January 1 to June 30, "fall" from July 1 to December 31), under the supervision of the same master distiller. It had to be at least four years old and bottled at 50 percent ABV (100° proof).

The label must bear the Distilled Spirits Plant (DSP) number of the distillery where it was distilled, and, if different, the DSP where it was bottled. DSP numbers are unique to a facility and issued by the federal government. They are not necessarily distilleries; they can be bottling or processing plants where spirits from other sources are bottled.

Bottled in bond also meant that it had to be aged in a bonded warehouse. At that time, "bonded" meant that access to the whiskey was under the scrutiny of a U.S. Treasury agent, who would live nearby and had the keys to one set of locks on the warehouse; the distillery had keys to a second set. Nothing happened until the agent unlocked the doors.

Starting in the 1980s, the locks started to disappear (I remember seeing a few remaining locks and hasps when I started visiting Kentucky distilleries in the 1990s; they might have been for show), and nowadays, "bonded" just means that the whiskey goes through an extra set of audits. It's still a requirement for bottled in bond, though.

The words *bottled in bond* on a whiskey label represented a government (and industry) guarantee that the bourbon was pure, unadulterated, and sufficiently aged. It was "the good stuff." You may have read that the Pure Food and Drug Act of 1906 was the nation's first consumer protection act, but whiskey drinkers know that honor belongs to the Bottled-in-Bond Act of 1897.

Sadly, by the time Bernie Lubbers came along in the 2000s, bottled-in-bond whiskeys were bottom-shelf relics, forgotten by most drinkers, and largely kept on as bargain whiskeys, and out of a lingering loyalty to the idea. I first discovered them late in the 1990s, and I was quite taken by the value they represented.

Bonded whiskeys were kind of a secret hand-shake for years, a whiskey we kept to ourselves and shared with friends. Then inevitably, they were discovered by the new whiskey groups. They jumped on them, and rightly so. Bonds got popular.

The market changed. New bonded whiskeys appeared for the first time in decades. Dickel and Jack Daniel produced two excellent bonded bottlings that were widely acclaimed and, happily, reasonably priced. Craft distillers produced bonded bottlings, which truly made my heart swell with pride that the old traditions had new adherents.

But what of the survivors? Some of the old bottlings disappeared, maybe to reappear in a year or two with new labels and new price tags. Some of them, the quietest, can still be found in far-flung markets, waiting to be discovered. I won't tell you where they are; you should go find them. It's the thrill of the hunt. In the meantime . . . stay bonded.

The Bottle on the Shelf

This last section is also somewhat subjective, though not entirely. The most subjective part is the effect of the packaging—the bottle shape and heft, the look of the label and the bottle closure, and any box or tube the bottle comes in—on your perceived impression of the whiskey's flavor.

Somewhat less subjective are any negative effects of transporting the whiskey and how it is stored. I know I've seen many bottles sitting on shelves in front of windows, subjected to bright sunlight for hours every day. I've read about bottles being stored in unventilated containers in the summer. You may have seen this yourself and wondered what that was doing to the whiskey.

Briefly, heat and light are bad for whiskey, but light is worse by far. Direct light from the sun or electric lights can cause flavor compounds in the whiskey to break down into smaller components. It also works on the molecules of color. Leave a whiskey in sunlight for a year or so, and you can be left with a substantially paler and significantly different-tasting spirit.

Heat seems to mostly shift the flavor of whiskey slightly in the direction of sweeter, richer. But if a whiskey bottle gets too hot, the alcohol could start to vaporize, and the resulting pressure inside the bottle could break the seal. Then the alcohol vapor escapes, and that's what makes open whiskey change flavor.

I had this happen once on an unexpectedly hot summer day. I was driving to a whiskey tasting out on Long Island from my Pennsylvania home and went to air-conditioning as the temperature outside climbed to almost 100°F (37.8°C). About 20 miles (32.2 km) east of Brooklyn, I started smelling whiskey. I stopped and found that a new bottle of whiskey had popped its cork, right through the shrink-wrapped plastic cover. From then on, I took care to always keep whiskey out of direct sunlight.

That's the kind of thing that could happen to a whiskey on even a relatively short trip from a wholesaler's warehouse to a bar, or from a store to your home. It doesn't hurt to take a moment to sniff around the seal of a new bottle. If you smell a noticeable aroma of whiskey, you probably want to leave that one alone on the chance that the seal's been compromised.

On a more subjective note, a fancy or heavy bottle can lead to expectations of quality that will color your perception of a whiskey's flavor. That's human nature and the distillers certainly know that.

Think about picking up a new bottle of whiskey. Consider hefting a whiskey with a very plain label, a lightweight and generic-shape bottle, and then twisting open a plastic screw top. What are your expectations from that bottle? Do you even consider them?

(Continued on page 228)

HAZMAT WHISKEY

There's been a trend toward cask strength whiskeys recently, and a liquor store owner I know in Massachusetts, Gary Park of Gary's Liquors in Chestnut Hill, thinks he knows when it might have started.

"It all started with the [Buffalo Trace Antique Collection] George T. Stagg 2007," he said. "It came in at 144.8 proof, and TSA rules said that any alcohol over 140 proof was considered HAZMAT [hazardous material]. Well after that, the 2007 Stagg was referred to as HAZMAT!" I've seen it other places too, not just at Gary's.

Kind of fun, right? Kind of flammable, too, but kind of fun. Until Gary added this. "There were people ripping through my shelves trying to find 140+ proof bottles to say they had a HAZMAT bottle," he said. "I noticed more and more people were mainly concerned with how high the proof was before they even tasted the whiskey."

Cask-strength, barrel-proof bottlings are a great way to try out proofing as an experiment or to dial in a whiskey to just where you like it best, which may be higher or lower than the usual bottling. But buying a whiskey just for the numbers? Before you even taste it?

Whenever you buy whiskey, whenever you're thinking about whiskey, please remember this, above all: It's a drink, not an investment vehicle, not a status symbol. There's no whiskey on this earth that you *absolutely must have*.

Because there will always be another one. As I'm writing this, there was literally a new bourbon released today; I saw it on social media. There will almost certainly be a new one out next week, if not before. Keep that in mind.

One more thing, while we're talking about cask strength whiskeys. You'd think that "cask strength" or "barrel proof" on a label means exactly that: The whiskey is at the same proof that came out of the barrel when it was dumped. And it might be, but in section 5.87a of the standards of identity, it says those terms may be used "only when the bottling proof is not more than two degrees lower than the proof of the spirits when the spirits are dumped from the barrels."

So, probably close, but not necessarily exactly dumping proof. I assume this is so that when a brand is known as cask strength, and the label is preprinted, they can nudge the proof a bit to hit the number on the label. Not a big deal, but it is a thing.

Now, weigh a heavy-based bottle in your hand, feel the richly embossed label with a history of the distillery and details of the composition of the whiskey, and peel open the lead foil capsule around a cork-and-wood closure. You'll expect more from the second bottle, no matter what's inside it. As a friend of mine said about an expensive bottle we opened, "Of course it's going to taste great. At that price, it has to!"

We'll talk more about that later. For now, remember that it's part of the effect, and it's as real as gravity when you're drinking, and it's completely a nonfactor when you're doing a blind tasting.

Finally, what happens to the flavor of a whiskey when you do open it? Oxygen gets at the whiskey as soon as the seal is broken and really attacks the whiskey when you start to pour it and the liquid is agitated.

Is that all bad? Sometimes a whiskey will actually taste better, more complex, when a bit of aeration takes place. There are pouring devices that increase that aeration, forcing oxygen into the whiskey. Oxygenation is at the heart of most accelerated aging schemes, so there's definitely an effect.

Any positive effects of added oxygen, though, are pretty short-lived before loss of alcohol starts the inevitable downhill slide. As alcohol vapor escapes every time the bottle is opened, your whiskey will start to taste a bit dull, without all the lively notes of fruit and flowers that delighted you. It will taste less and less special, becoming a pale reminder of what it once was. This will take some months in a closed bottle, given normal conditions.

You can slow this process even more in a couple ways. The easiest is to use the same preservative gases that wine drinkers use to preserve an open bottle of wine. A quick puff of a spray can before closing the bottle tightly can help preserve the flavor. You can also carefully and slowly decant a half-full bottle to a smaller bottle so as to store the whiskey with less "headspace" and oxygen.

Eventually, though, as mentioned in the "Time in a Bottle" sidebar on page 233, you'll want to get down to the business of finishing that bottle while it still tastes great. Don't be in a rush, but do your whiskey a favor and say goodbye to it when it's still close to its best. That way, you'll have nothing but great memories of a great bottle, which is how all whiskeys should leave this world.

“As alcohol vapor escapes every time the bottle is opened, your whiskey will start to taste a bit dull.”

BOTTLE IT YOURSELF: PRIVATE BOTTLINGS

One of the most exciting changes in whiskey bottlings in recent years is not more cask strength whiskeys, or older whiskeys, or grain innovations: It's the huge increase in private bottlings.

Private bottling used to be a rare thing done by the wealthy. It involved wading through a swamp of regulations, with little help from distilleries because they didn't do it often enough for it to be normal. I remember writing an article on it twenty years ago, and I think we were able to find seven distilleries that offered it, mostly in Scotland.

Passionate individuals and large liquor stores with a strong focus on whiskey were doing it in America. I remember running into a liquor store manager I knew in a Heaven Hill warehouse back in 1997, tasting through twelve barrels of bourbon to make a selection. But it was relatively rare. It wasn't something that occurred to people, and it was considered expensive and a little nuts.

No more. Small liquor stores, whiskey clubs, bars, and restaurants are all doing private bottlings, and distilleries have programs to help them with everything from selection to taxes and regulatory bureaucracy to bottling and labeling. There's still a hefty up-front cost, but the per-bottle price is reasonable. And the prestige is significant for a restaurant or bar program that has their own whiskey brand that you can only get there.

Widely known as "picks," as in "store picks" or "club picks," the whiskey may be a slight variation on a standard bottling, like a ten-year-old version of a whiskey that's usually eight years old, and the label may reflect that, with only a subtle change or an overlay sticker. It may be a single cask of an established brand, picked from a selection of barrels. The distilleries will often send samples of the various barrels if you can't travel there to try it. Or it may be more involved; a whiskey finished in another barrel, a blend of bourbon and rye.

Small distillers do it too, of course. I helped pick a store's barrel of Dad's Hat rye whiskey a while back. Everyone at the distillery (all three of them) stopped working, and we all tasted through nine barrels. Three of them tasted pretty similar and got kicked out pretty early: good, but not exceptional. One had a distinct note of fresh peppers; the store didn't pick that one, but the distillery made a single barrel bottling of it. They finally picked two barrels: one exceptionally rich, the other one particularly spicy.

This reflects how important it is to the people making the pick that it be theirs alone, not just a different label on the same old stuff. It has to be noticeably different. The Maker's Mark Private Select program I told you about in Chapter 11 is a hugely successful program where groups can "build" their own unique pick by selecting a mix of finishing woods to their own taste.

The question I always had about these custom selections, and about single cask bottlings in general, is whether they're cutting the heart out of standard bottlings. If people are willing to pay a premium for great barrels of, for instance, the bourbons destined for Evan Williams, is there a chance that enough will be sold that there aren't enough to maintain the level of quality for the main brand?

I've heard rumblings about that . . . but I've heard plenty of rumors and rumblings (and grumblings) about whiskey quality in thirty years. Whiskey, as I mentioned in the previous chapter, is romantic . . . and somewhat prone to conspiracy theories. Store picks and club picks will continue, I suspect, until the next thing comes along.

Knob Creek Single Barrel Select Rye 5 Years Old, "The Old College Try Rye!" Selected by the Allen Street Grill, State College, Pennsylvania. Huge nose of sweet mint, pepper and grass, orange honey. Easy on the palate for the proof, an orange honey and pepper roar. Finish is warm, long, and a bit dry, finally some oak. Quite different from the standard seven-year-old Knob Creek Rye.

TIME IN A BOTTLE

I get this question all the time. "I have a bottle of Old Riverboat 12-year-old rye whiskey from 1965. That's 12 plus 55 years old, so this is a 67-year-old whiskey, right?" No, it's a 55-year-old bottle of 12-year-old whiskey.

While there are some changes that take place in a bottle, very slowly over many years, generally speaking, as long as the seal is intact and no large amount of evaporation is taking place, whiskey doesn't change in the bottle until it is opened. Whiskey needs either wood or oxygen to change flavor at that point, and there is a small amount of oxygen in a sealed bottle. But if you're not shaking the bottle, it's going to be a very slow and limited interaction.

Once you open the bottle, all bets are off. I have what I call a "forty and out" rule. Once I get down to about 40 percent of the whiskey left in the bottle, I try to finish it within six months. Otherwise it's going to be robbed of its liveliness. Drink up; whiskey's wasting.

Master Distiller
Jimmy Russell
WILD TURKEY
BOURBON
WILD TURKEY
BOURBON

15

All the People

I like to say that there's one important ingredient in making good whiskey that's crucial but hard to quantify. There's the grain, the yeast, the water, the still, the barrel and the time in it, and the climate. But there's something else that's so important that we often overlook it. That's the will, the intent, and the purpose of the people making the whiskey.

It's not just the brewers, distillers, blenders, and warehouse workers, either. It's everyone: the farmers and maltsters, the sawyers and coopers, the people who plan and build the warehouses. It may even include people whose influence continues after their retirement or death.

It includes the people in the chain who get that whiskey from the barrel to your palate as well: people like the bottlers and the folks who design those bottles and their packages. There are the marketers who decide it's time for a new bottling, the blenders and distillers who design and create it, and the sales staff who then get out there and buttonhole bar managers and store buyers. They in turn put it in front of you, and the brand ambassador may come along and awake a thirst for that whiskey in you.

Take away any of those people, take away their drive and execution, and that whiskey may never reach your tongue. That's important, very important stuff indeed. Let's have a close look at what these people do and how they advance the taste of whiskey till it lands where it needs to be.

Jimmy and Eddie Russell, father and son master distillers at Wild Turkey Distillery

Seeds

Whiskey starts with grain, and grain grows on a farm. There is more than one type of farmer who raises grain for whiskey. Some operate the big farms that raise tons and tons of grain. They plant and tend fields that are half a mile on a side, planting and harvesting with huge specialized machines.

Farming for them is about clean yield per acre, and they're very good at it. An Iowa farmer counts on a yield of over two hundred bushels of corn (over 11,000 pounds [4989.5 kg]) per acre of ground. The consistency of their crop makes the distillers' jobs easier and helps make the whiskey consistent.

There are the farmers who are growing smaller fields of specialized crops, maybe to organic or non-GMO standards. They may be "salt of the earth" types who do things the old way, with natural fertilizers, contour plowing, and forty-year-old tractors. They may be new-tech farmers, using Bluetooth-enabled moisture probes in every field to keep tabs on the crops, maybe even in individual rows. They are farmers who are willing to take a risk to produce something other than commodity grains. They're filling a precise need some distillers have for a "clean" grain that allows them to make a whiskey they can present as less processed, more natural than others. They may even be the distillers themselves, growing the grain to make their whiskey.

There are also farmers like Robert McDonald at Dancing Star Farm in Imler, Pennsylvania, who grows more than ten varieties of corn for seed, including Bloody Butcher, Wapsie Valley, Blue Dent, and Cocke's Prolific. He's growing for other farmers and working with distillers directly to make those relationships. I ran into him at the American Whiskey Convention in Pennsylvania a while back, and he was very happy with the response he was getting from the small distillers.

There are farmers who very much want to try farming like this, being able to make money with grain crops that aren't for everyone. I literally just spoke with one a couple weeks ago, ran into him in a local bar, and gave him Robert McDonald's number to talk it over.

This is what the farmer-distiller relationship looks like today. Small distillers want boosted, different flavor from a variety of sources, and they're willing to pay a premium for it.

Maltsters also work with the distillers. Forty years ago, it was just come to work, clean the seed, and make ton after ton of pale malt. As the market has changed, as the character of whiskey has changed, maltsters are reacting to market demands and trying to anticipate them.

The interesting thing for me here is that while there are small maltsters starting up in a variety of places, offering various custom services (see the sidebar on page 71), there are also moves by the very large maltsters to meet these needs. I visited the huge Great Western Malting in Vancouver, Washington; eighty years old and it's so big we had to drive around to see the different parts of the operation. They were serving the craft brewing and distilling industries at this immense place, making thirty-five different varieties of malt and working on new ideas in a very advanced pilot plant on-site. They're eager to find new flavors from grain.

Micro to macro, these people are making a difference in the flavor and character of new whiskeys. The farmers in Michigan and Pennsylvania and Colorado who buck the system at the request of some distillers and grow Rosen, Danko, Abruzzi, or other, older strains of rye that have fallen out of favor help make that difference. Robert McDonald growing a rainbow of different corn and selling seed to farmers across the country makes a difference. Maybe it's the folks at the Breadlab creating different crosses of grains to give great flavor at higher yields. Farm distilleries like Jeptha Creed in Kentucky that grow their own Bloody Butcher corn make a difference. Without their will to *do* something different, whiskeys would taste more and more alike.

Heaven Hill
Grain to Glass Rye

123.2°. Made with locally grown corn. Sweet, minty nose. Rollicking rye: sweet, bitter, mint, corn, dried fruit, varied and delicious. Moves directly to an oak-framed finish. Bold performance, gripping.

> "Small distillers want boosted, different flavor from a variety of sources, and they're willing to pay a premium for it."

FORGIVEN

In 2013, Wild Turkey Distilling Company released a blend of roughly three parts 6-year-old bourbon and one part 4-year-old rye. The blend was called "Forgiven," and the story was that distillery workers accidentally mixed the two whiskeys together.

Someone was going to get fired, until master distiller Eddie Russell tasted the mix and decided that it was more than good enough to sell. That's the story, anyway, and Eddie swears it's true.

Some things just happen. It might be by accident; it might be desperation; it might be a reaction to an outside force. The ones that don't work out, well, we probably don't hear about them. The ones that do become part of the lore, and flavor, of whiskey.

Wood

I once went out in the Missouri woods with a sawyer and his crew (and Buffalo Trace Distillery master distiller Harlen Wheatley, who actually cut down an oak tree that day). It was hot, and felling the tree involved a new chainsaw technique that went dead against everything I'd been taught about safety.

When I got back, I found six ticks crawling around on me. Going out and cutting down oak trees to make barrels takes the right kind of person. They also know what they're doing. These days, sawyers are cutting only the right oaks for barrels because they know the inspectors at the mills are only going to pay for the right ones. They have to be straight, 16 to 22 inches (40.6 to 55.9 cm) in diameter with no branches for the first 20 feet (6.1 m), about eighty to one hundred years old, and it's preferred that they be from northern-facing slopes.

Cut the right trees and you get the right wood for barrels, barrels that make whiskey with consistent character. Cut too many out of one area and the character of the barrels could shift as trees have to be harvested from nonoptimal areas or simply from areas where the flavors that come from the wood will be different. These are long-view decisions, and it likely helps that many of the small companies that do the logging for barrel making are family concerns.

The sawyer makes that decision, and the wood moves on to the mill. The workers at the mill mainly do a piece-by-piece job, and they do it well, aided by automation, laser-tracked saws, and video inspection. Their job is to make sure the wood is the same every time. The engineers who work with them may find new ways to cut the wood, make it come together more tightly, change the loss rate, and change how the whiskey matures. Chemists and tree scientists track the changes in oak caused by the length of time the wood is left out to season and dry, and what changes are brought by kilning. These days, there are always experiments going on to see what treatment makes a difference in flavor, retention, and cost.

The coopers who make the barrels are a fascinating cross of traditionalist keepers of the flame and laser-guided innovationists. They raise a barrel by eye and hand, they cut the wood with automated precision, and they hammer it into shape with a practiced skill.

We know that barrels impart a large amount of flavor to whiskey. The people in the labs at the cooperages work with the distilleries and experiment with the wood to find new ways to treat it, heat it, toast it, or char it to make a difference in that flavor.

Some of it is more physical. Brown-Forman makes their Coopers' Craft bourbon with a special coopering technique they call "chiseling" that leaves a series of grooves in the inside of the charred barrel. The wood that is chiseled out is left in the barrel. All of this is designed to get more surface contact with the wood and spirit. This is just the latest in a series of experiments over the years: cuts, saw-toothed staves, heavier charring.

People in many places are thinking every day about ways to work with wood—before it even touches the whiskey—that will get more flavor into the bottle, with different character.

Cooper's Craft Barrel Reserve 100 Proof

Grooves are chiseled in the barrel interior, and the wood shavings are left in for extra surface area. Bold oak and char aromas on a 100° proof heat wave; crisp Asian pear frames marshmallow and caramel; oak fires the finish.

Techs

Experiments bring data to mind, and the people who collect and track data have made a difference in whiskey and how it tastes in the same way they've made a difference in almost every industry.

The whiskey industry, in general, used to just move along, doing things as they'd always done. "Don't change a damned thing" is a watchword in the business.

There were exceptions and innovators, especially as new materials and technologies were developed. But computers led to an explosive number of changes, with easier and more certain ways of tracking the results of process changes. For instance, millions and millions of barrels of whiskey move through hundreds of warehouses around the globe, and almost every one of them is tracked from fill to dump, thanks to bar codes and data recording, and warehouse managers learn where in their warehouses particular types of whiskey come from.

That was just the beginning in wood science. Dendrochronologists studied the growth rings on the best barrels to see how the trees had grown. Sawyers and foresters were recruited to track the position of each tree felled: hill, valley, north or south facing, boggy or sandy soil. Chemical analysis of cut wood as it seasoned showed changes in structure and flavor precursors. Farmers have moisture probes in fields to determine what produces the best yield. Probes in the barrels tracked temperature and pressure of the aging whiskey over months and years. The results of wood treatments, different warehouse positions, and seasonal variations all come together in easily consulted records, and decisions are made.

Process has become more transparent. Temperatures of distillation, length of cook, time of fermentation, yeast cell counts, alcohol levels—every bit of data that can be recorded is becoming digitized. Once those data points are connected to sensory evaluations done by trained tasters and chemical testing done in the labs, changes in flavor can be tracked to changes in process.

Data is then applied back to those processes in the form of automation. Track all the still runs in a year and you'll find the best ones. Then a programmer writes a series of instructions for automated valves and probes to follow, and you can have the best run every time. You'll know where a tweak will make a difference or not.

Conversely, some distillers deliberately choose not to automate. Dickel, to go back there, was the most determinedly nonautomated large distillery I'd ever seen when I visited back in 2006, where every operation was done by hand, valves turned by people who were right there, not pushing a button somewhere else.

I caught up with Dickel master distiller Nicole Austin recently and asked her if that was still the case. Not quite . . . but close. "These days Dickel is more of a hybrid," she told me. "We've focused a lot on adding automation in support of sustainability, as well as safety (automatic shutoffs, etc.).

"A lot of the core 'whiskey-making functions' like managing mash temperatures, running the still," she noted, "are still largely manual in the sense that a person is next to the equipment and manually managing what is happening, but we've added functionality to automate the pump/valve motions. I see no romance in making an operator walk up and down four flights of stairs in a stillhouse in August when they can do the same thing with a screen." Well put.

If some distilleries have digital probes and servo-actuated valves run from a computerized control room while others are worked by hand and eye and sweat and memory, can we say if one way is better?

The relative merits of automation are a settled argument in most industries. Automation saves money, increases efficiency, and makes for a consistent product. But in the distilling business, tradition often trumps efficiency. Whiskey makers differ on the amount of automation they'll allow in the process, and they have good arguments for both sides.

If you automate your process and program your control system to re-create that best run every time, you've achieved consistency. You may miss the possibility of the occasional incredible run, but you've eliminated every one that might be below average. And still, even when the machines are opening and closing, stirring and steaming, they're mimicking what a very human person decided and did.

The coming of the technicians to the industry may seem to be creating whiskey without the human touch, a reduction of whiskey to numbers. But when the passion of a whiskey lover is combined with the techniques of a data cruncher, great things can happen. Data collection and retrieval systems, and the people who created and adapted those systems, who first saw the utility of them, have made an immense impact on the flavor of whiskey over the past forty years. The workers' contribution has not gone away. It is, if anything, amplified by data collection, which makes ever-finer adjustments possible.

On the other hand, there's the argument that the team that's working in a manually operated brewery and stillhouse knows what's going on, because they can smell it, hear it, feel it in the heat and the vibration. They've become attuned to the whole thing, and can arguably tweak it on the fly to improve it.

The big downside of manual operation is that there can be mistakes. But making whiskey, even for experienced people with a long-settled regimen, is inherently a process fraught with chaotic elements. Barrels are handmade from individual trees. Grain varies, not as much as grapes do for a vintner, but it's there. The weather can affect mashing and fermentation; climate affects aging. Whiskey ages differently in various warehouses or on different floors of the same warehouse. The blender has to bring it all together; what's one more random factor, really?

I find romance in this notion, and I believe in the value of variance. The industry needs this kind of multipath approach to making whiskey to provide the variety drinkers want. So long as there are distilleries with equipment that has been in place for fifty years or longer, I believe we will see hands-on distillers making whiskey. But as Austin notes, that doesn't mean we have to do every single thing by hand. Once again, it's a choice.

The Makers

Whiskey making is still largely an industry that relies on human senses to measure process.

The mill operator runs the mill to the accepted standards, but the operator still checks the grist for consistency, heat, and smell. A brewer may measure temperature and saccharification to see if fermentation is complete, but the brewer also checks on the bubbles and smell to know how it's progressing and when it's done.

The distiller relies on smell and taste to know when things are right with the cuts, and on sound to know the system is running smoothly. "You can't sneak up on a stillman," I've been told. "They hear anything that's out of place." Warehouse workers, the folks who move and check the barrels, can always tell you where the good barrels are because they know the smell of the different parts of the warehouses.

The people who do these jobs are largely maintaining the whiskey. They keep it on track; they know how things are supposed to smell, sound, feel, and taste; and they can stop it before things go off course. These are important jobs, but they're not making new flavors; they're keeping the ship on course. If they are making new flavors, they're probably not doing their jobs right.

The people who create new whiskeys are a smaller, heavily trained and experienced group. Credit must be given to the folks who often start the process, a group that is more often blamed than credited: the marketers, the folks in the offices, or out in the bars and stores, gathering information. They gauge the public taste, they look at the sales of current whiskeys against the stock of barrels needed to make those expressions, and they come up with an idea of how a whiskey should taste.

That's a particularly hard job these days, thanks to people like you and me. Maybe twenty-five years ago, the job was hard because there were stocks of aging whiskey that had to be bottled before they got too old and became undrinkable, or simply evaporated away to nothing. Then people like me and my colleagues helped get people like you and your friends excited about whiskey, and pretty soon the problem was that the stocks of aged whiskey were getting too low to make all the whiskeys we liked and could afford. Bottles got scarcer, prices went up, and marketers were called.

The marketers and their ilk dream up new whiskeys that the times call for, in their best estimation. We may like the whiskeys or not, but the marketers often have the first call on what they should be. After that, it is up to the other folks in this group—the master distillers, distillery managers, warehouse managers, and blenders—to make that concept into a whiskey, if possible. (In truth, all of these people, at different distilleries and whiskey companies, have had ideas for whiskeys that made it to the shelf.)

The distillers and distillery managers know what is possible with their whiskeys, with their physical plant, and with the barrels they can acquire. Their knowledge guides new projects over years of time as they experiment with new techniques, new mash formulations, new distilling paths, and new types

(Continued on page 246)

Ryan Maloney of Julio's Liquors (Westborough, MA)

"WATCH YOUR BUNGHOLE!"

The warehouse workers have a job that combines strength, control, and a quick eye for distances.

They steer the 500-pound (226.8 kg) barrels off the lifts and down the aisles of the warehouses, spinning and stopping them on a dime. That's part of the amazing utility of the modern barrel: One person can easily handle and move 500 pounds (226.8 kg) of freight, stop it, start it, spin it, and turn it.

The trick of the warehouse worker's job is "clocking" the barrels. That's rolling each barrel so that as it comes up against the last barrel in, the bunghole is at the top of the barrel. You don't want the poplar bung touching the whiskey. It's not oak, and it's slightly porous.

Say the first barrel into the rack rolls two and a half times to have the bung up; the barrel roller has to position the bung on the bottom of the barrel as they start the roll into the rack. But the next barrel needs to roll less, about a quarter turn less, but not exactly.

It's difficult and what makes it worse is when someone has to go into the rack and wrestle with a 500-pound (226.8 kg) barrel to fix it.

Once a year, the warehouse men and women show off their skills. The Barrel Relay at the Kentucky Bourbon Festival is the high point of the weeklong festival for the distillers. There are individual races and team races, with male and female teams. The barrels have to be rolled on a course that includes three 90-degree turns and then rolled into a rack.

But it's not just how long you take to get them in the rack. For every barrel that's clocked correctly, time is taken off the competitor's elapsed total. The focus on getting the bung topmost on every barrel leads to friends and family hollering, "Watch your bunghole!" It's a fun time, and the winners get bragging rights for the year.

The Maker's Mark women's team at the Kentucky Bourbon Festival Barrel Relay

of barrels. A different way of running a still can produce new make with a very different character, ready to age and blend with the standard make. Add a new grain to the mash, or a new peating level, or blend different yeasts, and you've got a new whiskey. One of the most far-reaching decisions can be where to build a warehouse and of what design. Whiskeys may age there over the course of two hundred years or more, with a definite influence on the flavor every day.

The warehouse managers would likely know if a new whiskey is possible immediately. They have their fingers on the flow of barrels in and out of every warehouse used for aging. The cliché that "at least 50 percent of the flavor comes from the barrel" tacitly acknowledges that part of that fraction isn't just the individual barrel; it's the warehouse microclimate where it ages. Most of the barrels in America are quite similar—new, charred white oak—but where they are aged can make an enormous difference.

The blender has an enormous potential effect on a whiskey's flavor. Even given a profile by the people in marketing, it's the blender's job to make that happen or to change it subtly to make it possible. An experienced blender knows all the potential flavor components of a distillery—often more than one distillery—and can pull together barrels to make whiskeys of different character and texture and perceptions of freshness or age. The silly little dabbling I've done in blending has made clear to me how difficult this job is.

When a blender is in place for decades, he has a deeply personal effect on a whiskey brand's shape and overall character. Parker Beam carved out a flavor profile over five decades for Heaven Hill's whiskeys that will last long after his death in 2017; Jimmy Russell still has input, and he started working at Wild Turkey seven years before I was born (and I'm 65).

The people who make the whiskey make the flavor. They defend that flavor from random effects, they aim it at a consistent target, and when the decision is made to create a new whiskey, they have the tools to do so readily at hand. They are the core team for flavor creation.

Flavor Delivery

The people who actually make the whiskey have an enormous effect on the flavor, of course. Not by semantic twisting either: "They make all the flavor; they make the whiskey!" But what about the people who manage the whiskey after it's in the bottle?

I won't kid you. Once the whiskey is dumped, blended, vatted, and proofed, it's going into a bottle and flavor creation is *done*. No matter how good the bottle looks, how it's presented to you, how you learn the whiskey's story, the flavor is set.

Mostly. Because flavor is always subjective. I've had the same single malt, from the exact same bottle, in two different settings taste significantly different. It was a combination of temperature, weather, ambient aromas, and probably the company. One setting brought the whiskey's sherry cask aging surging to the fore, while the other boosted my awareness of the brine and peat. We are humans, tasting what we feel in the moment. We are "the meat in the machine," as a stillman I talked to at a Scotch distillery referred to himself.

So our sensations of taste and pleasure can be influenced by other factors than the pure organoleptic. Try to deny this and you will, I believe, deny yourself some of the pleasures of this very human drink, this truly human accomplishment. Save that denial for the important job of quality control, tasting whiskey in a blank-white cubicle, from a blue glass, with pen in hand and silent concentration your only companion. At other times, why not taste what comes across your tongue and thus your brain?

Then the people who design the package, the bottle, the label, any kind of presentation box the bottle comes in, can have an effect on your whiskey's taste. If we're going to be honest, probably the people who set the whiskey's price have an effect as well. The reviewer whose opinions you read can affect your experience. The bartender or shop seller may tell you things about the whiskey that will set your expectations in one direction or another; they may even show you an entirely new way to imagine your whiskey. That's happened to me, and I spent hours talking to them and learning as we went.

A brand ambassador may lead you to expect to taste history in the glass or sun-warmed grain or the solid steadiness of a masonry warehouse. This person might take you through a tasting of several whiskeys, guiding your perception at each sip. It's done to sell whiskey, of course. But every brand ambassador I've ever met—and I have a large box full of their cards—has been a true whiskey lover as well, and they most often sincerely want to share that passion and make you a whiskey lover, too.

Even the sales representative you've never met or the store buyer you may never see has had an effect on how the whiskey tastes. After all, if the whiskey isn't there on the shelf, being poured at the bar, because the representative didn't make the sale, it doesn't have any flavor at all!

Whiskey doesn't just happen. The people involved in the process of whiskey making—every one of them—are crucial to the flavor of the whiskey in your glass. At some point in the process, as the whiskey's being made or maybe years before, people make decisions and the flavor of the whiskey changes. It might be huge; it might be as light as a bee's wing. But you can taste their decisions there in your glass. Think about them the next time you enjoy a drink.

Parker's Heritage Blend of Mash Bills 2012

A blend of rye and wheat mash bill bourbons. A nose that's sweet, somewhat floral, but not hot, even over 65 percent ABV. Lean and leathery, sweet in reserve, and miles of finish. Indelibly Parker Beam's palate.

Next spread: Pouring with care can set expectations that affect how your whiskey tastes. Believe it.

LOVE & WHISKEY
UNCLE NEAREST
UNCLE NEAREST RYE
UNCLE NEAREST SINGLE BARREL
UNCLE NEAREST 1884

UNCLE NEAREST
UNCLE NEAREST RYE

16

Intangibles

There are, I'm sure, people who'd rather see this chapter titled "Nonsense," "Make Believe," or maybe even "Bullshit." This is a chapter about the final additions that add or subtract flavor in whiskey—the ones that are not quantifiable. Any scientist will tell you that if you can't measure it or record it, it didn't happen.

But it isn't scientists who blend whiskeys, or if they do, they don't do it with high-performance liquid chromatography or a mass spectrometer. Whiskey is blended by hand and nose, by palate and memory, by the human perception of the blender. It can be measured using these tools, but it can't be duplicated. Not yet, anyway.

Once a whiskey is made, blended, and bottled, there's still no definitive set of numbers or words about how it tastes. That's because there are few things that are more subjective. We even have a saying about it that goes back to Roman times: *"De gustibus non disputandum est."* It literally means "taste should not be disputed/discussed." These days, we say, "There's no accounting for taste." You can see this played out on any given day in various online whiskey discussion forums, where if one person praises a whiskey, inevitably another will say that it is garbage and vice versa.

What makes this so? Much of it is personal taste, developed in many curious, even eccentric ways. I didn't drink Old Forester for years because it was the first whiskey I ever tried, and at age 11, it simply shocked me. I avoided "that rotten Old Forester" thereafter. Then I tried it again, at the urging of another writer, and I felt like a fool for all the years of drinking a good whiskey I'd wasted. It's hard to say how taste develops.

So personal taste, what whiskey you like and don't, is *by definition* intangible. It cannot be touched or truly explained. If that's so, what's hard to believe about flavors coming from intangible sources?

Keep an open mind and let's dive into the waters—
Are they murky? Are they clear? Are they even there?—
of the Intangibles.

Terroir

Let's start with something that's more than a bit controversial, even in the realm of wine, where it originates.

Terroir is a concept from wine making, the idea that the very place where the grapes are grown affects the flavor of the wine. The soil, the terrain and topography, the latitude and climate, the prevailing winds, perhaps even the local flora and fauna are all included.

Quantifying that is difficult, even with wine, and that's why it's such a controversial concept in whiskey making, which is more process oriented and includes more steps. If it's about where the ingredient is grown, most distillers don't use grain that is grown adjacent to them, or even within 10 miles (16.1 km). Some do, but not most. They may buy from "local" growers or in-state growers, but then which terroir is it?

Is it only about where the grain is grown? Whiskey is certainly an expression of the grain (or grains) but also the wood of the barrel and, quite arguably, the warehouse as well. As we discussed earlier, the type of oak and where it grows has a definite effect on the flavor of the whiskey. Whiskey ages in oak for quite a bit longer than wine, which is only in the wood for one or two years, so consideration of the oak's origins is reasonable. The warehouse's siting and surrounding terrain make for yet another consideration, affecting the barrels' heating cycle.

It gets more interesting when you consider the differences between the French winemaker's understanding of terroir versus the American winemaker's. The French include regional traditions that have established themselves over decades and centuries: the natural yeasts on the grapes (and in the bellies of the wasps that help pollinate the vines), the way the vines grow. Americans tend to a stricter interpretation: only what is natural, nothing that is man-made or changed by the hands of humans.

Some in the industry, who seem to hew more to the American idea, say that there is no terroir in whiskey. Whiskey is more man-made, more processed than wine is. Grain is malted, milled, hydrated, and cooked. It is then chilled, strained (or not), and fermented with carefully tended yeasts, after which it is subjected to distillation—eliminating all but the higher volatiles—and long aging. How could any influence of the soil be there?

Hillrock Estate Double Cask Rye

Made from rye grown organically on the distillery farm. Rye dominates: cinnamon-spiked mint candy on the nose, youthfully oily rye bursts on the tongue, supported by oak-borne vanilla. Distiller Dave Pickerell said this rye had a special minty character from these fields.

Others disagree, arguing that despite the different natures of wine and whiskey, there is a difference in whiskeys that comes down to locality: the same "taste of the earth" that winemakers talk about. Perhaps, because of that difference between wine and whiskey, there should be a different term for the local effects on flavor in whiskey. Maybe it isn't

Rye growing in Hillrock Estate's fields

so much that there is no terroir as it is that we don't discern that effect, because until very recently, most whiskey makers in the modern era were too big to discretely express the kinds of microeffects that terroir represents.

The late distiller Dave Pickerell, a man who kept a famously open mind about possible influences on whiskey flavor, was convinced that the rye grown in the fields around Hillrock Estate Distillery, in New York's Hudson Valley, lent a noticeable difference in flavor to the distillate. He believed that we were only at the beginning of recognizing such microdifferences, thanks to small batch distilling. He was also hoping to discover more differences that might be possible from using locally harvested peat for smoking the malt on-site.

I don't have an answer, nor do I have a suggested term for the combination of local effects on grain, oak, and warehouses that may or may not comprise "whiskey terroir." That's why we're in the chapter called "Intangibles," after all. But it is an intriguing and promising path for craft distillers to investigate.

George Dickel Rye

Dickel tags MGP's Indiana distillery as the source for their rye whiskey. Powerfully sweet nose with oak framing, and that's exactly what you get on the palate. And the truth leaves no distraction from doubt.

Age and Youth

As I grow older, I have to deal with young writers always nipping at my heels (I don't, actually, I love 'em, but it works with the narrative—humor me).

When they do, I remind myself that earned experience trumps youthful exuberance. It often does. That is why when I want a simply perfect beer, I head for Prague, Brussels, or Bavaria, and when I want a whiskey that's going to be zeroed in on my palate from the first sip, it's going to be from a distillery that's been operating for at least fifty years. No surprises, please.

There is a lot to be said for experience and consistency, especially when it's employed in the service of making top-notch whiskey. It can also get hijacked into a situation where it's used to make vast quantities of crashingly mediocre stuff, all of which has its place and market niche. But when you look at the whiskey shelves in even a moderately good spirits retailer, there are always some whiskeys there that you know, without hesitation, are 100 percent going to satisfy your desire for a glass of amber glory.

The legacy distillers are laden with this kind of experience. There are people working at most of those distilleries who've been there longer than you've been drinking whiskey. I'm no spring chicken, yet there are one or two people who've been working in the industry longer than I've been alive.

That kind of institutional memory and depth of experience has an effect on a whiskey's flavor that can't be expressed as anything more exciting than "consistent," unless you want to crank it all the way up to "perfect." Don't, though, because the best of these people know that there's always room to make it, as one distiller said to me with a wink, "perfecter."

Does that mean that the craft distillers are all behind the curve until they're fifty years old? Most definitely not. For one thing, some of the craft distillers lured those experienced folks out of retirement or across the street to their operations. Dave Pickerell, mentioned earlier, was the master distiller at Maker's Mark, then started a new career as a consulting distiller and started quite a few new outfits on the path to deliciousness. The late Dick Stoll, the man who made what was arguably some of the best bourbon in the modern era at the original Michter's distillery in Pennsylvania, came back after over twenty years to help establish the character of Stoll & Wolfe whiskey in Lititz, Pennsylvania.

Wyoming Barrel Strength Bourbon

The distilling experience of Bourbon Hall of Famer Steve Nally and master blender Nancy Fraley got this start-up sailing. A king bourbon nose: warehouse, corn, and oak. Both lively and solid on the tongue, minty and corn solid, framed in full-size oak.

The Russells tasting Wild Turkey in the warehouse

As far as that goes, if they're just making bourbon or just making malt whiskey or even making single pot still in the Irish style, and they're doing it the same way as the established distillers, they can't win. Even if they do it just as well—which is hard because of the experience gulf noted above—it's going to be almost impossible to do it for the same price: economies of scale, lower cost of capital for known businesses, and lower capital debt to begin with.

The smart thing to do is to be different, which is where that youthful exuberance comes in. Some of the stuff I've talked about in other chapters—types of stills, innovative or even crazy mash bills, wild yeasts, different barrels, and heritage grains—are all the result of someone saying, "Wait, I've never seen this before; how about we try this?"

It makes me think back to a green malt whiskey I tried from Coppersea Distilling near Hyde Park, New York. "We found an old Scottish distilling text," distiller Christopher Williams told me, "that mentioned making whiskey from unkilned, fresh malt; you grind it to a paste in a meat grinder. They essentially said, 'Don't do this; it's delicious, but it's really difficult.' That was all we needed to hear!" I still remember that whiskey: like a magic potion, sipped from an elf's jeweled flask, layer after layer of grassy, herbal spring freshness.

To be honest, the next batch of it I tried wasn't anywhere near as good. But that's part of craft distilling's wildly experimental designs, too. When you reach for the stars, sometimes you fall short. It's the ones that lift you out of your usual reality that make everything else worthwhile. What can exuberance add to the flavor of your whiskey? Anything!

"Perception Is Reality"

Lee Atwater was a brilliant American political strategist, something that has to be granted regardless of what you think of the people he worked for. Although Atwater died young, he left behind a legacy of political wisdom, and perhaps the brightest jewel in his hoard was this: "Perception is reality."

What it means is simple but deep. Atwater was saying that it didn't matter what reality, or the facts, actually were. What mattered was how people saw them. Before you dismiss this as the gimmickry of a political charlatan, remember that medical science backs him up by the admission of the placebo effect. Some medicines work because people think they're going to work, even when they're just sugar pills. Why should whiskey be any different?

If a whiskey is wrapped up in a fancy package, fancy words, or a top-shelf price, does that have an effect on the flavor? Several studies about the perceived price of wines suggest strongly that it does. If people perceive value in the package, they'll have a better opinion of the whiskey, often before they even try it.

I've seen it work in liquor stores. I've had whiskey makers admit it to me after they've redone packaging and seen sales (and positive comments) rise. If a new whiskey comes to market at a price that's equivalent to already well-regarded whiskeys of the same type, it stands a better chance of becoming well regarded itself.

23 Year Old
Pappy Van Winkle's
Family Reserve
Kentucky Straight Bourbon Whiskey
Bottle # P-2133
750ML • ALC 47.8% / VOL (95.6 PROOF)
Bottled By Old Rip Van Winkle Distillery • Frankfort, Ky

You'll also see a general climb in prices when the collector's market pays an outlandish price at auction for a particularly rare or stunningly packaged bottle. The prices on that brand's entire line may well creep up, or even for American whiskeys in general. It's the "halo effect," where the reputation (or price) of an exceptional bottle at the top of the range draws all prices along with it.

The funny thing with pricing, though, is that there seems to be a different scale for craft whiskeys. Because of a lack of economies of scale, pressing debt service needs, or a simple struggle to keep the lights on, you may see a two-year-old (or younger) craft whiskey priced the same as a twelve-year-old bourbon from a so-called legacy distiller. The craft whiskey will sell, even if it's notably younger in flavor.

I suspect that there are a few different factors at play here, all relatively intangible. First, craft whiskey is more popular with people who are new to the category, either new to drinking beverage alcohol or new to drinking whiskey. They are referred to as "naive drinkers," people who have very few preconceptions about what whiskey "should" taste like. If they try this new whiskey and it has flavors they like, that's exciting, and they'll stick with it.

There is also a "local hero" factor. Local producers are made much of these days—a trend I applaud, in general—and if a whiskey is made in your town or in your county, that's a plus. You'll be well disposed toward that whiskey and have a perhaps unrealized tendency to give it the benefit of the doubt when it comes to critique.

Those days are changing as craft distillers get more experienced, and their whiskeys are better-crafted and can afford to have a bit more age on them. There are good craft-distilled bottled-in-bond four-year-old bourbons that sell for less than twice as much as the bonded whiskeys from established distilleries, and that's a trend I'd like to see continue.

Packaging is another intangible that fits here. Does whiskey taste better when the bottle is heavy? Whiskey makers put corks in way too many bottles (in my opinion) when a good screw cap would make a better closure, simply because there's a perception that screw caps look cheap. "The good stuff always has a cork," one whiskey maker told me—and everyone wants to make the good stuff.

Such signaling abounds in variety. Some whiskeys have a tube, either cardboard or metal, that the bottle sits in like a loaded torpedo, ready for launch. Maker's Mark used to be unique with their wax-topped bottles, but you'll see plenty of them on shelves now. Heavy bottles imply seriousness, quality. A ceramic bottle may imply that a brand has a long history. Jugs and decanters appeal to collectors.

What flavor is added by things like this? Packaging and other visual and tactile cues make the whiskey taste "better." Even I can still be led into that occasionally.

Am I saying it's true? It can be. When you approach a whiskey that you know is expensive, rare, elegantly packaged, or particularly old, it's natural to have expectations. You can rely on your objectivity, you can rely on blind tasting (more on that in the next chapter), or you can simply enjoy the whiskey. After all, if all that stuff is combining to make the whiskey taste *better* to you, exactly who is being hurt in that transaction?

The Flip Side

All of this works the other way as well, of course. Put a great whiskey in a so-so package, and chances are it won't receive as much love from the aficionados. Why would a distiller want to do that?

There are various reasons. For marketing reasons, a distiller will often want to have a whiskey to sell in every price range, and one way to put a whiskey in the lower price brackets is to bottle it with a plastic screw cap, maybe even in a plastic bottle, with a simply printed label.

That kind of packaging won't get a whiskey much love from the critics, but it sure does make friends with a lot of everyday drinkers. Put it in a "handle" and put it on the shelf for a good price, and you'll have a ready audience.

I have an admission: I regularly buy bourbon and rye bottled that way. Why does a "pro" whiskey drinker get the bottom-shelf stuff? It is because I like a tall highball of rye and ginger when I grill in the summer, or a bourbon I can free-pour into a rocks glass with a few cubes while sitting on the porch contemplating life. And it's because I have friends who drop by who feel the same way. This is a good way to drink whiskey when it's "just a drink," and that's the solution to a problem I've noticed with the serious aficionado (or the aficionado who takes themself too seriously).

That problem is this: Some people don't seem to realize that whiskey does not have to be the focus every time you have a drink. We have a small whiskey club here in town; we get together and sample new whiskeys every few months. In between meetings, Dave and Rich may come by my house with some new whiskeys, and I'll pull out some as well. We'll taste, compare, and discuss. But when that's done, we'll pour one for drinking, and the conversation immediately turns to local politics, history, and food.

If I'm just sitting out on the front porch with my dogs, watching the day go by, or if I'm reading a book on a cool night, likely as not there's a screw cap bottle of whiskey by my side, and maybe an ice bucket if it's a hot day. Screw cap whiskey tastes fine—if maybe not fantastic—which is perfect, because I've got other things on my mind.

J. W. Dant Bonded

Poured from a screw-capped plastic bottle. Nose of allspice, cinnamon, and teaberry. Corn, oak, more teaberry-mint with solid heat into the finish.

MEET A SOURCER: DAVE SCHMIER

I happen to know one of the bigger independent bottlers of American whiskey, Dave Schmier. Dave owns Proof & Wood, which bottles the Deadwood and Tumblin' Dice bourbons, Roulette and The Senator rye whiskeys, and several other brands, plus a number of non-whiskey brands. Before that, Schmier owned (and then sold) the now well-known Redemption brand, which sold higher-proof, longer-aged rye whiskeys.

The reason why Schmier now refers to himself as an independent bottler gets to the heart of how they work. "Going back to Redemption," he told me, "I thought of myself as a brand owner; bought whiskey on Monday, bottled it on Tuesday."

In 2010, he started selecting barrels at the old Seagram's distillery in Lawrenceburg, Indiana, which is now owned by (and generally known as) MGP, a large Kansas-based company that specializes in grain products, including alcohol. At the time, the plant was cranking out whiskey to plan, and the plan was producing blending stock for Seagram's 7. Sales had been slowly declining, though, and there was a surplus of aged rye whiskey.

Schmier was one of the early brokers to come around and sample those surplus barrels. He liked what he tasted, and Redemption was born. I remember those early bottlings of Redemption, and they were exceptionally good. As rye whiskey became more popular—at least partially due to the education program Schmier put into place around his brand—other entrepreneurs came calling in Lawrenceburg. They built new brands and wanted more whiskey to fill their pipeline.

"Things changed as I realized we couldn't just buy aged whiskey and bottle it at will," he said. "That glut was going to dry up. The realization was [that we] had to buy new make whiskey and lay it down for the future." That's when he became more like an independent bottler, and less like a simple salesman.

At Proof & Wood, Schmier is buying both new make whiskey to lay down and aged whiskey for blending. "Aging and blending with intent is important to me," he said, about his new company. "As the name kind of implies, I don't distill, but I do have control of [the] age, the Wood, and the Proof, the ABV in the bottle."

He's not afraid of blending, either. We talked briefly about the possibility for better American blended whiskeys back in Chapter 3; Schmier's done it. Proof & Wood's Vertigo 2021 release blended two older light whiskeys, a rye whiskey, and a bourbon at 51.15 percent ABV, and it was brilliant. It can be done!

In a market where whiskey is in demand, how does he find aged whiskey to buy in bulk? Like any good trader, he's developed a network of people who are actively looking to sell and buy whiskey. A fair amount of his time is spent talking to those people and then "pouncing on opportunities when I see them, occasionally even buying intriguing stuff without even tasting." He's bottled a seven-year-old Polish rye whiskey, The Stranger, that I have to assume falls into that category.

But there is always whiskey available. "The challenge with whiskey," Schmier said, "is you need to predict and produce whiskey today for your demand years in the future. Inevitably you will get it wrong, so if a distiller produces too much whiskey, they will be motivated to sell it on the open market. Also, public companies might be motivated to sell whiskey at the end of a quarter to meet corporate forecasts . . . " and Dave Schmier will be there, waiting to pounce.

Proof & Wood
The Justice Bourbon

Barrel proof of 94.2° at fourteen years old. Nose: lots of well-integrated corn, oak, Juicy Fruit gum. Corn-bread-mellow on the tongue, sweet/spicy; finish continues to tell the same story. A classic old and easy drinker.

Truth

There's one more thing that seems to have an effect on the flavor of whiskey in an intangible kind of way: the truth. I mean the truth about where a whiskey is made, which is not as obvious as it may seem.

The first time you realize that the whiskey brand you've come to love *doesn't have a distillery* . . . it's maybe a little hard to swallow. A significant part of the experience of enjoying a whiskey, whether we like to admit it or not, is often wrapped up in the label and lore. Does feeling misled about that affect the flavor of the whiskey?

First, let's talk about how a whiskey ends up on the shelf with a label, and an age, and a proof, and, usually, some kind of story on the label, but without a home. Where did the whiskey come from? The label might say "Distilled in Indiana" and also "Bottled in Kentucky." That's a big hint that someone bought the whiskey somewhere and had it bottled for them.

So what? This is nothing new. People have been buying bulk whiskey and putting their own label, their own brand on it, almost as long as there's been whiskey. The original George Dickel was a bottler, not a distiller, for example.

There are a variety of reasons for this. One of them, more common today, is for a new distillery to buy aged whiskey in order to have something to put their name on and sell until they have whiskey of their own (and hope they taste similar).

But it usually comes down to money. Selling bulk whiskey for the distiller means cash in the hand instead of barrels in the warehouse, maybe right when you need some cash. Buying bulk whiskey means instantly owning barrels, without the huge cash outlay and investment needed for building and expanding a distillery and aging warehouses.

You can put different spins on that, but this is usually what's going on, and neither angle is illegal or unethical. It's a straight-up business transaction, not unlike when you buy a bottle of whiskey at the store.

The problem, in my opinion and others', is that not all of these brands make a point of telling us where they come from and may deliberately mislead consumers with vague language like "from an old family recipe" or "we make this whiskey the way we like it." It might be *someone's* old family recipe, and "make" can mean blending, or choosing, or even just naming.

But they're not telling you "we bought this from someone and put it in a bottle," and legally, they don't have to. Labeling regulations have a loophole for that; if the whiskey is made in the same state as the bottler, they don't even have to say the state on the label.

Some brands do say that they didn't actually distill the product, either on the label or on readily available information on their website or social media. They may or may not say the precise distillery, but they don't claim to be making it themselves.

So what? Does it make a difference in how it tastes if you know where the whiskey comes from? Aficionados say they want transparency, and while some of them mean, "I want to know every single detail about how you made this whiskey," most of them want to know who made it and where, more than they want to know how.

To hear some people talk, the truth about these questions has more impact on the flavor than anything else. They learn that a whiskey isn't what they thought it was, and suddenly it doesn't taste as good, the price is too high, and they don't want anything more to do with it.

Here's my take, and again, it's a choice, not right or wrong. I don't need to know everything about a whiskey; I don't even need to know exactly where it's from. All I ask of a sourced whiskey is that the whiskey maker is not actually lying to me about where it comes from, whether or not they actually made it or if they selected it.

If a whiskey label, a whiskey brand, does consistently lie or misdirect about where it's made, who makes it, what part the people putting the label on the whiskey actually had to do with putting the flavor into the whiskey, then it does change the taste for me. It makes it taste like lies and disappointment, and I'll probably find another brand, even if this one was something I liked.

The truth is perhaps more intangible than any other thing that goes into a whiskey. But there's no denying its importance. Stick to the truth.

17

It's in the Glass

We've finally put your whiskey together. Every flavor input, from the huge contributions of the barrel and the warehouse to the tiny tweaks of the mash hydration and the milling of the grain, has been included. It's all sitting in the bottle on the bar in front of you, just waiting to be unleashed. Years of work have gone into it, the contributions of many people, places, and machines.

What are you waiting for? Let's take it out for a spin!

If you want to have a simple drink, maybe a tot at the end of the day or something to celebrate a win, it's likely that you'll want to snap open that cap, pour a generous amount into a glass or two, and relax in a comfy chair with your partner or friends nearby. Good whiskey! Turn up the music and let your mind roll on.

But if you really want to get everything you can possibly taste out of this whiskey, in this moment, it's going to take a little bit of work on your part. That's not really asking that much after all the effort everyone else put into it. Once you've done the work, you'll reap the benefits in the future. Concentrate and find those little hints of violets, or the licorice hiding behind the stone fruits and spicy oak, and you'll find them waiting the next time you open this bottle.

Framing the Tasting

You have to prepare to get the most out of a whiskey. Part of that is physical preparation. First clear your mouth and hands of any food or cooking aromas, and try to sample in an area free of such smells. Some of the master blenders won't eat food with garlic even two days before they're going to be sampling whiskey, though that's asking a lot from ordinary folks like us.

Next, clear your perceptions of any other type of sensory distraction. Silence your phone; turn off the radio and television. If music helps you focus on other things, put some on. If it gets you singing along, turn it off for a while, since it's a good bet the whiskey is going to taste "better" because of it.

Get your glassware. I've made some suggestions in the sidebar on page 270.

If you can do a blind tasting, that's great. You'll find that not knowing what you're tasting will focus your senses tremendously. If that's not an option, there are benefits to an open-label tasting as well; you have context and a point of comparison. Don't worry about how you're tasting so much as what you're tasting.

That said, some folks still fear that they'll somehow "get it wrong" and not find what they're "supposed" to taste. Stop worrying, because every pro taster will come up with a different list of descriptors for a whiskey. That's simply how people work.

Be fearless, and write down what *you* smell and taste. Don't worry about getting it right; there is no right. As you get better, your list of scents and flavors will become more congruent with others. There will be some notes that every taster gets, but they will never be identical. That's the magic of self and the magic of whiskey. Taste it, write it, and move on.

To do that, you'll need some very simple equipment. Get a tumbler and some plain water, preferably not chilled. You may want an eyedropper or some kind of pipette to add small amounts of water to the whiskey when the time comes. Add some plain crackers or bread, something crusty, like a baguette. You'll want to clear your palate after each whiskey.

Get your note-taking setup: a pen and a notebook, a pencil and pad, a laptop or electronic tablet. You don't have to take notes, but I find that it helps me focus. Finally, get a piece of white paper and tape it to a vertical surface. You'll be able to hold the whiskey up to the paper to get a better eye on what color it is.

Pour the whiskey (or, if you're blind tasting, have your assistant pour it and bring it to you). Settle yourself. Relax. It's whiskey time.

BLIND VERSUS OPEN TASTING

Blind tasting doesn't require a blindfold, but it does require an assistant. You need at least two possible whiskeys to taste—more is better—and someone who can pick the whiskeys randomly and pour one or pour several and mark the glasses so the assistant knows which is which. Then you taste, record what you get from each whiskey, and only then have the assistant reveal what was in each glass.

What's the point? You may think you're able to taste a whiskey without prejudice, but you're not. It's because your brain is just too powerful. If you see a label or a distinctive bottle shape and you know what that whiskey is, your brain is already building expectations. You may think "Expensive whiskey! This will be great!" or "Cheap whiskey . . . boring," or "Ah, favorite whiskey—I love this." And you've already affected what you're going to taste and, by the way, cheated yourself out of a new experience.

At another level, if you're tasting for a competition, even something as simple as a local newspaper article about the "best local whiskey!" you want to protect the results from any taint of personal preference. I speak from sad experience: There's always someone out there who thinks a tasting is rigged. Do it blind and you've already greatly increased the confidence level about the results.

If you're feeling particularly objective, you can do a triangle test. Here your assistant has three different whiskeys and three glasses. They pour three samples and bring them to you—and the fun begins. Was it three different samples? Or two of Whiskey A and one of Whiskey C? Or maybe just three samples of Whiskey B? I've done triangle tests where I got two whiskeys and, unexpectedly, a brandy, and it threw me. Is there a lot of sherry cask influence here? What's all that vaporous fruit doing in my whiskey?

The point of blind tasting is to force you to focus directly on what you're smelling and tasting, and nothing else. Don't take into account the whiskey's name or reputation, the details of how it's made or where it's aged, or your own personal preferences. Just nose, taste, and linger with the whiskey, completely blind to anything else.

You can even get opaque glassware to take the whiskey's color out of consideration.

Or turn it on its head and do an open-label tasting. Bring everything you know to bear on the whiskey: where it's made and who makes it and how, what you know about previous bottlings you've tried. This will inform your experience more than a blind tasting can, and you'll look for what you know. Is it there? Is this a significant departure?

You can also do a tandem open-label tasting, comparing a new whiskey with a familiar one from the same maker or another. I find these tastings to be very revealing. They will hone my focus almost as sharply as a blind tasting as I try to tease out every difference, so much so that my subjectivity gets left behind.

SINGLE

> "Be fearless, and write down what *you* smell and taste. Don't worry about getting it right; there is no right."

Whiskey work

THE GLENCAIRN GLASS

When I drink whiskey, I usually take it in an old-fashioned glass, the solid-based low tumbler used to build that classic cocktail. It's heavy in my hand and feels solid, there's room for ice if it's a hot day, and there's also room for the volatile aromas to bloom.

When I taste whiskey with attention and effort, I taste it from the Glencairn glass, the product of Glencairn Crystal, a Scottish family glass business. Its design is the result of consultation and trial with master blenders and distillers and is widely accepted in the industry.

Why do I use the Glencairn? At first it was because I had a lot of them. They were the glass of choice at almost all the early whiskey festivals, mainly because they were the first glass designed specifically for nosing and tasting whiskey. Before I knew it, I had over two dozen.

It is also a good idea to try whiskeys from the same glass to eliminate any variable that different glassware might create. I'm not much of a believer in the idea that "the right glass" can make whiskey (or wine or beer) taste better. But I do believe they can deaden or obscure flavors.

So why have I stuck with the Glencairn? It's comfortable and holds the right amount of whiskey. There's a solid little base to grip it, a bowl to hold the whiskey and let the volatile aromas come off and gather, and then the signature chimney that brings those aromas directly to your nose.

There are other whiskey tasting glasses that have come along, but the Glencairn has served me well for years, and I've seen no real reason to change after trying the others. I'd encourage you to try them all out and find *your* favorite.

"Its design is the result of consultation and trial with master blenders and distillers and is widely accepted in the industry."

Nose and Tongue

Before you taste the whiskey, you'll want to smell it. It only makes sense, because your nose is a much, much more sensitive organ than your tongue.

While your tongue can really separate only five flavor types—salt, sweet, sour, bitter, and *umami*, the last of which is a sort of richness—your nose is capable, after training, of identifying hundreds of thousands of aromas. Just think of how many aromas you can identify for bananas alone: ripe banana, under-ripe banana, overripe, cooked, burnt, thawed; the scent of the peel, of the butt (they are different), of a green peel. That's at least nine scents just for one fruit!

As we've been discussing, there are many ways that aroma can be created in whiskey. They put all that together in the bottle, and then it's your job to tease it apart.

So close your eyes, relax, and bring the glass to your nose. Don't jam your nose into it; that's a good way to beat up your olfactory nerves with alcohol. Wave the glass gently under your nose, see what you get: perhaps corn, mint, berries, sharp oak, caramel?

Now, try something I was absolutely sure was nonsense when I first heard it. If you have a glass with a "chimney" top, like the Glencairn, tip it slowly near horizontal, then move your nose very slowly to the bottom rim of the glass, without touching it. Now, inhaling gently as you go, through several breathing cycles, move your nose upward (or the glass downward, your choice).

As you do, you'll get the heavier, sweeter aromas sliding up and over the edge at the bottom. In the middle you'll find lighter, maybe nutty and baked grain aromas, and then any light floral or fresh fruit aromas will be escaping at the top. (We're assuming there are no off aromas in this ideal glass.) It's essentially fractional distilling, the lighter vapor coming off the top, the heavier ones at the bottom, like the reflux in a pot still.

Got that? Good. Now stick your nose in the crook of your elbow and take a deep sniff. This is an old taster's trick. You're essentially smelling yourself, the background aromas of sweat, perfume, or laundry detergent that make up the smell you smell all day: your baseline. Smelling like that hits the reset button on your nose and sets you back to ground state, as it were.

Now smell the whiskey again, but take it easy. We've been talking about focusing your attention, but now you want to let it wander. There's an episode of the celebrated crime drama *The Wire* where they talk about the idea of looking at a crime scene with "soft eyes," a deliberate unfocusing of attention that opens your mind to seeing things out of place or finding patterns that a sharp look, focused on the individual components rather than the whole, won't find. You want to approach a new whiskey with a soft nose, not looking for anything in particular, but just letting it happen to you.

As you do, you'll smell things that are either immediately familiar—corn bread, vanilla, mint—or that might hang right on the edge of recognition: unspecified fruit, sweet, "spicy." Mull that over and see if any of them resolve. Look up one of the flavor wheels that are available on the web and see if the lists of descriptors jog a particular aroma for you: figs, maple, sawdust.

Don't smell too long or too deeply; you can overload your senses. Pause and think. Now try it again, this time with your mouth open, and breathing through both your nose and mouth. This engages the receptors in the connecting passages, and you may find more aromas coming to your attention.

Time to sip. You want to take a fairly small sip, spread it over your tongue, and swallow. The first one's really to get your tongue set up. Have some water. Now take another small sip and let it sit on your tongue for a few seconds. Roll it off your tongue and "chew" the whiskey, move it around in your mouth so it touches every part, and gently breathe in through pursed lips as you do it.

This isn't just about tasting but about spreading the whiskey around on all the warm skin in your mouth to heat it and bring out the volatiles. Feel those flavors and the alcohol heat in your mouth, feel the creaminess, the tannic grip, the oaky dryness.

At this point, you're not just tasting; you're also smelling, deeply, as the volatiles rise through the back of your mouth and touch the olfactory receptors in the back of your nose. This is the richest, most effective way to experience your whiskey—with taste, touch, and smell combined. As the eighteenth-century French gastronome Jean-Anthelme Brillat-Savarin put it: "The taste and the sense of smell form but one sense, of which the mouth is the laboratory and the nose the chimney."

All the flavors and aromas that have been built into your whiskey are here, but you still may not be able to taste them. If you'll remember what we talked about in Chapter 14 about proofing, the amount of water in a whiskey can hide or reveal flavors. Take your eyedropper (or carefully pour from a pitcher) and drop a small amount of water into the whiskey. Swirl it, have another sniff, and sip. You'll taste the whiskey differently now; some aromas move back or disappear, while others come to the fore. The heat will be less, and the "finish," the flavors and aromas that linger on the tongue after the swallow, will change as well.

Make your notes, have a few more sips, and sharpen your impressions. If you want, leave the whiskey for twenty minutes and come back to it: It will have changed again as it interacts with oxygen in your glass.

You've tasted the whiskey, all the flavors and aromas that took so long to develop and integrate. Now you can unlock them again any time you open the bottle.

Taste Everything

If you want to taste everything in a whiskey, I have some advice from an interview with Kermit Lynch, the wine importer (and author of *Adventures on the Wine Route*—get yourself a copy).

To paraphrase, Lynch said that you should pick a wine and learn everything you can about it: where it was made, what the countryside is like. Taste the grapes; ask who made the wine and how, what they're like and what other wines they make, how long wine's been made there, and what the other wines in the area are like. Then you will know that wine, and what it truly tastes like, better than you ever can by simply drinking a glass of juice.

Learn everything you can about a whiskey. Ask good questions and listen carefully to the answers. Travel to where it is made, walk the ground, watch the grain coming in, and smell that diffuse blanket of dusty sweetness. Enter the warehouses if you can and lay your hand on the barrels. Breathe deeply and take in that warehouse richness of slowly leaking barrels and decades-old oak beams. Smell the sweet tang of fermenting bourbon mash, the funky weirdness of the heads cut off a rye run in a hybrid still. Feel the heat in the warehouse; hear the quiet bubbling of the fermenting beer or the magic gush of water from any number of springs. Talk to the people who make it; hear their stories.

It has nothing to do with the flavor, seeing that, knowing that. It has everything to do with the enjoyment.

Enjoying the Best Whiskey

If you want to find the best whiskey, it's simple: Taste widely and decide what your favorite is.

There is no other way. You can't ask me (I don't even have a favorite!), you can't look at numeric ratings in magazines or online, and you certainly can't ask on a social media group: You'll get more opinions than there are whiskeys, and there are bound to be those that directly contradict each other.

Don't make up your mind too early. You'll only limit yourself, and that's never good. Don't let anyone else tell you, "I only drink X whiskey; it's the best!" I realize that there are a staggering number of whiskeys, often with staggering prices. But these days you'll have to take the price into account when you're deciding what your favorite whiskeys are.

Back in the 1990s, when I started drinking and writing about whiskey for a living (with a much more serious eye to flavor), whiskeys were substantially cheaper than they are now. It's not simple inflation; it's demand. Not many people wanted whiskey back then; now we do. I guess I did my job too well! There's nothing to be done about that outside of simply sighing for the good old days, and buying wisely.

Don't fall into the error of putting too much credence into the online opinions of whiskey wowsers, either.

They'll try to convince you that you have to spend a lot to get good whiskey, that popular whiskeys are trash, or that you need to constantly hunt for rare whiskeys.

My friends, I do this for a living. I've tasted rare and wonderful whiskeys from all over. The whiskeys I drink most often all cost under $70 a bottle, most of them under $50. Start with the popular bottlings and take direction from there. Don't take your driving lessons in a Ferrari.

Take tasting opportunities where you can find them. Bars often host tastings that will offer flights of small pours at a fraction of the price you would pay by the drink. Distillers often hold tasting events; get on their email lists and watch for one to come to your town.

There are whiskey clubs that will share the cost of a high-end bottle and some that have members who like nothing better than buying one of those rare or expensive bottles and sharing it with folks who might otherwise never get so much as a sniff. You can do it anywhere; I live in a town of nine hundred in deep rural Pennsylvania, and we have a twelve-member whiskey club that tastes some great whiskeys. All you have to do is find some other fans and get together on occasion to sip, sample, and talk whiskey.

When you've found some whiskeys you know you enjoy, expand your enjoyment by relaxing with them. Don't save them for a special occasion; make any occasion special by having a great whiskey!

Relax about how you drink them, too. If you want some water in your whiskey, add it. If you want a cube or two of ice, drop it in. (I'd advise you to skip the whiskey stones; they're tough on the teeth, and I broke a glass with them once.) And by all means, if you want to make a highball in the summer—or the winter!—get out the ice and the soda and have at it! I added a seltzer tap to my home bar just for high-balls. It's your whiskey; do what you want with it.

Of course, the best way to drink whiskey isn't neat, with ice, or in a cocktail. It's when you drink whiskey with friends, new or old. Whiskey shared is twice enjoyed, and there's something positively conspira-torial about sharing a whiskey, especially when you know other people aren't.

One of my favorite people in the industry, Wild Turkey's Jimmy Russell, told me something long ago (and I'm sure he's told lots of people, as have I): "We don't really care how you drink it," he said, with a grin, "just so long as you drink it."

I like that, but I think I like this one even more. I'm not certain, but I believe I was talking to the incom-parable Anthony Burnet, an early brand ambas-sador for Glenmorangie. We were talking about whiskey collectors, and he shook his head, and said, "Take it off the shelf. We make it to drink."

That's what I'd like to leave you with. Remember: The only reason they make whiskey, and the only reason you have whiskey, is to drink it. Do that and savor every drop, every bit of flavor that's been packed into it in so many different ways.

Cheers!

IT'S YOUR WHISKEY

One of the happiest conversations I ever had about whiskey was when my book *Tasting Whiskey* had just come out, and my agent got me booked to call into a bunch of radio shows across the country. I was doing a Los Angeles drive-time show, and the woman asked, "Are you going to tell me I can't drink my Glenlivet on the rocks?"

Truth be told, the way she asked it made it sound like people had already told her that, and she was feeling some shame for liking it that way. I asked her: "You said 'my Glenlivet.' You bought it, right? It's your whiskey, ma'am; you drink that anyway you want, and don't let *anyone* tell you different." She laughed out loud and said "*My* whiskey! That's right!" At the end of the segment, she thanked me, said I'd made her day, which surely made mine.

But let's talk a bit about how to get the most out of that enjoyment. As in, if you're going to add ice or water, what's the best way to go about that?

Why are you adding ice or water? Is it primarily to cool the whiskey, or to dilute it, or is it some of both? Or, also completely valid: You never really thought about it; you just like it that way. Let's think it through.

If you're cooling the whiskey, but you don't like the dilution, there's a simple solution. Chill the bottle. Keep your "drinking whiskey" in the fridge, and it's sitting at that cool temperature, ready to pour.

If it's for dilution, you'll want a good water to put in it. I'm lucky: Our tap water in this little town is amazing (this is a great trout-fishing area, and the town has a top-notch water plant to keep it that way; solar-powered, too!), and I can just add that. You might want to pick out a bottled water that's clean and fresh, maybe something with some lively minerality to it.

You can get picky about adding it, if you want. There are very reasonably priced pipettes and eyedroppers available for it; you can pour it by the capful off your bottled water, or you can simply eyeball it and pour some in. Be careful; you can't take water out, you can only add more whiskey . . . if that's an option.

If it's for both, that's when ice comes into play, and that's when things get a bit more complicated. Not because of some imagined right or wrong, but because homemade ice can be problematic. I have an icemaker in the main fridge. It uses our great tap water and then puts it through a filter (a really expensive one . . .), and it's, well, it's okay. Most fridge icemakers are okay more or less. I also have a countertop icemaker a friend gave me, and I can use the water I want and clean it as often as I like, and it makes good, cold, bullet ice that works great in a highball.

You can buy ice. Our local ice maker says on every bag, "We are proud to say that we have no taste," and it's true. It is extremely pure ice, with no off-flavors. I usually keep a small bag in the freezer, and we keep the freezer very cold. That's good enough for every day.

But sometimes I want something special, or I just want to sit on the porch with the bottle and keep pouring. So I did get some big cube molds, silicon molds that make cubes that are about 2 inches (5 cm) square. They won't fit in a Glencairn, but I'm not looking for that when I'm drinking on the rocks. I put one in a low old-fashioned glass, pour the whiskey right over it, and enjoy. Even on a hot day, that's usually good for three pours.

If you really do want to get crazy about your ice, you need to get *The Ice Book*, written by my friend Camper English. Camper has been obsessed with ice for years, and his presentations on it to bartenders are legendary. *The Ice Book*, however, presents his knowledge in usable form (and is fun, to boot). If you want perfect ice, it is attainable.

Don't overthink it. Find what works for you, find what's good. If that's Camper-level perfect ice? Do that. If some spring water or a couple nice cubes do it? Leave "perfect" for the obsessives among us. Enjoy the whiskey, most of all: It's your whiskey.

Acknowledgments

When a person who's never distilled a drop of whiskey in their life writes a book about making whiskey, you know they had a lot of help.

To the team at Buffalo Trace, my thanks for your continuing assistance, patience, and solid information: Mark Brown, Harlen Wheatley, and the late Elmer T. Lee, Ronnie Eddins, and Truman Cox, three men who are sorely missed. To the folks at Heaven Hill, past and present, who have graciously kept me on their sampling list and thereby hugely expanded my knowledge: much thanks. The good people at Beam Suntory have been very generous with time, information, and excellent whiskey. Nicole Austin at George Dickel has been hugely generous with information about Tennessee whiskey and kept me entertained with a smart sense of humor as well.

The craft distillers who've helped me are literally too many to mention. But I must single out Herman Mihalich at Dad's Hat, Paul Hletko at FEW Spirits, and Todd Leopold at Leopold Bros., all of whom have increased my knowledge of spirits enormously over the past ten years. Erik and Avianna Ponzi-Wolfe at Stoll & Wolfe introduced me to the late great Dick Stoll, for which I am forever grateful. Black Button Distilling in Rochester, New York, and Balcones Distilling in Waco, Texas, came through with last-minute samples for tasting notes. And a warm thank you to Sydney Jones, who absolutely made my day when she thanked me for encouraging her to become a distiller, and didn't she just!

To the very patient and knowledgeable people (not all Americans!) who submitted to thorough questioning on stuff I just did not get: Stuart MacPherson of the Edrington Group, Conor O'Driscoll of Heaven Hill, distilling consultant to the stars Liz Rhoades, Chris Morris of Brown-Forman, Greg Roshkowski of Brown-Forman Cooperage, Dr. Pat Heist of Wilderness Trail, Andrew Wiehebrink at International Stave Company, Hank Ingram at O.H. Ingram, chemists Bob Simpson and Scott Spolverino, Jay Erisman of New Riff, and Dr. Don Livermore of Wiser's. I'm indebted to the independent bottlers and blenders who have shared their knowledge and whiskeys over the years, especially Dave Schmier at Proof & Wood and Adam Polonski and Nora Ganley-Roper at Lost Lantern.

There are a number of folks who have helped me over the past twenty-odd years, learning about whiskey and whiskey making, and as my parish priest used to say on Christmas Eve, I apologize to the ones I know I forgot. Thanks to Jeff Arnett, Jimmy and Eddie Russell; Fred Noe and his father, the late Booker Noe; Jim Rutledge; Jerry Dalton; the late Parker Beam and his son Craig Beam; Dave Scheurich; Greg Davies; Bill and Rob Samuels; Marianne Eaves; Jane Bowie; Denny Potter; Matt Hoffmann; Bruce Joseph; Christian Krogstad; Alan Bishop; Rob Cassell; and thanks to Robert Mohr for pointing out that weird little regulation about cask strength bottlings. Almost forgot: thanks to Chris Peters at the Allen Street Grill for letting me taste that great Knob Creek pick (and a few others that . . . just happened to get poured).

Whiskey is a business, and there are folks in that business I owe gratitude to. Thanks to Joe Magliocco of Michter's; Robin Robinson, Frank Coleman, and the crew at the Distilled Spirits Council of the U.S.; Josh Hafer; Larry Kass; Lauren Cherry; Kylie Flett; Alexandra Clough; Monique Huston; Mike Miller; John Cooper; and Ryan Maloney.

My colleagues, the whiskey writers and editors I work with, have taught me a lot, and I owe them. Thanks to Dave Broom, Chuck Cowdery, Wayne Curtis, Camper English, Davin de Kergommeaux, John Hansell, Maggie Kimberl, Fred Minnick, Noah Rothbaum, Mike Veach, David Wondrich, Max Watman, and Liza Weisstuch. You are more than colleagues, you are friends . . . and sometimes co-conspirators.

I owe special thanks also to a couple of very good friends. Marty Duffy, the U.S. brand representative for the Glencairn Glass, was my travel companion when we did a fun series of whiskey presentations with the late Tom Johnson, whose discussions of the craft of writing I sorely miss. Marty and I also did a podcast with Liz Rhoades during the pandemic, *A Sip of Knowledge*, that was a great education, and a whole lot of fun.

Sam Komlenic isn't just a good friend and solid drinking buddy, he's also an authority on Pennsylvania distilling history and a stickler for proper grammar and punctuation, which has made him invaluable to me as my First Reader. Thanks, Sam!

I'd be remiss if I didn't mention my local whiskey club, the Camp David Discords. Good friends all, who never forget that drinking whiskey may have serious moments (like when Jen, the chemical engineer, delivered an impromptu lecture on column distillation that had me taking notes), but it's always about having a good time. Special thanks to fellow "executive committee" member Dave Dreese, for his help with the illustrations.

I do owe thanks to the people who got the book from my mind into your hands: my agent, Marilyn Allen, and my editor at Quarto, Jennifer Kushnier. It's been a pleasure, thanks!

My family has always been a great support, and there is no way I could do it without them. My children, Thomas and Nora, who have grown to be capable critics of my writing, and our dogs, Pippin and young Samwise. Most of all my wife, my partner, my strong heart, Cathy. You make it possible; you make it worthwhile. I'm back, honey; I know book-writing time is rough!

Finally, I dedicate the book to the memory of my mother, Ruth Bryson. I know she never expected her son to be a booze writer, but she never wavered in her support. Love you, Mum; miss you.

About the Author

Lew Bryson has been writing about beer and spirits full-time since 1995. He was the managing editor of *Whisky Advocate* magazine from 1996 through 2015. Bryson is the author of *Tasting Whiskey* (Storey Publishing 2014), a broad survey of the whiskeys of the world. He is a columnist for *Craft Spirits* magazine and produces *Seen Through a Glass*, a podcast about central Pennsylvania food and drink. He has served as a judge for the American Craft Spirits Association, the New York State Brewers Association, and the Great American Beer Festival.

Lew lives in central Pennsylvania with his wife and two Welsh Corgis.

DISTILLING
COMPANY
OSP-NY-21026
NYR 7-22-16-6

Index

F

G

H

I

J

Photo Credits

Jack Sorokin Photography: pages 15, 25, 45, 82, 92, 95, 98, 99, 118, 120, 123, 126, 138, 139, 142, 148, 150, 155, 159, 163, 164, 169, 179, 187, 190, 218, 250, 262, 264, 268, 271

Glenn Scott Photography: pages 26, 43, 48, 57, 117, 125, 145

Courtesy of the author: pages 14, 29, 61, 113, 129, 136, 144, 161, 180, 183, 213, 231, 234, 242, 255

Courtesy of West Overton Village & Museum: pages 8, 223

Courtesy of Uncle Nearest Premium Whiskey: pages 17, 104, 248

Courtesy of Cedar Ridge Distillery: page 52

Courtesy of Black Button Distilling: page 63

Courtesy of Jordan Bush and Stoll & Wolfe: page 75

Courtesy of Heaven Hill Brands: pages 100, 115

Judd Brook/Courtesy Elizabeth Rhoades: page 103

Courtesy of Balcones Distilling: page 131

"Bulletin relative to production of distilled spirits." United States. Internal Revenue Service. Washington: Government Printing Office, 1912: page 147

Courtesy of Ingram River Aged: pages 170, 189

Jason Tinacci/Courtesy of St. George Spirits: page 195

Courtesy of Michter's: page 201

Courtesy of Lost Lantern: page 216

Courtesy of Bernie Lubbers: page 225

Courtesy of ISC Barrels: page 245

Courtesy of Hillrock Estate Distillery: page 253

Courtesy of Buffalo Trace Distillery: page 257

Courtesy of David Schmier: page 261

David Handschuh: page 281

Shutterstock: pages 2, 6, 12, 23, 35, 39, 64, 67, 68, 69, 73, 76, 78, 80, 91, 106, 132, 141, 172, 204, 209, 229, 232, 277

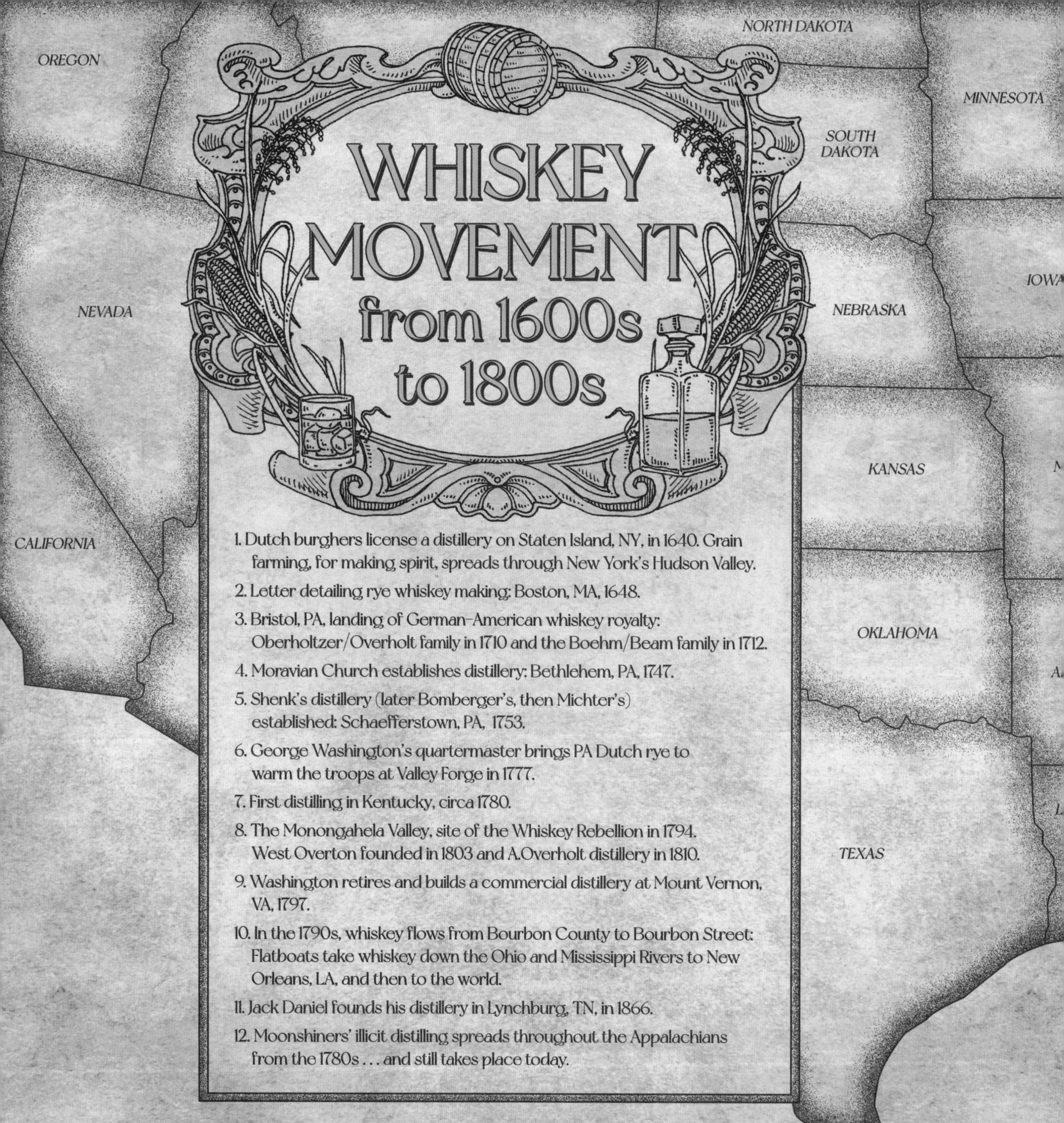
OREGON
NORTH DAKOTA
MINNESOTA
SOUTH DAKOTA
IOWA
NEVADA
NEBRASKA
CALIFORNIA
KANSAS
OKLAHOMA
TEXAS
WHISKEY MOVEMENT from 1600s to 1800s
1. Dutch burghers license a distillery on Staten Island, NY, in 1640. Grain farming, for making spirit, spreads through New York's Hudson Valley.
2. Letter detailing rye whiskey making: Boston, MA, 1648.
3. Bristol, PA, landing of German-American whiskey royalty: Oberholtzer/Overholt family in 1710 and the Boehm/Beam family in 1712.
4. Moravian Church establishes distillery: Bethlehem, PA, 1747.
5. Shenk's distillery (later Bomberger's, then Michter's) established: Schaefferstown, PA, 1753.
6. George Washington's quartermaster brings PA Dutch rye to warm the troops at Valley Forge in 1777.
7. First distilling in Kentucky, circa 1780.
8. The Monongahela Valley, site of the Whiskey Rebellion in 1794. West Overton founded in 1803 and A.Overholt distillery in 1810.
9. Washington retires and builds a commercial distillery at Mount Vernon, VA, 1797.
10. In the 1790s, whiskey flows from Bourbon County to Bourbon Street: Flatboats take whiskey down the Ohio and Mississippi Rivers to New Orleans, LA, and then to the world.
11. Jack Daniel founds his distillery in Lynchburg, TN, in 1866.
12. Moonshiners' illicit distilling spreads throughout the Appalachians from the 1780s . . . and still takes place today.